PUB
QUIZ

Published by Collins
An imprint of HarperCollins Publishers
Westerhill Road
Bishopbriggs
Glasgow G64 2QT
www.harpercollins.co.uk

First Edition 2014

10 9 8 7 6 5 4 3 2 1

© HarperCollins Publishers 2014

ISBN 978-0-00-758008-8

Collins® is a registered trademark of
HarperCollins Publishers Limited

www.harpercollins.co.uk

Typeset by Davidson Publishing
Solutions, Glasgow

Printed in Great Britain by Clays Ltd,
St Ives plc

A catalogue record for this book is
available from the British Library.

If you would like to comment on any
aspect of this book, please contact
us at the above address or online.
E-mail: puzzles@harpercollins.co.uk

AUTHOR
Chris Bradshaw

Introduction

'Healthy body, healthy mind,' so the saying goes. We can't do much about the body part (unless you plan on doing ten press-ups after every correct answer) but we can certainly help with the latter.

Think of the *Sun Pub Quiz* as a general-knowledge workout to build up your brainpower and tone up your trivia talents. We've got questions on all manner of subjects aimed at everyone from the beginner right up to the Olympian quizzer.

Whether it's the quizzing equivalent of a leisurely stroll round the block, a brisk workout at the mental gym, or a full-on question marathon, there's something for everyone.

So are you ready? Take your marks, set, quiz!

The quizzes

The book is divided into 200 different quizzes. Half of them are based on classic quizzing categories ranging from art to architecture, food to football, TV to transport, and pretty much anything you could imagine in between. The other 100 quizzes are pot luck and contain a little bit of everything.

The quizzes are grouped together depending on how tricky they are. The easy ones come first, followed by medium and finally difficult.

Easy

Think of the easy questions as a gentle warm-up. You should be able to stroll through these without expending too much mental energy. A tricky question or two may trip up the odd unsuspecting competitor, though.

Medium

After limbering up with the easy questions it's time for something a little more challenging. The medium section is full of testers to give you a serious general knowledge workout. There are some sneaky hurdles to clear to keep things competitive.

Difficult

If the easy questions are like an easy stroll, think of the difficult quizzes as a 10,000m race with Mo Farah. Some of them will have you gasping, but think of the satisfaction when you come up with the right answer. Get all of these right and it's a real gold-medal-winning performance.

The answers

The answers to each quiz are printed at the bottom of the following one. For example, the answers to Quiz 1 appear at the bottom of Quiz 2. The exception to this rule is the last quiz in every level. The answers to these quizzes appear at the bottom of the very first quiz of the level.

Running a quiz

As any top athlete will tell you, every great performance requires preparation. The same goes for hosting a successful quiz. A little bit of effort beforehand will go a long way to making an event run smoothly.

❖ Rehearse: don't just pick this book up and read out the questions cold. Go through all the quizzes you're going to be asking by yourself beforehand. Check for any potentially tricky pronunciations. Note down all the questions (notes look better in a quiz environment than reading from a book) and answers. Every effort has been made to ensure that all the answers in the *Sun Pub Quiz* are correct. Despite our best endeavours, mistakes may still appear. If you see an answer you are not sure is right, or if you think there is more than one possible answer, then check.

❖ Paper and writing implements: do yourself a favour and prepare enough sheets of paper for everyone to write on. The aim of the game here is to stop the mad impulse certain people feel to 'help'. They will spend ten minutes running around looking for 'scrap' paper, probably ripping up your latest novel in the process. The same problem applies to pens. Ideally, have enough for everyone. Remember, though, that over half of them will be lost forever once you've given them out.

❖ Prizes: everyone likes a prize. No matter how small, it's best to have one on offer.

Good luck! We hope you enjoy the *Sun Pub Quiz*!

Contents

Easy Quizzes

Medium Quizzes

Difficult Quizzes

EASY QUIZZES

Quiz 1: Pot Luck

1. Which English football team plays its home matches at Old Trafford?

2. Mr Carson is the name of the butler in which popular TV costume drama?

3. Charles de Gaulle airport serves which European capital?

4. Comedy duo Ant and Dec are originally from which English city?

5. In the medical profession, what do the initials 'GP' stand for?

6. Which German football team won the Champions League in 2013?

7. Maris Piper and King Edward are varieties of what?

8. H_2O is the chemical formula for what?

9. Which English king married six times?

10. Which British newspaper is nicknamed the 'currant bun'?

11. Whom did David Cameron succeed as the British prime minister?

12. In a game of football, how long does each half last?

13. Brandenburg, Bremen and Lower Saxony are states in which European country?

14. Which football manager celebrated his 1000th game in charge of Arsenal in March 2014?

15. Complete the title of the play by Shakespeare – 'The Merchant of...'?

16. Silly mid off, beamer and googly are terms used in which sport?

17. By what name is the TV adventurer Edward Michael Grylls more commonly known?

18. Summer Bay is the setting for which TV soap?

19. A milliner is a maker of what?
    a) carpets
    b) hats
    c) mints

20. New York City comprises how many boroughs?
    a) 3
    b) 4
    c) 5

Answers to Quiz 67: Pot Luck

1. Atlantic
2. Wind speed
3. Élysée Palace
4. New York
5. Neighbours
6. Saudi Arabia
7. Jupiter
8. Triangle
9. 1966
10. 64
11. Tea
12. Donkey
13. Casablanca
14. Westminster Abbey
15. Dublin
16. John Major
17. Los Angeles
18. Bram Stoker
19. Canary Wharf Tower
20. The Orange Prize

Quiz 2: Television

1. DCI John Barnaby is the central character in which popular detective drama?

2. Nurses Cynthia Miller, Trixie Franklin and 'Chummy' Noakes are characters in which medical drama?

3. Which duo host 'I'm a Celebrity ... Get Me Out of Here'?

4. In 'The Simpsons', who is older – Lisa or Bart Simpson?

5. 'Nice to see you, to see you nice' is the catchphrase of which veteran broadcaster?

6. 'BGT' are the initials of which TV talent show?

7. The Woolpack is a fictional pub in which British soap?

8. Which chat-show host and radio DJ won National Television Awards in 2013 and 2014 for his show 'For the Love of Dogs'?

9. Which actor is the host of TV quiz show 'The Chase'?

10. Who is missing from this list – Darcey Bussell, Len Goodman and Bruno Tonioli?

11. Who is the host of TV panel show 'Celebrity Juice'?

12. Idris Elba plays the title character in which hard-hitting detective drama?

13. What is the name of the popular Channel 4 series that watches people watching television?

14. David Tennant, Christopher Eccleston, Matt Smith have all played which TV time-traveller?

15. Dave Lamb provides sarcastic commentary on which culinary TV show, where contestants take turns to host a dinner party?

16. Which classic TV comedy was set in Slade Prison?

17. DI Humphrey Goodman is the central character in which Caribbean-set crime drama?

18. Which comedian hosts TV panel show '8 out of 10 Cats'?

19. Matt Lucas and David Walliams starred in which TV sketch show?
    a) Little Britain
    b) Little England
    c) Little World

20. What is the first name of Mrs Brown of 'Mrs Brown's Boys' fame?
    a) Agnes
    b) Bridget
    c) Violet

Answers to Quiz 1: Pot Luck

1. Manchester United	11. Gordon Brown
2. Downton Abbey	12. 45 minutes
3. Paris	13. Germany
4. Newcastle upon Tyne	14. Arsene Wenger
5. General practitioner	15. Venice
6. Bayern Munich	16. Cricket
7. Potato	17. Bear Grylls
8. Water	18. Home and Away
9. Henry VIII	19. Hats
10. The Sun	20. 5

Quiz 3: Pot Luck

1. What do the initials 'UFO' stand for?

2. Which fictional sleuth was played on TV for 25 years by David Suchet?

3. Which British classical violinist represented Thailand in a skiing event at the 2014 Winter Olympics?

4. Brie and Camembert are types of which food?

5. Jeans are made from which material?

6. Which stage and screen musical was based on a book called 'The Story of the Trapp Family Singers'?

7. In the classic pirate novel 'Treasure Island', what type of animal is Captain Flint?

8. Hospital drama 'Casualty' is set in which fictional city?

9. 'Aloha' is a greeting used by people in which American state?

10. 'Sunflowers' is a painting by which Dutch artist?

11. Yom Kippur is a festival celebrated by followers of which religion?

12. Complete the title of the hit romantic comedy – 'When Harry Met...'?

13. Prior to joining the euro, what was the currency of Portugal?

14. 'Joyeux anniversaire' means happy birthday in which langauge?

15. What type of creature lives in an apiary?

Answers – page 9

16. In London, what can be found at Spitalfields, Portobello Road and Camden?

17. Which British artist is famous for his spot paintings?

18. A rugby union team is made up of how many players?

19. Europe covers approximately what percentage of the Earth's land area?
    a) 7%
    b) 17%
    c) 27%

20. Which New York thoroughfare is famous for its theatres?
    a) Broadway
    b) Fifth Avenue
    c) Wall Street

EASY

Answers to Quiz 2: Television

1. Midsomer Murders	11. Keith Lemon
2. Call the Midwife	12. Luther
3. Ant and Dec	13. Gogglebox
4. Bart Simpson	14. Dr Who
5. Bruce Forsyth	15. Come Dine with Me
6. Britain's Got Talent	16. Porridge
7. Emmerdale	17. Death in Paradise
8. Paul O'Grady	18. Jimmy Carr
9. Bradley Walsh	19. Little Britain
10. Craig Revel Horwood	20. Agnes

Quiz 4: Fill in the Blank – Movies

Fill in the missing word from the titles of the following Oscar-winning films:

1. The ____ Speech (2010)

2. The ____ Locker (2009)

3. No ____ For Old Men (2007)

4. Million Dollar ____ (2004)

5. The Lord of the Rings: The ____ of the King (2003)

6. American ____ (1999)

7. The English ____ (1996)

8. The Silence of the ____ (1991)

9. Dances With ____ (1990)

10. Out of ____ (1985)

11. Chariots of ____ (1981)

12. One Flew Over the ____ Nest (1975)

13. The ____ Connection (1971)

14. In the Heat of the ____ (1967)

15. The ____ of Music (1965)

EASY

16. Around the World in ____ Days (1956)

17. On the ____ (1954)

18. From Here to ____ (1953)

19. The Greatest ____ on Earth (1952)

20. Gone with the ____ (1939)

Answers to Quiz 3: Pot Luck

1. Unidentified Flying Object
2. Hercule Poirot
3. Vanessa-Mae
4. Cheese
5. Denim
6. The Sound of Music
7. Parrot
8. Holby
9. Hawaii
10. Vincent van Gogh
11. Judaism
12. Sally
13. Escudo
14. French
15. Bee
16. Markets
17. Damien Hirst
18. 15
19. 7%
20. Broadway

Quiz 5: Pot Luck

1. Pearl Harbor, scene of a famous military attack, is in which American state?

2. A rugby union match lasts how many minutes?

3. Which British patron saint is celebrated annually on 1 March?

4. What colour flag is awarded to a beach that meets high standards for cleanliness, safety and water quality?

5. The airline Qantas is based in which country?

6. A millennium is a period of how many years?

7. Pantomimes traditionally take place at what time of the year?

8. A dermatologist is a doctor who specializes in diseases affecting what part of the body?

9. Which actor plays the magician-turned-detective Jonathan Creek?

10. Aussie soap 'Neighbours' is set in which city?

11. Which TV duo invite viewers to join them for a 'Saturday Night Takeaway'?

12. In which religion is Krishna a god?

13. In which sport are there playing positions called flanker, fly half and tight-head prop?

14. Which gas, which has the chemical symbol N, is the most common element in the earth's atmosphere?

15. Giant home furnishing retailer Ikea was founded in which country?

16. What boy's name is also the capital of the Falkland Islands?

17. TV comedy 'Dad's Army' was set during which conflict?

18. Stilton, Wensleydale and Yarg are types of which food?

19. The River Taff flows through which city?
    a) Cardiff
    b) Dublin
    c) Edinburgh

20. How many legs does a spider have?
    a) 6
    b) 8
    c) 10

EASY

Answers to Quiz 4: Fill in the Blank – Movies

1. The King's Speech
2. The Hurt Locker
3. No Country For Old Men
4. Million Dollar Baby
5. The Lord of the Rings: The Return of the King
6. American Beauty
7. The English Patient
8. The Silence of the Lambs
9. Dances With Wolves
10. Out of Africa
11. Chariots of Fire
12. One Flew Over the Cuckoo's Nest
13. The French Connection
14. In The Heat of the Night
15. The Sound of Music
16. Around the World in 80 Days
17. On the Waterfront
18. From Here to Eternity
19. The Greatest Show on Earth
20. Gone with the Wind

Quiz 6: History

EASY

1. In which decade did Queen Elizabeth II become the British monarch?

2. Lee Harvey Oswald assassinated which political figure?

3. Which sporting event was founded by Baron Pierre de Coubertin?

4. J Edgar Hoover was the founder and long-time head of which American organization?

5. In which year did the September 11 attacks on the East coast of America take place?

6. Which country was known by the Romans as Hibernia?

7. In which year did the Falklands War take place?

8. Which Italian fascist leader was known as 'Il Duce'?

9. Who was the first British monarch to have the title 'Empress of India'?

10. In which century did the first postage stamp come into use?

11. Who was the last leader of the Soviet Union?

12. Who is Britain's longest-serving Labour prime minister?

13. Roundheads and Cavaliers were the on the opposing side in which conflict?

14. In which country was Adolf Hitler born?

15. In 1066, William the Conqueror became king of England after beating Harold's forces in which battle?

16. Which English monarch was the father of Elizabeth I?

17. Han, Ming and Qing were ruling dynasties in which country?

18. In 1958, 23 people were killed after the plane carrying the Manchester United football team crashed at an airport in which city?

19. What was the only part of the British Isles that was occupied by Germany during World War II?
    a) Channel Islands
    b) Isle of Man
    c) Isle of Wight

20. What was the name of the British policy in the 1930s that allowed Hitler to expand German territory?
    a) Advancement
    b) Allowance
    c) Appeasement

EASY

Answers to Quiz 5: Pot Luck

1. Hawaii	11. Ant and Dec
2. 80	12. Hinduism
3. St David	13. Rugby union
4. Blue	14. Nitrogen
5. Australia	15. Sweden
6. 1000	16. Stanley
7. Christmas	17. World War II
8. Skin	18. Cheese
9. Alan Davies	19. Cardiff
10. Melbourne	20. 8

Quiz 7: Pot Luck

1. The phrase 'three strikes and you're out' originates from which sport?

2. Which English city is often abbreviated to Soton?

3. Which mountain range forms a natural border between France and Spain?

4. Shannon Airport is in which European country?

5. Nora Batty was a character in which long-running TV comedy?

6. Murrayfield Stadium is in which British city?

7. In which sport may a player score a birdie, eagle or albatross?

8. Goal shooter, goal attack and wing attack are playing positions in which sport?

9. The underwater city of Bikini Bottom is the setting for which popular children's cartoon?

10. Colombo is the largest city of which Asian country?

11. Which sci-fi character has been played on the big screen by Leonard Nimoy and more recently by Zachary Quinto?

12. How many English monarchs have been called Edward?

13. In Tolkien's 'The Hobbit', what type of fictional creature is Smaug?

14. Carrow Road is the home ground of which English football team?

15. The 'Financial Times' newspaper is printed on what colour paper?

Answers – page 17

16. For what is 'the dunny' an Australian slang term?

17. The Canary Islands are a region of which country?

18. In the popular video game series, what type of animal is Sonic?

19. Jim Robinson was a character in which TV soap?
    a) Coronation Street
    b) EastEnders
    c) Neighbours

20. On Valentine's Day 2014 Simon Cowell became a father for the first time. What is his son's name?
    a) Ernie
    b) Eric
    c) Ronnie

EASY

Answers to Quiz 6: History

1. 1950s	11. Mikhail Gorbachev
2. John F Kennedy	12. Tony Blair
3. The Olympic Games	13. The English Civil War
4. The FBI	14. Austria
5. 2001	15. The Battle of Hastings
6. Ireland	16. Henry VIII
7. 1982	17. China
8. Mussolini	18. Munich
9. Queen Victoria	19. Channel Islands
10. 19th	20. Appeasement

Quiz 8: Places

1. The Algarve is a popular tourist location in which country?

2. Berlin is the capital of which country?

3. Which country is bounded by the Atlantic Ocean, English Channel and the Mediterranean Sea?

4. Which European capital city sits on the banks of the River Liffey?

5. The volcano Mount Etna lies on which Mediterranean island?

6. Which two English counties traditionally make up the region of East Anglia?

7. What name is shared by a town in Lincolnshire and the capital of the US state of Massachusetts?

8. Which arm of the Mediterranean Sea lies between the Italian and Balkan peninsulas?

9. Canberra is the capital city of which Commonwealth country?

10. Lazio, Sardinia and Sicily are regions of which country?

11. Which ocean is connected to the Atlantic Ocean by the Panama Canal?

12. Tenerife and Lanzarote are part of which group of islands?

13. Home to many technology companies, Silicon Valley is in which American state?

14. The Apennines are a mountain range in which European country?

15. The Midlands town of Stratford sits on which river?

16. Chicago is the largest city in which American state?

17. The Azores are an island territory belonging to which European country?

18. Which Greek island gives its name to a type of lettuce?

19. What man's name is also the name of a Welsh port town in the Vale of Glamorgan?
    a) Barry
    b) Garry
    c) Harry

20. The Atlas Mountains are in which continent?
    a) Africa
    b) Europe
    c) South America

EASY

Answers to Quiz 7: Pot Luck

1. Baseball
2. Southampton
3. The Pyrenees
4. Ireland
5. Last of the Summer Wine
6. Edinburgh
7. Golf
8. Netball
9. SpongeBob SquarePants
10. Sri Lanka
11. Mr Spock
12. Eight
13. Dragon
14. Norwich City
15. Pink
16. The toilet
17. Spain
18. Hedgehog
19. Neighbours
20. Eric

Quiz 9: Pot Luck

EASY

1. Greens, fairways and bunkers are part of the setting for which sport?

2. Which UK city was the venue for the 2014 Commonwealth Games?

3. Molineux is the home ground of which English football team?

4. Water Lilies is a painting by which French artist?

5. Ramsay Street is the setting for which TV soap?

6. The Great Barrier Reef lies off the coast of which country?

7. In 2014, which singer and musician launched a range of eyewear under the brand 'ill.i.Optics'?

8. On a tournament dartboard, what colour is the bullseye?

9. Which European capital is known as the 'Eternal City'?

10. Which pair of superheroes are known as the 'Dynamic Duo'?

11. Alf Stewart is a character in which TV soap?

12. What are made and repaired by a cobbler?

13. Which Olympic sport takes place in a velodrome?

14. Which joint connects the foot to the leg?

15. In London what are Tate Modern, Tate Britain and White Cube?

16. What name is shared by a brass musical instrument and a type of ice-cream cone?

17. Prior to joining the euro, what was the currency of Spain?

18. Which American city was also the title of a 2002 Oscar-winning film starring Catherine Zeta-Jones and Richard Gere?

19. What item, useful in the rain, provided the title of a hit single for Rihanna?
    a) Headscarf
    b) Raincoat
    c) Umbrella

20. How many legs does a scorpion have?
    a) 6
    b) 8
    c) 10

EASY

Answers to Quiz 8: Places

1. Portugal	11. Pacific
2. Germany	12. The Canary Islands
3. France	13. California
4. Dublin	14. Italy
5. Sicily	15. River Avon
6. Norfolk and Suffolk	16. Illinois
7. Boston	17. Portugal
8. Adriatic Sea	18. Cos
9. Australia	19. Barry
10. Italy	20. Africa

Quiz 10: Britain

1. Aintree racecourse is in which city?

2. Coniston Water and Derwent Water are part of which UK National Park?

3. Speaker's Corner is a feature of which London park?

4. Harley Street in London is commonly associated with which profession?

5. What is the national flower of Wales?

6. Ringway airport serves which British city?

7. Which fortification stretches from Bowness-on-Solway to Wallsend?

8. St Mungo's Cathedral is in which Scottish city?

9. Glyndebourne is associated with which type of music?

10. The Balti Triangle is an area of which British city?

11. The Derby is held at which English racecourse?

12. Which English county is known as 'Shakespeare's County'?

13. Which London suburb gave its name to a series of film comedies including 'The Ladykillers' and 'The Lavender Hill Mob'?

14. The naked horse-rider Lady Godiva is associated with which English city?

15. Which Suffolk town is known as the home of thoroughbred horseracing?

16. The Clifton Suspension Bridge spans which river?

17. Which district of London is home to a major flower show each May?

18. Ynys Mon is the Welsh name for which island?

19. All distances from London are measured to which point?
    a) Charing Cross
    b) Leicester Square
    c) Greenwich

20. Bara brith is a dish that originates from which part of Britain?
    a) England
    b) Scotland
    c) Wales

EASY

Answers to Quiz 9: Pot Luck

1. Golf
2. Glasgow
3. Wolverhampton Wanderers
4. Claude Monet
5. Neighbours
6. Australia
7. Will.I.Am
8. Red
9. Rome
10. Batman and Robin
11. Home and Away
12. Shoes
13. Cycling
14. Ankle
15. Art galleries
16. Cornet
17. Peseta
18. Chicago
19. Umbrella
20. 8

Quiz 11: Pot Luck

1. By population, what is the largest city in Scotland?

2. The soap opera 'Brookside' was set in which city?

3. Freestyle and Greco-Roman are disciplines of which Olympic sport?

4. Quebec is a province in which Commonwealth country?

5. In which quiz show do contestants answer a 'starter for 10'?

6. Niall Horan, Zayn Malik, Liam Payne, Harry Styles and Louis Tomlinson are members of which band?

7. What was the name of the operatic boy band that won 'Britain's Got Talent' in 2014?

8. R.I. are the initials of which American state?

9. A round of championship golf consists of how many holes?

10. The cricket ground Trent Bridge is in which English city?

11. The province of Rioja, which gives its name to the famous drink, is in which country?

12. Ibrox Stadium and Celtic Park are football grounds in which British city?

13. Trumpet, trombone and French horn of members of which family of musical instruments?

14. Which department of the British government is responsible for promoting and protecting UK interests overseas?

15. The Latin phrase 'Utrinque Paratus' is the motto of which regiment of the British Army?

Answers – page 25

16. The guilder was the former currency of which European country?

17. Which of tennis' four major championships is played on clay?

18. If an event is biannual how many times a year does it take place?

19. Complete the title of a popular BBC sitcom from the 1980s – 'Ever Decreasing...'?
    a) Circles
    b) Squares
    c) Triangles

20. What was the maiden name of American singer Beyoncé?
    a) Davis
    b) Knowles
    c) Meo

Answers to Quiz 10: Britain

1.	Liverpool	11.	Epsom
2.	The Lake District	12.	Warwickshire
3.	Hyde Park	13.	Ealing
4.	Medicine	14.	Coventry
5.	Daffodil	15.	Newmarket
6.	Manchester	16.	Avon
7.	Hadrian's Wall	17.	Chelsea
8.	Glasgow	18.	Anglesey
9.	Opera	19.	Charing Cross
10.	Birmingham	20.	Wales

Quiz 12: Movies

The following movies all have a number in their title. Fill in the blank.

1. 'The Magnificent ____' (1960)

2. 'The ____ Steps' (1935 and 1959)

3. '____ Weddings and a Funeral' (1994)

4. 'The ____ Year Old Virgin' (2005)

5. 'Zero Dark ____' (2012)

6. '____ First Dates' (2004)

7. '____ Hour Party People' (2002)

8. 'Gone in ____ Seconds' (2000)

9. 'The Taking of Pelham ____' (2009)

10. '____ Angry Men' (1957)

11. '____ Days Later' (2002)

12. '____ Men and a Baby' (1987)

13. '____ : A Space Odyssey' (1968)

14. '____ to ____' (1980)

15. 'The ____ Year Itch' (1955)

16. '____ Jump Street' (2012)

17. '(____) Days of Summer' (2009)

18. '____ Things I Hate About You' (1999)

19. 'District ____' (2009)

20. '____ Hours' (2010)

EASY

Answers to Quiz 11: Pot Luck

1. Glasgow
2. Liverpool
3. Wrestling
4. Canada
5. University Challenge
6. One Direction
7. Collabro
8. Rhode Island
9. 18
10. Nottingham
11. Spain
12. Glasgow
13. Brass
14. Foreign Office
15. Parachute Regiment
16. The Netherlands
17. French Open
18. Twice
19. Circles
20. Knowles

Quiz 13: Pot Luck

EASY

1. Which is the only tennis major tournament to be played on grass?

2. TV drama 'The Smoke' centres on which of the emergency services?

3. Which Spice Girl won the Designer of the Year award at the 2011 British Fashion Awards?

4. A pug is a breed of which domestic pet?

5. Which European capital city is known in its native language as Praha?

6. Motor manufacturer Toyota is based in which country?

7. Which British athlete was the first man to run a mile in under four minutes?

8. Which actress, best known for playing TV sleuth Jessica Fletcher, was made a Dame in 2014?

9. What colour beret is worn by members of the Royal Marines?

10. What name is shared by a famous Scottish golf course and a football ground in the English Midlands?

11. What does the G in the initials 'GMT' stand for?

12. Which actor played the antique-loving title character in the TV drama 'Lovejoy'?

13. Which northern English city was known in Roman times as Deva?

14. Calcio is the Italian word for which sport?

15. Dick Grayson is the alter ego of which comic-book superhero sidekick?

16. Which outdoor sport is played at Lord's?

17. GTA are the initials of which best-selling video game?

18. The hit film and stage musical 'The Commitments' is set in which city?

19. The word 'antipodean' is used to refer to people from which of the following countries?
    a) America
    b) Australia
    c) Canada

20. Which of the following is a group of prestigious American universities?
    a) Holly League
    b) Ivy League
    c) Mistletoe League

EASY

Answers to Quiz 12: Movies

1.	Seven	11.	28
2.	39	12.	Three
3.	Four	13.	2001
4.	40	14.	Nine to Five
5.	Thirty	15.	Seven
6.	50	16.	21
7.	24	17.	500
8.	Sixty	18.	10
9.	123	19.	9
10.	12	20.	127

Quiz 14: Science

1. At what temperature in Celsius does water boil?

2. Which travels faster, light or sound?

3. Solar energy is made from heat or light from what?

4. Which English naturalist first proposed the theory of evolution?

5. What is the fourth planet from the sun?

6. NaCl is the chemical formula of which common substance?

7. Botany is the scientific study of what?

8. By what name is ethanol more commonly known?

9. In the human body, saddle, ball-and-socket, hinge and pivot are types of what?

10. True or false – alkalis have a pH level below 7?

11. What is the most abundant element in the universe?

12. The thalamus, cerebrum and cerebellum are found in which organ of the body?

13. What is measured using the decibel scale?

14. The patella is the scientific name for which bone of the human body?

15. Which English scientist's three laws of motion explain the relationship between a body and the forces acting upon it?

16. What is the branch of medicine that deals with the manufacture of artificial body parts?

17. The ulna and humerus are bones in which part of the body?

18. Which planet of the Solar System orbits closest to the sun?

19. Au is the chemical symbol for which metal?
    a) aluminium
    b) gold
    c) silver

20. Rickets is caused by a deficiency of which vitamin?
    a) A
    b) B
    c) D

EASY

Answers to Quiz 13: Pot Luck

1. Wimbledon
2. Fire brigade
3. Victoria Beckham
4. Dog
5. Prague
6. Japan
7. Sir Roger Bannister
8. Angela Lansbury
9. Green
10. St Andrews
11. Greenwich
12. Ian McShane
13. Chester
14. Football
15. Robin
16. Cricket
17. Grand Theft Auto
18. Dublin
19. Australia
20. Ivy League

Quiz 15: Pot Luck

EASY

1. Greenwich Village is a neighbourhood in which American city?

2. How many signs of the zodiac are there?

3. Joanne Kathleen are the forenames of which best-selling author?

4. CIA are the initials of which American organisation?

5. Europe is separated from Africa by which sea?

6. What Italian city is known locally as Napoli?

7. Nairobi is the capital city of which African country?

8. How many legs does an insect have?

9. Boy band One Direction found fame after appearing in which TV talent show?

10. Which unit of length is abbreviated to cm?

11. The Canary Islands lie off the coast of which continent?

12. Stade de France is a famous stadium in which city?

13. In terms of area, what is the largest country in South America?

14. The samba, fandango and bossa nova are types of what?

15. What is the world's largest dog show?

16. True or false – a bee can only sting once?

17. Which actor and comedian caused controversy in 2013 after saying that 'the overthrow of the current political system is the only way I can be enthused about politics'?

18. What does the 'MI' in 'MI6' stand for?

19. The National Exhibition Centre is located in which English city?
    a) Birmingham
    b) Manchester
    c) Newcastle

20. Which comedy family lived at Number 42?
    a) The Kumars
    b) The Steptoes
    c) The Trotters

EASY

Answers to Quiz 14: Science

1. 10°C
2. Light
3. The sun
4. Charles Darwin
5. Mars
6. Salt
7. Plants
8. Alcohol
9. Joints
10. False

11. Hydrogen
12. The brain
13. The loudness of sound
14. Kneecap
15. Sir Isaac Newton
16. Prosthetics
17. The arm
18. Mercury
19. Gold
20. Vitamin D

Quiz 16: Food and Drink

1. Teriyaki is a cuisine associated with which country?

2. The name of which dessert translates into English as 'burnt cream'?

3. The juice of which fruit is fermented to make cider?

4. What type of Italian spicy sausage derives its name from the Latin word for salt?

5. Emmental cheese originates from which country?

6. What shape is fusili pasta?

7. Anjou, Clapp's Favourite and Concorde are varieties of which fruit?

8. Which food is known in French as 'frites'?

9. On which day of the year are hot cross buns traditionally eaten?

10. Which area of Manchester gives its name to a cake filled with dried fruit?

11. Which nut is used to flavour the alcoholic drink amaretto?

12. Which vegetable is also known as ladies' fingers?

13. What name connects a famous British soldier and statesman and a dish of beef that is wrapped and cooked in pastry?

14. What is the main ingredient in the Indian drink lassi?

15. Hock wine comes from which country?

16. The name of which type of thin spaghetti translates into English as 'little worms'?

17. The Japanese alcoholic drink sake is made from the fermented juice of what?

18. Which town in Germany gives its name to a pink and yellow, quartered sponge cake?

19. Which spirit is used to make a screwdriver cocktail?
    a) gin
    b) vodka
    c) whisky

20. Smokies are associated with which Scottish town?
    a) Arbroath
    b) Dundee
    c) Inverness

EASY

Answers to Quiz 15: Pot Luck

1. New York City
2. 12
3. JK Rowling
4. Central Intelligence Agency
5. Mediterranean Sea
6. Naples
7. Kenya
8. Six
9. The X Factor
10. Centimetre
11. Africa
12. Paris
13. Brazil
14. Dance
15. Crufts
16. True
17. Russell Brand
18. Military Intelligence
19. Birmingham
20. The Kumars

Quiz 17: Pot Luck

1. By population, what is the second largest city in England?

2. Which religious leader was named 'Time' magazine's 'Person of the Year' for 2013?

3. What is the maximum speed a car is allowed to travel on a UK motorway?

4. In which novel by Charles Dickens did a character called the Artful Dodger appear?

5. Fill in the missing word from this famous Shakespearean quote: 'Now is the ____ of our discontent'?

6. Which culinary TV talent shows features rounds called Signature Challenge, Technical Challenge and Showstopper Challenge?

7. Which sign of the zodiac is represented by the ram?

8. What do the initials 'HMRC' stand for?

9. Who created the fictional detective Hercule Poirot?

10. Arachnophobia is the fear of what type of creatures?

11. Elland Road is the home ground of which English football team?

12. The long-running sitcom 'Frasier' was set in which American city?

13. Which English team beat Bayern Munich in the 2012 Champions League final?

14. Basil Rathbone, Jeremy Brett and Benedict Cumberbatch have all played which fictional character?

15. Ruby Walsh and Tony McCoy are notable performers in which sport?

16. What does the 'M' in the initials 'GMT' stand for?

17. Richie Benaud, Henry Blofeld and Charles Colville are commentators on which sport?

18. Former prime minister Gordon Brown lost the sight in one eye after an accident playing which sport?

19. John Thaw played which TV detective?
    a) Frost
    b) Morse
    c) Taggart

20. What is the nickname of the Argentina national rugby team?
    a) The Gazelles
    b) The Hounds
    c) The Pumas

EASY

Answers to Quiz 16: Food and Drink

1. Japan
2. Crème brûlée
3. Apple
4. Salami
5. Switzerland
6. Corkscrew
7. Pear
8. Chips
9. Good Friday
10. Eccles
11. Almond
12. Okra
13. Wellington
14. Yoghurt
15. Germany
16. Vermicelli
17. Rice
18. Battenberg
19. Vodka
20. Arbroath

Quiz 18: Alias Smith and Jones

1. Which British actress married Michael Douglas in 2000?

2. Which two-time Oscar-winning actress plays Violet Crawley, Dowager Countess of Grantham in TV drama 'Downton Abbey'?

3. Which footballer-turned-actor was once sent off just three seconds into a game?

4. Which Mancunian actor played Les Battersby in TV soap 'Coronation Street'?

5. Which Jamaican singer and actress played May Day in the James Bond film 'A View to a Kill'?

6. The 1998 hit 'I Don't Want to Miss a Thing' was the only UK top-ten single for which American rock band?

7. Dean Jones, Simon Jones and Geraint Jones were all internationals at which sport?

8. Which actor received an Oscar nomination for his portrayal of Muhammad Ali in the 2001 film 'Ali'?

9. Which member of the Rolling Stones drowned in a swimming pool at the age of 27 on 3 July 1969?

10. What name is shared by a veteran Welsh singer and the title character in a classic 18th-century novel by Henry Fielding?

11. Jones is the most common surname in which country of the UK?

12. Which female singer, who topped the charts in 2002 with the album 'Come Away with Me', is the daughter of sitar player Ravi Shankar?

13. Who was the controversial lead singer with Manchester band The Smiths?

14. Who was the first woman to win five athletics medals at a single Olympic Games but later returned them after admitting using banned substances?

15. Which 18th-century Scottish philosopher and economist wrote 'The Wealth of Nations'?

16. Vickie Lynn Hogan was the real name of which American model and TV personality who married an oil mogul 62 years her senior and died in 2007 aged 39?

17. Which England footballer's career took in stops at Leeds United, Manchester United, Newcastle United and Milton Keynes Dons?

18. Smith and Wesson is a famous manufacturer of what?

19. What is sold at Smithfield Market?
    a) fish   b) flowers   c) meat

20. Which Scandinavian popsters topped the charts in 1998 with Doctor Jones?
    a) Aqua   b) Whigfield   c) Abba

Answers to Quiz 17: Pot Luck

1. Birmingham
2. Pope Francis
3. 70mph
4. Oliver Twist
5. Winter
6. The Great British Bake Off
7. Aries
8. Her Majesty's Revenue and Customs
9. Agatha Christie
10. Spiders
11. Leeds United
12. Seattle
13. Chelsea
14. Sherlock Holmes
15. Horse racing
16. Mean
17. Cricket
18. Rugby union
19. Morse
20. The Pumas

Quiz 19: Pot Luck

1. What is the largest city in Northern Ireland?

2. Claustrophobia is the fear of what?

3. In relation to the US TV drama, what do the initials 'CSI' stand for?

4. Palermo is the capital and largest city of which Mediterranean island?

5. Bollywood is a name given to films from which country?

6. What in London are Barts, Guy's and St Thomas'?

7. The famous 'To be or not to be' speech appears in which Shakespeare play?

8. Tom-tom, snare and bass are types of what musical instrument?

9. A chess board has how many squares?

10. 'Louis, I think this is the beginning of a beautiful friendship' is the last line of which classic movie?

11. An equilateral triangle has how many sides of the same length?

12. Which item of women's clothing is also the name of a cut of beef?

13. Which star sign is represented by a bull?

14. Which is longer – one metre or one yard?

15. What does the 'A' in the medical condition 'ADHD' stand for?

16. An animal called Simba is the central character in which film and musical franchise?

17. Old Trafford cricket ground is in which city?

18. Michael O'Leary is the CEO of which Irish airline?

19. Tripe is a meat dish that comes from which part of an animal?
    a) brain
    b) breast
    c) stomach

20. China is a slang word for what?
    a) enemy
    b) mate
    c) brother

EASY

Answers to Quiz 18: Alias Smith and Jones

1. Catherine Zeta-Jones
2. Dame Maggie Smith
3. Vinnie Jones
4. Bruce Jones
5. Grace Jones
6. Aerosmith
7. Cricket
8. Will Smith
9. Brian Jones
10. Tom Jones
11. Wales
12. Norah Jones
13. Morrissey
14. Marion Jones
15. Adam Smith
16. Anna Nicole Smith
17. Alan Smith
18. Guns and firearms
19. Meat
20. Aqua

Quiz 20: Return of the Mac

EASY

1. The Golden Arches are the symbol of which global company?

2. Which American actor won an Oscar in 2014 for his performance in 'Dallas Buyers Club'?

3. Who was the presenter of TV show 'Big Brother' between 2000 and 2010?

4. Which tennis player won the Men's Singles at Wimbledon in 1981, 1983 and 1984?

5. Which actor played Gandalf in the 'Lord of the Rings' film series?

6. 'The Big Impression' was a TV show that starred which British mimic?

7. 'Five Colours in Her Hair', 'Obviously' and 'I'll Be OK' were number-one hit singles for which British band?

8. Mount McKinley is the highest mountain in which continent?

9. Which team won eight Formula One constructors' titles between 1974 and 1998?

10. Between 1997 and 2011 Mary McAleese was the President of which country?

11. Which play by Shakespeare is known as 'the Scottish play'?

12. The final series of TV's 'Pop Idol' was won by which Scottish singer?

13. In the 'Star Wars' film series, Obi-Wan Kenobi has been played by Sir Alec Guinness and which Scottish actor?

EASY

14. 'Pipes of Peace' was the only solo UK number-one single by which pop legend?

15. John McClane is the central character in which action film franchise?

16. Which supermodel was nicknamed 'The Body'?

17. Barack Obama beat which Republican Party candidate to win the US presidency in 2008?

18. Which Northern Irish golfer won the 2012 US PGA Championship?

19. Who was the British prime minister from 1957 until 1963?

20. Which character in the 'Star Trek' film franchise has been played by DeForest Kelley and Karl Urban?

Answers to Quiz 19: Pot Luck

1. Belfast
2. Small, confined spaces
3. Crime Scene Investigation
4. Sicily
5. India
6. Hospitals
7. Hamlet
8. Drum
9. 64
10. Casablanca
11. Three
12. Skirt
13. Taurus
14. One metre
15. Attention
16. The Lion King
17. Manchester
18. Ryanair
19. Stomach
20. Mate (from China plate)

Quiz 21: Pot Luck

1. Km is an abbreviation to denote what distance?

2. Which celebrity couple have children called Brooklyn, Romeo, Harper and Cruz?

3. The religions Hinduism, Buddhism, Jainism and Sikhism all originated in which country?

4. Ricky Gervais played David Brent in which TV comedy?

5. Ibracadabra is the nickname of which European footballing superstar?

6. S4C is a television station in which part of the UK?

7. Which common domestic pet is known in French as 'un lapin'?

8. What is Britain's longest-running TV soap?

9. What do the initials 'CCTV' stand for?

10. What name is given to the person who directs an orchestra using hand and arm gestures?

11. In measurement, a gallon is equal to how many quarts?

12. What type of establishments are Wormwood Scrubs, Strangeways and Winson Green?

13. What nationality is the multiple major-winning golfer Ernie Els?

14. In the TV show 'The Simpsons', what is the name of the family that lives next door to Homer and Marge Simpson?

15. The Garda Síochána is the name of the police force in which country?

16. What is the only city in Cornwall?

17. Twins represent which sign of the zodiac?

18. Which popular British game show is known in America as 'Family Feud'?

19. What phrase is used to describe an elected official whose time in office is due to end shortly?
    a) lame cat
    b) lame dog
    c) lame duck

20. Portman Road is the home ground of which English football club?
    a) Aston Villa
    b) Derby County
    c) Ipswich Town

EASY

Answers to Quiz 20: Return of the Mac

1. McDonald's	11. Macbeth
2. Matthew McConaughey	12. Michelle McManus
3. Davina McCall	13. Ewan McGregor
4. John McEnroe	14. Sir Paul McCartney
5. Sir Ian McKellen	15. Die Hard
6. Alistair McGowan	16. Elle Macpherson
7. McFly	17. John McCain
8. North America	18. Rory McIlroy
9. McLaren	19. Sir Harold MacMillan
10. Republic of Ireland	20. Dr Leonard 'Bones' McCoy

Quiz 22: Reality TV

1. Which Take That star has appeared on the judging panel of 'The X Factor'?

2. What is the maximum total score a couple can receive for a single dance on 'Strictly Come Dancing'?

3. What type of animal was Pudsey, who was part of the winning act in 'Britain's Got Talent' in 2012?

4. Kian Egan, the winner of 'I'm a Celebrity ... Get Me Out of Here' in 2013, was a member of which Irish boy band?

5. In which series do the professionals David Whiston, Frankie Poultney and Brianne Delcourt appear?

6. Who was the first female winner of 'The X Factor'?

7. Fran Newman-Young, Victoria Baker-Harber and Spencer Matthews feature in which scripted reality show?

8. A nightclub called 'The Sugar Hut' features in which scripted reality show?

9. Which former 'Brookside' actor was later a runner-up on 'The X Factor' and a winner of 'Dancing on Ice'?

10. Which female singer won 'The X Factor' in 2013?

11. Which 'Strictly Come Dancing' judge appeared in the video for Elton John's song 'I'm Still Standing'?

12. Which Pussycat Doll joined the judging panel on 'The X Factor' in 2012?

13. Who is the male presenter of 'Dancing on Ice'?

14. Sharon Osbourne threw a glass of water over which fellow judge during the second series of 'The X Factor'?

15. Which choirmaster and broadcaster was awarded an OBE in 2012 for his services to music?

EASY

16. Who was Bruce Forsyth's regular co-presenter on 'Strictly Come Dancing'?

17. 2007 'Dancing on Ice' winner Kyran Bracken was a professional at which sport?

18. Harry Judd, the winner of the 2011 series of 'Strictly Come Dancing' is a member of which pop group?

19. 'Strictly Come Dancing' star Brendon Cole is from which country?
    a) Australia
    b) New Zealand
    c) South Africa

20. Which of the following was not a judge in the first series of 'The X Factor'?
    a) Simon Cowell
    b) Louis Walsh
    c) Pete Waterman

Answers to Quiz 21: Pot Luck

1. Kilometre
2. David and Victoria Beckham
3. India
4. The Office
5. Zlatan Ibrahimovic
6. Wales
7. Rabbit
8. Coronation Street
9. Closed circuit television
10. Conductor
11. Four
12. Prisons
13. South African
14. The Flanders
15. Republic of Ireland
16. Truro
17. Gemini
18. Family Fortunes
19. Lame duck
20. Ipswich Town

Quiz 23: Pot Luck

1. Which famous fictional detective is noted for wearing a deerstalker hat?

2. In 1947 India gained independence from which country?

3. What nationality is darts champion Michael Van Gerwen?

4. Which former member of the band Mis-Teeq went on to become a judge on 'Strictly Come Dancing' and 'Britain's Got Talent'?

5. A pentagon is a shape with how many sides?

6. What nationality is the multiple Formula One world champion Sebastian Vettel?

7. What item of formal clothing is sometimes abbreviated to DJ?

8. In which reality TV series do competitors earn treats for completing the 'Dingo Dollar Challenge'?

9. Schnauzer is a breed of which domestic animal?

10. Which TV soap was originally set in the village of Beckindale?

11. What position in rugby is also a slang term for a prostitute?

12. What name is shared by a dating show hosted by Paddy McGuinness and a song by indie rock band Franz Ferdinand?

13. What two-word French phrase is said when wishing someone a good journey?

14. In relation to home improvements, what do the initials 'DIY' stand for?

15. What style of sunglasses is also another name for a pilot?

16. What unit of weight is abbreviated to 'lb'?

17. Which European mountain translates into English as 'White Mountain'?

18. In March 2013, Justin Welby succeeded Rowan Williams in which religious post?

19. By what name are Belgium, Luxembourg and The Netherlands known collectively?
    a) The High Countries
    b) The Low Countries
    c) The Narrow Countries

20. What was the first name of the composer Beethoven?
    a) Frederic
    b) Ludwig
    c) Wolfgang

Answers to Quiz 22: Reality TV

1. Gary Barlow	11. Bruno Tonioli
2. 40	12. Nicole Scherzinger
3. Dog	13. Phillip Schofield
4. Westlife	14. Louis Walsh
5. Dancing on Ice	15. Gareth Malone
6. Leona Lewis	16. Tess Daly
7. Made in Chelsea	17. Rugby union
8. The Only Way Is Essex	18. McFly
9. Ray Quinn	19. New Zealand
10. Sam Bailey	20. Pete Waterman

Quiz 24: Religion

1. The pope is the leader of which Christian denomination?

2. Hinduism, Judaism, Christianity, Sikhism and Islam were all founded on which continent?

3. According to the Bible, Jesus was born in which town?

4. In which religion are the most important duties known as the 'Five Pillars'?

5. A small skullcap called a kippa is worn by some followers of which religion?

6. Which Christian festival marks the resurrection of Jesus Christ?

7. The most senior clergyman in the Church of England is the Archbishop of which city?

8. What is the holy book of Islam?

9. Muslims fast during the ninth month of the Islamic calendar. What is that month called?

10. Taoism is a religion native to which Asian country?

11. When praying, muslims are supposed to face which city?

12. True or false – in the 2011 UK census 176,632 people identified their religion as Jedi?

13. In the Bible, the Wise Men brought which three gifts to honour the birth of Christ?

14. The Jewish sabbath begins on which day of the week?

15. In Christianity, what is the period of 40 days prior to Easter known as?

Answers – page 51

16. Which religion was founded in the 16th century by Guru Nanak?

17. In the Bible, what is the first book of the Old Testament?

18. And what is the first book of the New Testament?

19. Purim is a new-year festival celebrated in which religion?
    a) Buddhism
    b) Islam
    c) Judaism

20. With over two billion followers worldwide, what is the largest religion in the world?
    a) Christianity
    b) Islam
    c) Judaism

EASY

Answers to Quiz 23: Pot Luck

1. Sherlock Holmes
2. Britain
3. Dutch
4. Alesha Dixon
5. Five
6. German
7. Dinner jacket
8. I'm a Celebrity ... Get Me Out of Here
9. Dog
10. Emmerdale
11. Hooker
12. Take Me Out
13. Bon voyage
14. Do it yourself
15. Aviator
16. Pound
17. Mont Blanc
18. Archbishop of Canterbury
19. The Low Countries
20. Ludwig

Quiz 25: Pot Luck

EASY

1. In measurement, how many inches are in one foot?

2. What nationality are the fashion designers Dolce & Gabbana?

3. Who is singer Lily Allen's famous father?

4. What is the name of Paul McCartney's fashion designer daughter?

5. Who is the head judge on TV talent show 'Strictly Come Dancing'?

6. Tom Daley is an Olympic medal winner in which sport?

7. Which British singer won an Oscar in 2013 for the theme song to the James Bond film 'Skyfall'?

8. Which famous sitcom family lived in Nelson Mandela House?

9. A Francophile is a lover of the culture of which country?

10. A rhombus is a shape with how many sides?

11. Curveball, left-field and heavy hitter are terms that derive from which sport?

12. Xenophobia is an irrational fear of what?

13. In TV quiz show 'University Challenge', each team is made up of how many contestants?

14. In which decade was hospital drama 'Casualty' broadcast for the first time?

15. The name of which planet features in the name of a 2014 Brit award-winning musician?

16. In poker, which of the 'face' cards has the lowest value?

17. How many English kings have been called George?

18. Model and reality TV star Abbey Clancy is married to which footballer?

19. The Golden Gate Bridge is in which American city?
    a) Los Angeles
    b) New York
    c) San Francisco

20. Which of the following was used to describe an ancient trade route that linked China with the west?
    a) Cotton Road
    b) Silk Road
    c) Wool Road

EASY

Answers to Quiz 24: Religion

1. Roman Catholicism
2. Asia
3. Bethlehem
4. Islam
5. Judaism
6. Easter
7. Canterbury
8. The Qu'ran
9. Ramadan
10. China
11. Mecca
12. True
13. Gold, frankincense and myrrh
14. Friday
15. Lent
16. Sikhism
17. Genesis
18. The Gospel According to St Matthew
19. Judaism
20. Christianity

Quiz 26: Numbers

1. Which conflict started in 1914 and ended in 1918?

2. 'Second Coming' was an album by which Manchester indie rockers?

3. By what name was the German state known between 1933 and 1945?

4. Oliver Stone won the Oscar for Best Director in 1989 for which Vietnam War film starring Tom Cruise?

5. What was the name of the 2013 film starring Benedict Cumberbatch as Wikileaks founder Julian Assange?

6. Which 1999 film featured Haley Joel Osment as a boy who communicated with spirits that didn't know they were dead?

7. Complete the phrase that means a state of extreme happiness – seventh...

8. Which English king was born in 1491 and died in 1547?

9. What wood, often used to make cricket bats, is the traditional gift for a ninth wedding anniversary?

10. Which actor in 2005 became the tenth actor to play 'Dr Who'?

11. To leave something until the last minute is to do it at the eleventh...?

12. What term is used to describe the first day of the grouse shooting season in Great Britain?

13. What day and date is considered to be especially unlucky?

14. Born in 1935 in Tibet, Tenzin Gyatso is the 14th person to hold which religious position?

15. Which war was fought between the houses of York and Lancaster during the latter half of the 15th century?

16. With the symbol S, which bright yellow solid is the 16th element of the periodic table?

17. On what date is St Patrick's Day celebrated?

18. The 18th Amendment to the US Constitution banned the manufacture or sale of what?

19. Which British monarch sat on the throne for more than half of the nineteenth century?

20. 'Lincoln', 'Life of Pi' and the 'Star Wars' films were all made by which film studio?

EASY

Answers to Quiz 25: Pot Luck

1. 12
2. Italian
3. Keith Allen
4. Stella
5. Len Goodman
6. Diving
7. Adele
8. The Trotters
9. France
10. Four
11. Baseball
12. Strangers or foreigners
13. Four
14. 1980s
15. Mars (Bruno)
16. Jack
17. Six
18. Peter Crouch
19. San Francisco
20. Silk Road

Quiz 27: Pot Luck

EASY

1. Which former BBC newsreader was runner-up in the 2013 series of 'Strictly Come Dancing'?

2. What do the initials 'VIP' stand for?

3. Which sign of the zodiac is represented by a crab?

4. What type of animal is known in French as 'un oiseau'?

5. The stories featuring fictional detective Wallander are set in which Scandinavian country?

6. In UK finance, what does the acronym 'ISA' stand for?

7. What is the capital city of India?

8. Complete the title of the BBC sitcom starring Adil Ray – 'Citizen...'

9. Which planet of the Solar System is sometimes known as 'the red planet'?

10. How often does a quadrennial event take place?

11. Who is the host of the TV panel show 'QI'?

12. On what date do children traditionally go 'trick or treating'?

13. What surname is shared by a presenter of TV motoring show 'Top Gear' and the first winner of talent show 'American Idol'?

14. In which decade was the first man-made satellite launched into space?

15. English breakfast and darjeeling are varieties of which drink?

16. Zoe Hanna, Tess Bateman and Kathleen 'Dixie' Dixon are characters in which British medical drama?

17. Which rank in the Royal Air Force is abbreviated as 'Sqn Ldr'?

18. 'The Firm', 'The Chamber' and 'The Rainmaker' are novels by which American thriller writer?

19. A 20th anniversary edition of which classic album was released in 2014?
    a) Definitely Maybe
    b) The Stone Roses
    c) The Bends

20. What is the nickname of the city of Chicago?
    a) The Rainy City
    b) The Snowy City
    c) The Windy City

EASY

Answers to Quiz 26: Numbers

1. First World War
2. The Stone Roses
3. The Third Reich
4. Born on the Fourth of July
5. The Fifth Estate
6. The Sixth Sense
7. Heaven
8. Henry VIII
9. Willow
10. David Tennant
11. Hour
12. The Glorious Twelfth
13. Friday the 13th
14. Dalai Lama
15. The War of the Roses
16. Sulphur
17. 17th March
18. Alcohol
19. Queen Victoria
20. 20th Century Fox

Quiz 28: Politics

1. Which politician's first ever tweet was, 'I'm starting Conference with this new Twitter feed about my role as Conservative Leader. I promise there won't be "too many tweets..."'?

2. On which day of the week do UK general elections take place?

3. What colour are the benches in the House of Commons?

4. And what colour are the benches in the House of Lords?

5. The holder of which post is responsible for the the UK's economic and financial policy?

6. Which American president was assassinated on 22 November 1963?

7. Who was Britain's first female prime minister?

8. Whom did Barack Obama succeed as president of the USA?

9. In which year did David Cameron become prime minister?

10. FCO are the initials of which UK government department?

11. In 2013, who was elected as the Chancellor of Germany for a third time?

12. What do the initials 'UKIP' stand for?

13. Which American president was forced to resign due to his involvment in the 'Watergate' scandal?

14. Which veteran Labour politician and diarist died in March 2014 at the age of 88?

15. In 2012, François Hollande succeeded Nicolas Sarkozy as the president of which country?

16. US presidential elections are held on which day of the week?

17. What colour is the front door at 10 Downing Street?

18. In which American state was US president Barack Obama born?

19. 11 Downing Street is the residence of the holder of which political office?
    a) Chancellor of the Exchequer
    b) Foreign Secretary
    c) Home Secretary

20. In British politics, what name is given to an official who maintains discipline in a party?
    a) hammer
    b) vice
    c) whip

EASY

Answers to Quiz 27: Pot Luck

1. Susanna Reid
2. Very Important Person
3. Cancer
4. Bird
5. Sweden
6. Individual Savings Account
7. New Delhi
8. Khan
9. Mars
10. Every four years
11. Stephen Fry
12. 31st October
13. Clarkson
14. 1950s
15. Tea
16. Casualty
17. Squadron Leader
18. John Grisham
19. Definitely Maybe
20. The Windy City

Quiz 29: Pot Luck

1. Grand Central Terminal is a railway station in which US city?

2. Who is TV presenter Tess Daly's famous husband?

3. According to the proverb, what 'is the lowest form of wit'?

4. What name is shared by the actor who played the title character in the 'Captain America' film franchise and a British DJ and broadcaster?

5. Cartoon character Yogi Bear lived in which park?

6. Which organization's flag features 12 gold stars on a dark blue background?

7. Tapas is a style of cuisine associated with which country?

8. In music, what do the initials 'R&B' stand for?

9. The didgeridoo is a musical instrument associated with which country?

10. Which word connects an actor appearing in a crowd scene in a movie and a score in cricket that isn't attributed to a batsman?

11. The motor-racing circuit Estoril is in which country?

12. The Canaries is the nickname of which English football team?

13. 'Hang on a minute lads, I've got a great idea' is the last line of which 1967 crime caper?

14. What does the 'C' in the honour 'CBE' stand for?

15. In UK banking, how many numbers does a sort code have?

16. In the book of the same name, what type of creature was Moby Dick?

EASY

17. 'La Boheme' is an opera by which composer?

18. Complete the title of a famous play by Arthur Miller – 'Death of a...'

19. Opening round matches at the World Snooker Championship are played over the best of how many frames?
    a) 9
    b) 13
    c) 19

20. A synod is a gathering of whom?
    a) bishops
    b) lawyers
    c) surgeons

Answers to Quiz 28: Politics

1. David Cameron
2. Thursday
3. Green
4. Red
5. Chancellor of the Exchequer
6. John F Kennedy
7. Margaret Thatcher
8. George W Bush
9. 2010
10. Foreign and Commonwealth Office
11. Angela Merkel
12. United Kingdom Independence Party
13. Richard Nixon
14. Tony Benn
15. France
16. Tuesday
17. Black
18. Hawaii
19. Chancellor of the Exchequer
20. Whip

Quiz 30: Fill in the Blank – Pop Music

Fill in the missing word from the titles of the following UK number one singles:

1. 'When We ____' – Matt Cardle (2010)

2. '____ Face' – Lady Gaga (2009)

3. 'I ____ a Girl' – Katy Perry (2009)

4. 'All ____ Long' – Kid Rock (2008)

5. 'Just Like a ____' – Pink (2002)

6. 'Somethin' ____' – Robbie Williams and Nicole Kidman (2001)

7. 'No Matter ____' – Boyzone (1998)

8. 'Return of the ____' – Mark Morrison (1996)

9. '____ to a Child' – George Michael (1996)

10. 'Things Can Only Get ____' – D:Ream (1994)

11. 'Rhythm is a ____' – Snap (1992)

12. 'World in ____' – England New Order (1990)

13. 'One ____ in Time' – Whitney Houston (1988)

14. 'I Should Be So ____' – Kylie Minogue (1988)

15. 'The Final ____' – Europe (1986)

16. 'Eye of the ____' – Survivor (1982)

17. 'A Town Called ____' – The Jam (1982)

18. '____ Love' – Soft Cell (1981)

19. 'The Tide is ____' – Blondie (1980)

20. 'What's Another ____' – Johnny Logan (1980)

Answers to Quiz 29: Pot Luck

1.	New York	11.	Portugal
2.	Vernon Kay	12.	Norwich City
3.	Sarcasm	13.	The Italian Job
4.	Chris Evans	14.	Commander
5.	Jellystone	15.	Six
6.	European Union	16.	Whale
7.	Spain	17.	Puccini
8.	Rhythm and blues	18.	Salesman
9.	Australia	19.	19
10.	Extra	20.	Bishops

Quiz 31: Pot Luck

1. Which newsreader was the original host of TV quiz show 'Eggheads'?

2. 'Der Hund' is the German name for what domestic animal?

3. Which sign of the zodiac is represented by a lion?

4. Footballer Frank Lampard started his professional career with which London club?

5. Which two countries are separated by the Tasman Sea?

6. Sheldon Cooper and Howard Wolowitz are characters in which hit US comedy?

7. True or false – TV presenter Vernon Kay and comedian Peter Kay are brothers?

8. In New York City, what colour are taxis?

9. Perkins and Giedroyc are the surnames of which comedy duo?

10. 'I'm Too Sexy' was a US number one single for which British band?

11. Which national daily newspaper is often abbreviated to 'the FT'?

12. British Honduras is the former name of which Central American country?

13. The so-called 'Great Train Robber' Ronnie Biggs spent many years on the run in which South American country?

14. Wien is the local name for which European capital city?

15. What type of food is tagliatelle?

Answers – page 65

16. A mysterious character called 'The Stig' is a regular on which TV show?

17. Which Welsh singer was knighted in 2006 for his services to music?

18. On the TV panel show 'QI' what do the initials 'QI' stand for?

19. Complete the title of the 2006 film – 'The Fast and the Furious...'
    a) Beijing Drift
    b) Singapore Drift
    c) Tokyo Drift

20. Which coffee shop chain sponsors a British book prize?
    a) Costa
    b) Pret a Manger
    c) Starbucks

EASY

Answers to Quiz 30: Fill in the Blank – Pop Music

1.	Collide	11.	Dancer
2.	Poker	12.	Motion
3.	Kissed	13.	Moment
4.	Summer	14.	Lucky
5.	Pill	15.	Countdown
6.	Stupid	16.	Tiger
7.	What	17.	Malice
8.	Mack	18.	Tainted
9.	Jesus	19.	High
10.	Better	20.	Year

Quiz 32: Sport

EASY

1. What colour shirts are worn by members of the British and Irish Lions rugby team?

2. How many dogs take part in a greyhound race?

3. Over what distance is the marathon run?

4. Who won the Grand National for the first time in 2010 riding a horse called Don't Push It?

5. Golf's US Masters takes place annually at which course?

6. Leighton Rees was the first World Champion in which sport?

7. Who captained the Australian team that won the Ashes in 2013/14?

8. Pittodrie is the home ground of which Scottish football team?

9. La Grande Boucle is the nickname of which major sporting event?

10. Over what distance is an Olympic steeplechase run?

11. Which football club won its first major English trophy in 2013 after beating Bradford City in the League Cup final?

12. The French Open tennis tournament is hosted at a stadium named after which World War I pilot?

13. Which sport is played at venues called The Rose Bowl, The Riverside and Grace Road?

14. Who was the first Spaniard to win the Formula One Drivers' Championship?

15. At its centre, how high in feet is a tennis net?

16. Which country won the 2013 Rugby League World Cup?

17. True or false – live pigeon shooting was once an Olympic sport?

18. Mo Farah was one of two British athletes to win a gold medal at the 2013 World Athletics Championship. Who was the other?

19. What nationality is the Formula One racing driver Kevin Magnussen?
    a) Danish
    b) Finnish
    c) Swedish

20. The classic horse race The Derby is run over how many furlongs?
    a) 10   b) 12   c) 14

EASY

Answers to Quiz 31: Pot Luck

1. Dermot Murnaghan
2. Dog
3. Leo
4. West Ham United
5. Australia and New Zealand
6. The Big Bang Theory
7. False
8. Yellow
9. Mel and Sue
10. Right Said Fred
11. Financial Times
12. Belize
13. Brazil
14. Vienna
15. Pasta
16. Top Gear
17. Tom Jones
18. Quite Interesting
19. Tokyo Drift
20. Costa

Quiz 33: Pot Luck

EASY

1. The Baker Street Irregulars were a group of street urchins who occasionally helped which fictional detective?

2. Barcelona footballer Lionel Messi plays international football for which country?

3. The headquarters of the United Nations are in which city?

4. A burka is worn by followers of which religion?

5. What were the first names of comedy duo Morecambe and Wise?

6. The Red Devils is the nickname of which regiment of the British Army?

7. The rand is the currency of which Commonwealth country?

8. Which Coronation Street character committed suicide in January 2014 after giving up her struggle against cancer?

9. Widow Twankey is a character in which pantomime?

10. Which famous ship was discovered in the Atlantic in 1872, minus its crew and lifeboat?

11. When appearing on a contract, what do the initials 'T&Cs' stand for?

12. Mrs McCluskey, Mr Bronson and Mr Robson were teachers at which fictional school?

13. Wayne Rooney started his professional football career with which club?

14. Which controversial singer won a Grammy in 2014 for the album 'Unapologetic'?

15. Complete the proverb: 'Birds of a feather...'

16. Jeremy Piven plays the title character in which shop-set TV drama?

17. In a car, what is usually measured using a dipstick?

18. The PFA is a union for people in which occupation?

19. St Helier is the largest town on which island?
    a) Guernsey
    b) Isle of Man
    c) Jersey

20. In which sport can a team use a nightwatchman?
    a) cricket
    b) ice hockey
    c) rugby union

EASY

Answers to Quiz 32: Sport

1.	Red	11.	Swansea City
2.	Six	12.	Roland Garros
3.	26 miles 385 yards	13.	Cricket
4.	Tony McCoy	14.	Fernando Alonso
5.	Augusta National	15.	Three feet
6.	Darts	16.	Australia
7.	Michael Clarke	17.	True
8.	Aberdeen	18.	Christine Ohuruogu
9.	Tour de France	19.	Danish
10.	3000m	20.	12

Quiz 34: Royalty

EASY

1. What is the official London residence of the British monarch?

2. Diana, Princess of Wales died in a car crash in which city?

3. How many grandchildren does Queen Elizabeth II have?

4. Which member of the Royal Family was born on 22 July 2013?

5. Zara Phillips is married to which former rugby international?

6. Prince William worked as a search and rescue pilot on which Welsh island?

7. In which country of the UK is the royal residence Balmoral Castle?

8. True or false – Queen Elizabeth II is a fluent French speaker?

9. Who is the first female in the line of succession?

10. In which year was Prince William born?

11. Which member of the Royal Family caused controversy after being snapped wearing a Nazi uniform at a party?

12. Who was Queen Elizabeth II's only sibling?

13. Which parade marks the Queen's official birthday?

14. Prince Phillip was born in which European country?

15. Who was the first British prime minister to serve under Elizabeth II?

16. Prince William is a supporter of which English football team?

17. What was the name of the royal yacht that was decommissioned in 1997?

18. The Duke and Duchess of Cambridge both studied at which Scottish university?

19. How old was the Queen Mother when she died?
    a) 99
    b) 100
    c) 101

20. In which year was Queen Elizabeth II born?
    a) 1920
    b) 1926
    c) 1932

EASY

Answers to Quiz 33: Pot Luck

1.	Sherlock Holmes	11.	Terms and conditions
2.	Argentina	12.	Grange Hill
3.	New York	13.	Everton
4.	Islam	14.	Rihanna
5.	Eric and Ernie	15.	Flock together
6.	Parachute Regiment	16.	Mr Selfridge
7.	South Africa	17.	Oil
8.	Hayley Cropper	18.	Footballers
9.	Aladdin	19.	Jersey
10.	Mary Celeste	20.	Cricket

Quiz 35: Pot Luck

EASY

1. What is the name of the tactile writing system that enables blind and visually impaired people to read?

2. What is the main ingredient in guacamole?

3. Risotto is usually made using which type of rice?

4. The alcoholic drink tequila takes its name from a town in which country?

5. In computing, what do the initials 'www' stand for?

6. In children's literature, which character's favourite meal was marmalade sandwiches?

7. The cry of 'Fee, Fi, Foe, Fum, I smell the blood of an Englishman' appears in which pantomime?

8. Which sign of the zodiac is represented by a maiden?

9. 'Solanum tuberosum' is the scientific name for what food plant?

10. 'i.am...i.can...i.will' is the Twitter biography of which musician?

11. True or false – broadcaster Jeremy Vine is the brother of comedian Tim Vine?

12. Who was the only member of the Beatles to receive a knighthood?

13. € is the symbol of which currency?

14. Which musical instrument is played by Jools Holland?

15. Which Asian country was formerly known as Persia?

16. What is the main ingredient in the Indian dish dal?

17. Hollywood, home of the US film industry, is a suburb of which city?

18. Which nut is traditionally used in a Waldorf salad?

19. In 2014, Prince Harry completed a trek with a group of injured servicemen to where?
a) Mount Everest
b) North Pole
c) South Pole

20. Which English county is known as 'The Garden of England'?
a) Essex
b) Kent
c) Yorkshire

Answers to Quiz 34: Royalty

1. Buckingham Palace
2. Paris
3. Eight
4. Prince George
5. Mike Tindall
6. Anglesey
7. Scotland
8. True
9. Princess Beatrice
10. 1982
11. Prince Harry
12. Princess Margaret
13. Trooping the Colour
14. Greece
15. Winston Churchill
16. Aston Villa
17. Britannia
18. St Andrews
19. 101
20. 1926

Quiz 36: Animals

1. What type of creature is a black widow?

2. Bactrian and dromedary are species of which animal?

3. What creature lives in a formicary?

4. True or false – penguins can be found at the North Pole?

5. Abyssinian, Balinese and Persian are breeds of which domestic animal?

6. Which animal appears on the logo for the World Wide Fund for Nature?

7. Friesian, Red Poll and Daisy Shorthorn are breeds of what animal?

8. Which American mammal is known for expelling a foul-smelling fluid when attacked?

9. Which animal lives in a nest called a drey?

10. By what name is the North American caribou more commonly known?

11. Squab is a name given to the young of which bird?

12. Cougar and mountain lion are alternative names for which member of the cat family?

13. 'Canis lupus familiaris' is the scientific name for which domestic animal?

14. Chinchillas are native to which continent?

15. Vulpine means something relating to what species of animal?

16. Which bird is an international symbol of peace?

EASY

17. What boy's name is also given to a young kangaroo?

18. 'Un canard' is the French for which animal?

19. The turkey is native to which continent?
    a) Asia
    b) Europe
    c) North America

20. Batrachian means something relating to what animal?
    a) birds
    b) fish
    c) frogs

Answers to Quiz 35: Pot Luck

1. Braille
2. Avocado
3. Arborio
4. Mexico
5. World wide web
6. Paddington Bear
7. Jack and the Beanstalk
8. Virgo
9. Potato
10. Will.I.Am
11. True
12. Sir Paul McCartney
13. Euro
14. Piano
15. Iran
16. Lentils
17. Los Angeles
18. Walnut
19. South Pole
20. Kent

Quiz 37: Pot Luck

1. Which London borough is home to the Houses of Parliament, St James' Palace and Buckingham Palace?

2. Which long-running radio drama is set in the village of Ambridge?

3. England cricketers Matt Prior, Andrew Strauss and Jonathan Trott were all born in which country?

4. On what part of the body would a person wear a coronet?

5. A water carrier represents which sign of the zodiac?

6. Are the stripes on the Dutch flag horizontal or vertical?

7. Which Olympic swimming technique is also the name of an insect?

8. 'All Shook Up' was the first UK number one from which legendary rock and roller?

9. What unit of length is abbreviated to 'mm'?

10. What is sodium chloride more commonly known as?

11. Assam and Ceylon are varieties of which drink?

12. Which pantomime is based on a 14th-century Lord Mayor of London?

13. 'Who do you think you are kidding, Mr Hitler?' is the theme song to which classic TV comedy?

14. What is the largest state of Germany?

15. James Gandolfini, who died in 2013, is best known for playing which TV gangster?

16. Which short-lived TV soap opera was set in the fictional Spanish town of Los Barcos?

17. Which word meaning 'the mechanism used to fire a gun' was also the name of a character in 'Only Fools and Horses'?

18. Which joint that links the upper and lower arm is also the name of a best-selling band from Manchester?

19. Complete the title of a classic Monty Python film – 'The Life of ...'
    a) Brian
    b) Keith
    c) Kevin

20. Which London thoroughfare is famous for tailors?
    a) Fleet Street
    b) Savile Row
    c) Goodge Street

Answers to Quiz 36: Animals

1. Spider	11. Pigeon
2. Camel	12. Puma
3. Ant	13. Dog
4. False	14. South America
5. Cat	15. Fox
6. Panda	16. Dove
7. Cattle	17. Joey
8. Skunk	18. Duck
9. Squirrel	19. North America
10. Reindeer	20. Frogs

EASY

Quiz 38: Connections part 1

EASY

1. 'Careless Whisper' and 'Fast Love' were UK numbers ones for which male singer?

2. Who was elected the Member of Parliament for Witney in Oxfordshire for the first time in 2001?

3. Which best-selling writer of detective stories also wrote a number of romantic novels using the pseudonym Mary Westmacott?

4. 'The Sound of Laughter' is the title of which Lancastrian comedian's best-selling autobiography?

5. Which star of classic sitcom 'The Good Life' was made a dame in 2014?

6. Which actor played Chandler in the TV comedy 'Friends'?

7. Who was the youngest member of The Beatles?

8. Which jockey-turned-author wrote over 40 thrillers set in the world of horse racing?

9. Which England striker joined Liverpool from Newcastle for £35m in 2011 before moving to West Ham United in 2013?

10. 'Know what I mean, Harry' was a catchphrase of which British boxer?

11. Which businessman is the chairman of Newcastle United FC?

12. Who is the famous other half of David Furnish?

13. Which former Manchester United captain has managed Huddersfield Town, Birmingham City, Wigan Athletic, Crystal Palace, Sunderland and Hull City?

14. Which actor played secret agent Jason Bourne in 'The Bourne Identity', 'The Bourne Supremacy' and 'The Bourne Ultimatum'?

EASY

15. Harry Webb is the real name of which veteran British singer?

16. Which actor starred in TV sitcom 'Home Improvement' and provided the voice of Buzz Lightyear in the 'Toy Story' films?

17. Jamie Foxx won an Oscar in 2005 for his performance in a film biopic about which legendary soul singer?

18. Which award-winning film composer is best known for writing the soundtracks to 11 'James Bond' films?

19. The musical 'Cats' is based on the poetry of which Anglo-American writer?

20. What is the connection between all the answers?

Answers to Quiz 37: Pot Luck

1. Westminster
2. The Archers
3. South Africa
4. On the head
5. Aquarius
6. Horizontal
7. Butterfly
8. Elvis Presley
9. Millimetre
10. Salt
11. Tea
12. Dick Whittington
13. Dad's Army
14. Bavaria
15. Tony Soprano
16. Eldorado
17. Trigger
18. Elbow
19. Brian
20. Savile Row

Quiz 39: Pot Luck

EASY

1. A hijab is a headscarf worn by followers of which religion?

2. Someone who is teetotal refrains from what?

3. @DjokerNole is the Twitter handle of which international sports star?

4. What type of animal is known in French as 'un cheval'?

5. Which character was played on TV in the 1980s by Dirk Benedict and in a 2010 film by Bradley Cooper?

6. GX11 1AA is the postcode used for all addresses in which British overseas territory?

7. Which British politician is known by the initials IDS?

8. Which comedian hosts the sporting comedy panel show 'A League of Their Own'?

9. In internet slang, what do the initials 'BRB' stand for?

10. Which actress famously sang 'Happy Birthday, Mr President' to John F Kennedy at Madison Square Garden in 1962?

11. The historic city of Canterbury is in which English county?

12. Which actor, best known for appearing in the TV comedy 'Happy Days' was awarded the Freedom of the City of London in early 2014?

13. The 1971 hit 'Your Song' was the first top ten single by which British singer and musician?

14. What was the name of the comedy partner of Griff Rhys Jones, who died in July 2013, at the age of 60?

15. True or false – the Tropic of Cancer is south of the equator?

16. Mike Dean, Michael Oliver and Mark Clattenburg are match officials in which sport?

17. Venison is the name of meat from which animal?

18. On what date do Americans celebrate Independence Day?

19. Holy Week is the week leading up to which Christian festival?
    a) Christmas
    b) Easter
    c) Epiphany

20. Nichiyobi, Getsuyobi and Kayob are days of the week in which language?
    a) Arabic
    b) Hindi
    c) Japanese

Answers to Quiz 38: Connections part 1

1. George Michael
2. David Cameron
3. Agatha Christie
4. Peter Kay
5. Penelope Keith
6. Matthew Perry
7. George Harrison
8. Dick Francis
9. Andy Carroll
10. Frank Bruno
11. Mike Ashley
12. Elton John
13. Steve Bruce
14. Matt Damon
15. Cliff Richard
16. Tim Allen
17. Ray Charles
18. John Barry
19. TS Eliot
20. They all feature people whose surname is also a Christian name

Quiz 40: Football part 1

1. Hillsborough is the home ground of which English club?

2. Which team won the Champions League in 2006, 2009 and 2011?

3. Who became manager of the England national team in May 2012?

4. Who said, 'I wouldn't say I was the best manager in the business. But I was in the top one'?

5. What colours are the stripes of the home kit of Italian giants AC Milan?

6. Which Scottish team plays its home games at Ibrox Stadium?

7. Who holds the record for the most appearances by a Manchester United player?

8. The Premier League is made up of how many teams?

9. Which is the only country to have taken part in every World Cup competition?

10. The Toffeemen is the nickname of which English club?

11. Football manager Jose Mourinho is from which country?

12. The famous Maracana Stadium is in which city?

13. In 2009, who became the first footballer to be sold for a fee of £80m?

14. Which country won the World Cup for the first time in 2010?

15. What are the seven clubs to have been in the Premier League for every season since its creation?

16. Which team won its first, and so far only, Premier League title in 1994/95?

17. In yards, how far is the penalty spot from the goal line?

18. Fill in the missing name: ____, Roy Hodgson, Kenny Dalglish, Brendan Rodgers

19. Ashton Gate and the Memorial Ground are football grounds in which English city?
    a) Birmingham
    b) Bristol
    c) Nottingham

20. What is English football's oldest professional club?
    a) Derby County
    b) Notts County
    c) Stockport County

Answers to Quiz 39: Pot Luck

1. Islam
2. Alcohol
3. Novak Djokovic
4. Horse
5. Templeton 'Face' Peck (from The A-Team)
6. Gibraltar
7. Iain Duncan Smith
8. James Corden
9. Be Right Back
10. Marilyn Monroe
11. Kent
12. Henry Winkler
13. Elton John
14. Mel Smith
15. False
16. Football
17. Deer
18. 4th July
19. Easter
20. Japanese

Quiz 41: Pot Luck

1. Bangkok is the largest city in which country?

2. Which two colours feature on the flag of Canada?

3. E20 5RH is the postcode of which fictional address?

4. Profiteroles are made using what type of pastry?

5. Which tennis star became the father of twins for the second time in less than five years in May 2014?

6. @grimmers is the Twitter handle of which radio DJ?

7. The fictional detective Rebus was created by which Scottish author?

8. A cricket team is made up of how many players?

9. The Torah is a sacred text to followers of which religion?

10. Which seaside town is sometimes known as the 'Queen of the English Riviera'?

11. Which sign of the zodiac is represented by a fish?

12. How many stars appear on the flag of Australia?

13. The pasty is associated with which English county?

14. Buttons is a character in which pantomime?

15. Which festival is celebrated in America on the fourth Thursday of November?

16. Skeletor was the arch-enemy of which cartoon character?

17. What is the name of the belt awarded to British boxing champions?

Answers – page 85

18. What type of animal is a Pekingese?

19. At the World Snooker Championship, the final is played over the best of how many frames?
    a) 19
    b) 27
    c) 35

20. Which of the following countries does not have red on its national flag?
    a) Estonia
    b) Poland
    c) Portugal

EASY

Answers to Quiz 40: Football part 1

1. Sheffield Wednesday
2. Barcelona
3. Roy Hodgson
4. Brian Clough
5. Red and black
6. Rangers
7. Ryan Giggs
8. 20
9. Brazil
10. Everton
11. Portugal
12. Rio de Janeiro
13. Cristiano Ronaldo
14. Spain
15. Manchester United, Liverpool, Everton, Arsenal, Tottenham Hotspur, Chelsea and Aston Villa
16. Blackburn Rovers
17. 12
18. Rafael Benitez (Liverpool managers)
19. Bristol
20. Notts County

Quiz 42: Football part 2

1. In 2013, Real Madrid paid a €100m fee for which British footballer?

2. Selhurst Park is the home ground of which football club?

3. Which striker was the first man to score 100 goals in the Premier League?

4. England lost their first World Cup penalty shoot-out in 1990 to which team?

5. Which English team won the Europa League in 2013?

6. 'The Blaydon Races' is a song associated with supporters of which club?

7. The Henri Delaunay Cup is awarded to the winner of which competition?

8. What connects Bolton Wanderers and the sitcom 'Only Fools and Horses'?

9. The Holte End is a feature of which football ground?

10. What is the most easterly club in England's top four divisions?

11. Which was the first country to win the World Cup three times?

12. Which two countries that took part in the 2014 World Cup have names starting with the letter A?

13. In which year was the Premier League formed?

14. Who were the last winners of the old First Division before it became the Premier League?

15. Fill in the missing name: Eriksson, ____, Capello, Hodgson

16. Somerset is home to a single Football League club. Name it.

17. The Rams is the nickname of which English team?

18. In which year did Scotland most recently qualify for the World Cup finals?

19. Which team won the first five European Cup finals?
    a) AC Milan
    b) Barcelona
    c) Real Madrid

20. Which team won the FA Cup for the first and so far only time in 1987?
    a) Coventry City
    b) Derby County
    c) Luton Town

Answers to Quiz 41: Pot Luck

1. Thailand
2. Red and white
3. Albert Square in EastEnders
4. Choux
5. Roger Federer
6. Nick Grimshaw
7. Ian Rankin
8. 11
9. Judaism
10. Torquay
11. Pisces
12. Six
13. Cornwall
14. Cinderella
15. Thanksgiving
16. He-Man
17. Lonsdale Belt
18. Dog
19. 35
20. Estonia

Quiz 43: Pot Luck

1. The acronym KISS advises people to 'Keep It...' what?

2. Which European country is sometimes nicknamed 'The Boot' because of its distinctive shape?

3. Which word describes a large artificial lake that is used to store water?

4. Which European country borders the North Sea to the north and west, Belgium to the south, and Germany to the east?

5. Which politician is the subject of a 2014 West End play called 'Handbagged'?

6. Which footballer scored the notorious 'Hand of God' goal?

7. 'Seventy-Seven: My Road to Wimbledon Glory' is the title of which sportsman's 2013 autobiography?

8. Which TV soap took its name from a mythical city of gold?

9. Which German city is known locally as München?

10. AVB are the initials of which football manager?

11. According to the proverb, what 'abhors a vacuum'?

12. Prince Charming is a character who appears in which pantomime?

13. Bournville, home of a famous chocolate factory, is in which English city?

14. What is the most westerly county of England?

15. Which bumbling hunter was the arch-nemesis of Bugs Bunny?

16. In a game of Test cricket, how many umpires are on the field?

17. Which animal is known in French as 'une vache'?

18. What is the only Scandinavian country to have yellow on its national flag?

19. What is the name of the detective played by Roger Allam in the TV drama 'Endeavour'?
    a) Fred Wednesday
    b) Fred Thursday
    c) Fred Friday

20. Which of the following is an island in New York?
    a) Long Island
    b) Short Island
    c) Wide Island

Answers to Quiz 42: Football part 2

1. Gareth Bale
2. Crystal Palace
3. Alan Shearer
4. West Germany
5. Chelsea
6. Newcastle United
7. European Championships
8. Trotters (Bolton's nickname)
9. Villa Park
10. Norwich City
11. Brazil
12. Argentina and Algeria
13. 1992
14. Leeds United
15. McClaren (England managers)
16. Yeovil Town
17. Derby County
18. 1998
19. Real Madrid
20. Coventry City

Quiz 44: Soaps part 1

1. Which Coronation Street character made his debut on 11 October 1976 and said farewell thirty years later on 7 April 2006 after 2,383 episodes?

2. Hollyoaks is set in which English city?

3. In which soap was a character called Tom King murdered?

4. Sue Nicholls plays which Coronation Street stalwart?

5. In 'Neighbours', what is Jarrod Rebecchi's aquatic-sounding nickname?

6. Characters called Marcus Tandy, Bunny Charlson and the Lockhead family appeared in which soap?

7. What was the name of the character played by Kylie Minogue in 'Neighbours'?

8. Joanna Lumley, Sir Ben Kingsley and Sir Ian McKellen have all appeared in which soap?

9. Which Hollywood star played Mike Young in 'Neighbours'?

10. In 'EastEnders', which of the Mitchell brothers is older – Grant or Phil?

11. 'Coronation Street' was originally broadcast how many times a week?

12. Kym Valentine and Michala Banas both played which 'Neighbour'?

13. True or false – Russell Crowe briefly appeared in 'Home and Away'?

14. Which veteran 'Hollyoaks' character is played by Nick Pickard?

15. Which Coronation Street character was run over by a Blackpool tram in 1989?

Answers – page 91

16. Which 'EastEnder' stole the Christmas club money and died while tending his allotment?

17. What was the name of the actor who played Coronation Street killer Richard Hillman?

18. Heroin addict and all-round troublemaker Rob Hawthorne was a character in which soap?

19. In which year was 'Coronation Street' broadcast for the first time?
    a) 1960
    b) 1964
    c) 1968

20. In 'EastEnders', how did Barry Evans die?
    a) car crash
    b) drowned
    c) pushed off a cliff

EASY

Answers to Quiz 43: Pot Luck

1. Simple Stupid
2. Italy
3. Reservoir
4. The Netherlands
5. Margaret Thatcher
6. Diego Maradona
7. Andy Murray
8. Eldorado
9. Munich
10. Andre Villas Boas
11. Nature
12. Cinderella
13. Birmingham
14. Cornwall
15. Elmer Fudd
16. Two
17. A cow
18. Sweden
19. Fred Thursday
20. Long Island

Quiz 45: Pot Luck

1. Are the stripes on the Russian flag horizontal or vertical?

2. How often does an event that is triennial take place?

3. What type of artwork uses small pieces of glass and stone to make a larger image?

4. Which English football team won the European match known as 'the miracle of Istanbul'?

5. At what time of the year is a cake called stollen traditionally eaten?

6. RTE is the state broadcaster in which European country?

7. Which reality TV star said during the 2013 series of 'I'm a Celebrity … Get Me Out of Here', 'I can't blow my nose. I've never learned how'?

8. The Solheim Cup is a competition in which sport?

9. On which date do the French celebrate Bastille Day?

10. Before joining the euro, what was the currency of Italy?

11. What is the motto of the British army unit, the SAS?

12. Which common pet is known in French as 'un chien'?

13. Which British artist is known for ceramic pots and vases and for his outlandish cross-dressing?

14. What is made by a farrier?

15. What does the 'F' in the acronym 'BAFTA' stand for?

16. The Beatles were from which British city?

Answers – page 93

17. Who is the famous husband of actress and comedian Jennifer Saunders?

18. Which Scottish poet is known as 'The Bard of Ayrshire'?

19. According to the proverb, two of what 'are better than one'?
    a) eyes
    b) heads
    c) legs

20. Which two colours appear on the flag of the United Nations?
    a) pale blue and white
    b) green and white
    c) red and white

EASY

Answers to Quiz 44: Soaps part 1

1. Mike Baldwin
2. Chester
3. Emmerdale
4. Audrey Roberts
5. Toadfish
6. Eldorado
7. Charlene
8. Coronation Street
9. Guy Pearce
10. Phil
11. Two
12. Libby Kennedy
13. False
14. Tony Hutchinson
15. Alan Bradley
16. Arthur Fowler
17. Brian Capron
18. Hollyoaks
19. 1960
20. Pushed off a cliff

Quiz 46: Fill in the Blank

EASY

1. Genesis, ____, Leviticus, Numbers

2. Bob Monkhouse, Max Bygraves, ____, Andy Collins

3. James Callaghan, Margaret Thatcher, ____, Tony Blair

4. France, Brazil, ____, Spain

5. Sean Connery, George Lazenby, Roger Moore, ____

6. ____, Edward VIII, George VI, Elizabeth II

7. Raiders of the Lost Ark, The Temple of Doom, ____,
    Kingdom of the Crystal Skull

8. Michael Keaton, Val Kilmer, George Clooney, ____

9. Australia, ____, China, United Kingdom

10. Mercury, ____, Earth, Mars

11. Rook, knight, ____, queen

12. Sandie Shaw, Lulu, Brotherhood of Man, Bucks Fizz, ____

13. Alex McLeish, George Burley, Craig Levein, ____

14. France, ____, Germany, South Africa

15. ____, (What's the Story) Morning Glory?, Be Here Now,
    Standing on the Shoulder of Giants

16. White, red, yellow, orange, green, blue, brown, ____

17. Phi, chi, psi, ____

18. Star Wars, The Empire Strikes Back, Return of the Jedi, ____

19. Chelsea, ____, Chelsea, Wigan Athletic

20. Richard Nixon, ____, Jimmy Carter, Ronald Reagan

EASY

Answers to Quiz 45: Pot Luck

1. Horizontal
2. Every three years
3. Mosaic
4. Liverpool
5. Christmas
6. Republic of Ireland
7. Joey Essex
8. Golf
9. 14th July
10. Lira
11. Who Dares Wins
12. Dog
13. Grayson Perry
14. Horseshoes
15. Film
16. Liverpool
17. Ade Edmondson
18. Robert Burns
19. Heads
20. Pale blue and white

Quiz 47: Pot Luck

1. In which sport can a player be run out, stumped or caught behind?

2. Which cheeky TV chef invited readers to 'Shop Smart, Cook Clever, Waste Less' in a bestselling 2013 book?

3. Ellie Simmonds is a multiple Paralympic medallist in which sport?

4. What sort of lines featured in the title of a best-selling 2013 single by Robin Thicke featuring TI and Pharrell Williams?

5. Which music and TV mogul is the founder of a company called Syco Entertainment?

6. Which former Liverpool footballer is a team captain on comedy panel show 'A League of Their Own'?

7. By what name is Cardinal Jorge Mario Bergoglio more commonly known?

8. The TV show 'I'm a Celebrity ... Get Me Out of Here!' is filmed in which country?

9. The NFL is the governing body of which sport?

10. Beth Tweddle won an Olympic medal in 2012 in which sport?

11. Which veteran politician died at the age of 95 in his Johannesburg home in December 2013?

12. The villainous King Rat is a character in which pantomime?

13. What does the 'T' in the acronym 'BAFTA' stand for?

14. Fidel Castro was the long-time leader of which Caribbean country?

15. 'The Immaculate Collection' was a 1990 album by which American singer?

16. Rucking and mauling are features of which team sport?

17. In 2014, David Beckham launched a football team in which American city?

18. A mastectomy is an operation to remove which part of the body?

19. A blue plaque honouring Robbie Williams was unveiled in February 2014 in which English city?
    a) Liverpool   b) Manchester   c) Stoke-on-Trent

20. Which of the following is the title of a school-based BBC drama?
    a) Euston Road   b) Victoria Road   c) Waterloo Road

Answers to Quiz 46: Fill in the Blank

1. Exodus (first four books of the Old Testament)

2. Les Dennis (hosts of Family Fortunes)

3. John Major (British prime ministers)

4. Italy (World Cup winners 1998 to 2010)

5. Timothy Dalton (James Bond actors)

6. George V (British monarchs)

7. The Last Crusade (Indiana Jones films)

8. Christian Bale (Batman actors)

9. Greece (Olympic host countries 2000 to 2012)

10. Venus (planets in order from the sun)

11. Bishop (chess pieces moving out to in)

12. Katrina and the Waves (winning UK entries at the Eurovison Song Contest)

13. Gordon Strachan (managers of the Scotland national football team)

14. Japan/South Korea (World Cup host countries 1998 to 2010)

15. Definitely Maybe (albums by Oasis)

16. Black (judo belts in order of skill)

17. Omega (last four letters of the Greek alphabet)

18. The Phantom Menace (Star Wars films in order of release)

19. Manchester City (FA Cup winners 2010 to 2013)

20. Gerald Ford (US presidents 1969 to 1989)

Quiz 48: Music

EASY

1. Who topped the charts in 2014 with 'Happy'?

2. Complete the title of a 1979 number one by Blondie – 'Heart of...'

3. Which soul legend 'Just Called to Say I Love You' in 1984?

4. Which female singer endured a 'Bad Romance' in 2009?

5. 'Summer Nights' and 'You're the One That I Want' were chart-toppers from the soundtrack to which film?

6. Noddy Holder was the lead singer with which glam rock band?

7. 'No Matter What' was the only million-selling single by which Irish boy band?

8. Elton John was formerly the chairman of which English football club?

9. Which British singer went 'Sailing' in 1975?

10. 'Midnight Matters' was a best-selling album in 2013 for which boy band?

11. What colour was The Beatles' submarine?

12. Which member of the Spice Girls was famous for her Union Jack dress?

13. Which regal-sounding band topped the charts in 2008 with 'Sex On Fire'?

14. 'The Man in Black' was the nickname of which country singer?

15. Which female singer discovered a 'Genie in a Bottle' in 1999?

16. What London thoroughfare was also the title of a 1969 album by The Beatles?

17. Who is the only Welsh artist to have a UK million-selling single?

18. Simon Le Bon, John Taylor and Nick Rhodes were members of which 1980s New Romantic band?

19. What was the name of veteran rock and roller Bill Haley's backing band?
    a) The Comets
    b) The Meteors
    c) The Planets

20. Which of the following was a guitarist with classic disco band Chic?
    a) Amazon Rodgers
    c) Nile Rodgers
    c) Trent Rodgers

Answers to Quiz 47: Pot Luck

1. Cricket
2. Jamie Oliver
3. Swimming
4. Blurred
5. Simon Cowell
6. Jamie Redknapp
7. Pope Francis
8. Australia
9. American football
10. Gymnastics
11. Nelson Mandela
12. Dick Whittington
13. Television
14. Cuba
15. Madonna
16. Rugby union
17. Miami
18. Breast
19. Stoke-on-Trent
20. Waterloo Road

Quiz 49: Pot Luck

1. LSE are the initials of which British university?

2. Michael Phelps won 18 Olympic medals in which sport?

3. A tricolour is a flag containing how many coloured stripes?

4. TV drama 'Doc Martin' is set in which English county?

5. Which common pet is known in French as 'un poisson rouge'?

6. Which Olympic gold medal-winning athlete is famous for his 'Mobot' celebration?

7. 'Stay Another Day' was a Christmas number one in 1994 for which band?

8. Which actor and politician is also the author of a book called 'The New Encyclopedia of Modern Bodybuilding'?

9. Melbourne is the largest city in which Australian state?

10. What colour shirts are traditionally worn by the the Dutch football team?

11. Which British band were the biggest-selling recording artists in the world in 2013?

12. Which British military honour is awarded for extreme bravery in the face of the enemy?

13. Which Liverpudlian comedian is famous for his tickling sticks?

14. In relation to taxation, what do the initials 'PAYE' stand for?

15. What colour is the cross on the Finnish flag?

16. The best-selling album of all time in the UK is the 'Greatest Hits' of which rock band?

17. Which children's animated TV show features a rabbit called Rebecca, a sheep called Suzy, and an elephant called Emily?

18. Mandy was the nickname of which former Labour MP, now a member of the House of Lords?

19. The musical 'Chitty Chitty Bang Bang' was based on a novel by which author?
    a) Ian Fleming
    b) Frederick Forsyth
    c) Roald Dahl

20. Roquefort is a cheese from which country?
    a) France
    b) Italy
    c) Spain

EASY

Answers to Quiz 48: Music

1. Pharrell Williams
2. Glass
3. Stevie Wonder
4. Lady Gaga
5. Grease
6. Slade
7. Boyzone
8. Watford
9. Rod Stewart
10. One Direction
11. Yellow
12. Geri Halliwell
13. Kings of Leon
14. Johnny Cash
15. Christina Aguilera
16. Abbey Road
17. Tom Jones
18. Duran Duran
19. The Comets
20. Nile Rodgers

Quiz 50: Connections part 2

1. Carrie Bradshaw, Samantha Jones, Charlotte York and Miranda Hobbes were the main characters in which TV comedy drama?

2. On what day of the week does Prime Minister's Questions take place?

3. What is the national flower of Scotland?

4. Ilyena Lydia Vasilievna Mironoff is the real name of which Oscar-winning British actress?

5. Annie Walker, Fred Elliott and Natalie Barnes have all run which famous fictional pub?

6. Albert Finney played detective Hercule Poirot in a 1972 film version of which Agatha Christie novel?

7. Who won an Oscar in 2007 for his performance as Idi Amin in 'The Last King of Scotland'?

8. What is the official London residence of the Archbishop of Canterbury?

9. What was the first UK number one for The Pet Shop Boys?

10. What is name of the fabric pattern, popular with golfers, that features overlapping diamond or lozenge shapes?

11. What is the world's fourth largest country by area?

12. What was the only UK number one single by ska band The Specials?

13. Which cousin of the Queen Elizabeth II was born on Christmas Day, 1936?

14. Country singer Kenny Rogers has had two UK number one singles: 'Lucille' was one, what was the other?

15. Complete the title of the debut album from the rock band Babyshambles: 'Down In ...'

16. What was the nickname of the medieval nobleman, and a central character in the Shakespeare play 'Henry IV Part I', Sir Henry Percy?

17. What trophy is awarded to the winners of North America's NHL ice hockey competition?

18. What word may describe a large country house of Roman times or a continental European holiday home?

19. Jason Lee Scott, Zack Taylor, Billy Cranston, Trini Kwan, Kimberly Ann Hart and Tommy Oliver were characters in which 1990s children's TV show?

20. What is the connection between all the answers?

Answers to Quiz 49: Pot Luck

1. London School of Economics
2. Swimming
3. Three
4. Cornwall
5. A goldfish
6. Mo Farah
7. East 17
8. Arnold Schwarzenegger
9. Victoria
10. Orange
11. One Direction
12. Victoria Cross
13. Ken Dodd
14. Pay as you earn
15. Blue
16. Queen
17. Peppa Pig
18. Peter Mandelson
19. Ian Fleming
20. France

Quiz 51: Pot Luck

1.   An Olympic decathlon is made up of how many events?

2.   Which vegetable is known in America as the eggplant?

3.   A circle is made up of how many degrees?

4.   Which UK motorway runs from Liverpool to Hull?

5.   Which branch of the British armed forces was founded in 1918?

6.   A herbivore is a creature that only eats what?

7.   Which word connects part of a loaf of bread and the outer layer of the Earth's surface?

8.   'Let's Go Fly a Kite' and 'Chim Chim Cher-ee' are songs from which film musical?

9.   George Michael and Andrew Ridgeley were members of which band?

10. Miles Davis and John Coltrane are associated with which genre of music?

11. Apartheid was a system of racial segregation that operated in which country?

12. Which former England cricketer is a regular team captain on TV panel show 'A League of Their Own'?

13. At the start of a frame of snooker, how many red balls are on the table?

14. 'Sound of the Underground' was a Christmas number one in 2002 for which group?

15. Which Olympic legend created the 'To Di World' celebration pose?

16. Which star sign is represented by a goat?

17. Ron Burgundy is the central character in which film franchise?

18. Which animal lives in a sett?

19. In the puppet adventure series 'Thunderbirds', what was the name of Lady Penelope's butler and chauffeur?
a) Barker
b) Larker
c) Parker

20. What is the name of the annual speech delivered by the president of the USA? 'State of the ...'
a) Country
b) Nation
c) Union

EASY

Answers to Quiz 50: Connections part 2

1. Sex and the City
2. Wednesday
3. Thistle
4. Helen Mirren
5. The Rovers Return
6. Murder on the Orient Express
7. Forest Whitaker
8. Lambeth Palace
9. West End Girls
10. Argyle
11. United States of America
12. Ghost Town
13. Princess Alexandra
14. Coward of the County
15. Albion
16. Hotspur
17. Stanley Cup
18. Villa
19. Mighty Morphin Power Rangers
20. They all contain the last word in the name of a British football team

Quiz 52: Chart-Toppers of the 1960s

Idenifty the artist or band who topped the charts with the following songs:

1. 'My Old Man's a Dustman' (1960)

2. 'Only the Lonely' (1960)

3. 'Runaway' (1961)

4. 'Walkin' Back to Happiness' (1961)

5. 'Summer Holiday' (1963)

6. 'I Like It' (1963)

7. 'House of the Rising Sun' (1964)

8. 'You Really Got Me' (1964)

9. 'Mr Tambourine Man' (1965)

10. '(I Can't Get No) Satisfaction' (1965)

11. 'Keep On Running' (1966)

12. 'You Don't Have to Say You Love Me' (1966)

13. 'Reach Out I'll Be There' (1966)

14. 'I'm a Believer' (1967)

15. 'Mighty Quinn' (1968)

16. 'Baby Come Back' (1968)

17. 'Those Were The Days' (1968)

18. 'Bad Moon Rising' (1969)

19. 'Sugar Sugar' (1969)

20. 'Where Do You Go to (My Lovely)?' (1969)

EASY

Answers to Quiz 51: Pot Luck

1. Ten
2. Aubergine
3. 360
4. M62
5. The RAF
6. Plants
7. Crust
8. Mary Poppins
9. Wham!
10. Jazz
11. South Africa
12. Andrew Flintoff
13. 15
14. Girls Aloud
15. Usain Bolt
16. Capricorn
17. Anchorman
18. Badger
19. Parker
20. Union

Quiz 53: Pot Luck

1. In which two field events do athletes stand in a cage?

2. The Norwegian flag is made up of which three colours?

3. Who was the first foreign manager of the England football team?

4. Which technology company was founded by Steve Jobs and Steve Wosniak in 1976?

5. What name is given to an animal that eats only meat?

6. At what time of the year would someone in Spain wish you 'Feliz Navidad'?

7. In which sport can a player score a duck, a pair and a king pair?

8. In the Disney film 'Dumbo', what type of animal was the title character?

9. Who was the captain of the England cricket team that lost the 2013/14 Ashes series in Australia 5-0?

10. Chef Delia Smith is a supporter of which English football club?

11. What type of dishes are korma, dopiaza and rogan josh?

12. The alter ego of which comic-book superhero was derived from the names of Hollywood stars Clark Gable and Kent Taylor?

13. The Lone Star State is the nickname of which American state?

14. In online slang, what does the acronym ROFL stand for?

15. The Museo CR7 in Madeira is a museum devoted to which superstar footballer?

Answers – page 109

16. Ali Campbell, Mickey Virtue and Astro were founder members of which Birmingham reggae band?

17. An hour is made up of how many seconds?

18. Neville, Bomber, Moxie and Oz were character in which 1980s TV drama?

19. In a game of chess, each player starts with how many pawns?
    a) 2
    b) 4
    c) 8

20. La Coruña is a city in which country?
    a) France
    b) Italy
    c) Spain

Answers to Quiz 52: Chart-Toppers of the 1960s

1. Lonnie Donegan
2. Roy Orbison
3. Del Shannon
4. Helen Shapiro
5. Cliff Richard and the Shadows
6. Gerry and the Pacemakers
7. The Animals
8. The Kinks
9. The Byrds
10. The Rolling Stones
11. The Spencer Davis Group
12. Dusty Springfield
13. The Four Tops
14. The Monkees
15. Manfred Mann
16. The Equals
17. Mary Hopkin
18. Creedence Clearwater Revival
19. The Archies
20. Peter Sarstedt

Quiz 54: Soaps part 2

1. The Dingle family feature in which TV soap?

2. Which unlucky-in-love soap character has had wives called Cindy, Melanie, Laura and Jane?

3. Simon Gregson plays which character in 'Coronation Street'?

4. Which pop singer first found fame playing Nina Tucker in 'Neighbours'?

5. In which soap could visitors go for a drink at The Waterhole, Chez Chez, Lou's Place and Scarlet Bar?

6. In 'Emmerdale' what is the ocupation of Paddy Kirk?

7. The Birmingham suburb of Letherbridge is the setting for which daytime soap?

8. Ray Meagher plays which long-serving soap character?

9. True or false – Dannii Minogue appeared in 'Neighbours'?

10. In which year was 'EastEnders' first broadcast?

11. Which actor, who appeared in American dramas 'The OC' and 'Ugly Betty', is best known to British viewers for playing Jim Robinson in 'Neighbours'?

12. 'Emmerdale' is set in which English county?

13. What is the name of the actor who plays 'Coronation Street's' Tyrone Dobbs?

14. 'Hollyoaks' first hit TV screens in which year?

15. Which veteran 'Neighbours' character is played by Jackie Woodbourne?

16. US soap 'Dynasty' was set in which city?

17. A mobile shop called The Moby regularly appeared in which soap?

18. The Albert Memorial hospital was the setting for which soap that ran from 1976 until 1983?

19. Paul Usher played which Brookside rogue?
    a) Barry Grant
    b) Gary Grant
    c) Harry Grant

20. What was the name of the actor who played Curly Watts in 'Coronation Street'?
    a) John Kennedy
    b) Kevin Kennedy
    c) Stuart Kennedy

Answers to Quiz 53: Pot Luck

1. Discus and hammer
2. Red, white and blue
3. Sven Goran Eriksson
4. Apple
5. Carnivore
6. Christmas
7. Cricket
8. Elephant
9. Alastair Cook
10. Norwich City
11. Curry
12. Superman (Clark Kent)
13. Texas
14. Rolling On the Floor Laughing
15. Cristiano Ronaldo
16. UB40
17. 3600
18. Auf Wiedersehen, Pet
19. 8
20. Spain

Quiz 55: Pot Luck

EASY

1. The International Convention Centre is in which English city?

2. How many millilitres make up one litre?

3. Which range of hills is known as 'the backbone of England'?

4. In the British police, what do the initials 'CID' stand for?

5. 'Stillness and Speed' was the title of a 2013 biography of which former Arsenal and Netherlands footballer?

6. Which Olympic gold-medal-winning athlete missed the 2014 Commonwealth Games because she was pregnant?

7. What is the only vowel on the second row of a standard computer keyboard?

8. A vintner is a seller of what?

9. Which game is played at Twickenham?

10. Zlatan Ibrahimovic plays international football for which country?

11. Which actor, best known for playing fictional MP Alan B'Stard in 'The New Statesman' and Richie in 'Bottom', died in June 2014 at the age of just 56?

12. A major music festival takes place on the August Bank Holiday weekend each year in which Berkshire town?

13. In snooker, which ball is worth six points?

14. The Capitol Building is in which American city?

15. What was singer Cheryl Cole's maiden name?

16. What does the acronym 'NIMBY' stand for?

17. The Mojave Desert is in which country?

18. Colonel Gaddafi was the long-time leader of which country?

19. In 1978, Reinhold Messner and Peter Habeler became the first climbers to reach the summit of Mount Everest without what?
    a) oxygen
    b) maps
    c) ropes

20. What is the first discipline in an Olympic triathlon race?
    a) cycling
    b) running
    c) swimming

EASY

Answers to Quiz 54: Soaps part 2

1. Emmerdale
2. Ian Beale
3. Steve McDonald
4. Delta Goodrem
5. Neighbours
6. Vet
7. Doctors
8. Alf Stewart (in Home and Away)
9. False
10. 1985
11. Alan Dale
12. Yorkshire
13. Alan Halsall
14. 1995
15. Susan Kennedy
16. Denver
17. Brookside
18. The Young Doctors
19. Barry Grant
20. Kevin Kennedy

Quiz 56: Chart-Toppers of the 1970s

Idenifty the artist or band who topped the charts with the following songs:

1. 'Bridge Over Troubled Water' (1970)

2. 'In the Summertime' (1970)

3. 'Chirpy Chirpy Cheep Cheep' (1971)

4. 'Maggie May' (1971)

5. 'School's Out' (1972)

6. 'Puppy Love' (1972)

7. 'Blockbuster' (1973)

8. 'Kung Fu Fighting' (1974)

9. 'Gonna Make You a Star' (1974)

10. 'Down Down' (1975)

11. 'Space Oddity' (1975)

12. 'You to Me Are Everything' (1976)

13. 'When I Need You' (1977)

14. 'Name of the Game' (1977)

15. 'I Feel Love' (1977)

16. 'Uptown Top Ranking' (1978)

17. 'Hit Me with Your Rhythm Stick' (1979)

18. 'Cars' (1979)

19. 'Sunday Girl' (1979)

20. 'We Don't Talk Anymore' (1979)

Answers to Quiz 55: Pot Luck

1. Birmingham
2. 1000
3. The Pennines
4. Criminal Investigation Department
5. Dennis Bergkamp
6. Jessica Ennis-Hill
7. A
8. Wine
9. Rugby union
10. Sweden
11. Rik Mayall
12. Reading
13. Pink
14. Washington DC
15. Tweedy
16. Not in my back yard
17. USA
18. Libya
19. Oxygen
20. Swimming

Quiz 57: Pot Luck

1. Which controversial comedian won 'Celebrity Big Brother' in January 2014?

2. How many days are in a leap year?

3. 'Lone Missile' is an anagram of the name of which footballing superstar?

4. Which three colours feature on the flag of the Czech Republic?

5. Which friend of Ricky Gervais and Stephen Merchant is the star of the TV show 'An Idiot Abroad'?

6. Which artist was noted for his paintings of 'matchstick men'?

7. Which National Park stretches from Chesterfield to Buxton and from Ashbourne to Glossop?

8. Tyke is a nickname used to describe people from which English county?

9. One of the Seven Wonders of the World, the Great Pyramid of Giza is in which modern-day country?

10. What is the national speed limit for cars on UK dual carriageways?

11. RNLI are the initials of which charitable rescue organization?

12. Which planet of our solar system is named after the messenger of the Roman gods?

13. Estadio Santiago Bernabeu is the home ground of which European football club?

14. Razor was the nickname of which portly footballer-turned-reality TV star?

15. Which massive musical festival is hosted near the village of Pilton in Somerset?

16. Under what plant do revellers traditionally kiss at Christmas?

17. What was the first name of the naval commander Lord Nelson?

18. What is the sixth planet from the Sun?

19. In which decade was the children's TV show 'Blue Peter' first broadcast?
    a) 1950s
    b) 1960s
    c) 1970s

20. Perth is the capital city of which Australian state?
    a) Queensland
    b) South Australia
    b) Western Australia

Answers to Quiz 56: Chart-Toppers of the 1970s

1. Simon and Garfunkel
2. Mungo Jerry
3. Middle of the Road
4. Rod Stewart
5. Alice Cooper
6. Donny Osmond
7. Sweet
8. Carl Douglas
9. David Essex
10. Status Quo
11. David Bowie
12. The Real Thing
13. Leo Sayer
14. Abba
15. Donna Summer
16. Althea and Donna
17. Ian Dury and the Blockheads
18. Gary Numan
19. Blondie
20. Cliff Richard

Quiz 58: Anagrams

Rearrange the letters to make the name of a recent England football international.

1. We Annoy Yore

2. Render Gravest

3. Vim Hacked Bad

4. Alley Echos

5. Grab Thy Rear

6. Droll Canary

7. Ladders Intrigue

8. Farm Pal Drank

9. Hear Jot

10. Neck End Bylaw

11. Royals Kerbs

12. Procure Tech

13. A Hilly Crag

14. Welch Tattoo

15. Lick Here Jaws

Answers – page 119

16. Jean Slimmer

17. Defame Joiner

18. Click Hair Cream

19. Stranded On Snow

20. A Jag Pike Hill

Answers to Quiz 57: Pot Luck

1. Jim Davidson
2. 366
3. Lionel Messi
4. Red, white and blue
5. Karl Pilkington
6. LS Lowry
7. The Peak District
8. Yorkshire
9. Egypt
10. 70mph
11. Royal National Lifeboat Institution
12. Mercury
13. Real Madrid
14. Neil Ruddock
15. Glastonbury
16. Mistletoe
17. Horatio
18. Saturn
19. 1950s
20. Western Australia

Quiz 59: Pot Luck

1. In a game of rugby union, what is the only playing position that is named after a number?

2. What does the 'DC' in 'Washington, DC' stand for?

3. How long in metres is an Olympic-sized swimming pool?

4. Damascus is the capital city of which country?

5. True or false – the Hundred Years' War lasted longer than 100 years?

6. Which 1987 film comedy was a remake of a French film called 'Trois Hommes et un Couffin'?

7. R-Patz is the nickname of which Hollywood star?

8. What ocean stretches from the west coast of America to the east coast of Asia?

9. In chess, what piece can move only diagonally?

10. Bodrum is a popular seaside resort in which country?

11. Which European country's name translates into English as 'low lands'?

12. In April 2014, Peter Moores was appointed coach of the England national team in which sport?

13. A 'score' is slang for how much money?

14. The line 'Friends, Romans, countrymen, lend me your ears' appears in which Shakespeare play?

15. Which body of water is east of Britain, west of Norway, Sweden and Germany and north of Holland, Belgium and France?

Answers – page 121

16. Prior to Barack Obama, who was the last US President whose surname started with a vowel?

17. What is the largest of the Channel Islands?

18. In text speak, what do the initials 'AFAIK' stand for?

19. Prior to entering politics, what was Tony Blair's occupation?
    a) doctor
    b) lawyer
    c) teacher

20. The word 'spa', meaning a health resort, takes its name from a town in which country?
    a) Belgium
    b) France
    c) Switzerland

EASY

Answers to Quiz 58: Anagrams

1. Wayne Rooney
2. Steven Gerrard
3. David Beckham
4. Ashley Cole
5. Gareth Barry
6. Andy Carroll
7. Daniel Sturridge
8. Frank Lampard
9. Joe Hart
10. Danny Welbeck
11. Ross Barkley
12. Peter Crouch
13. Gary Cahill
14. Theo Walcott
15. Jack Wilshere
16. James Milner
17. Jermain Defoe
18. Michael Carrick
19. Andros Townsend
20. Phil Jagielka

Quiz 60: Famous Dans

1. Who made his debut as 007 in the 2006 film 'Casino Royale'?

2. 'Now that's magic' is a catchphrase of which magician?

3. Which film director was the artistic director of the opening ceremony of the 2012 London Olympics?

4. 'Angels and Demons' and 'Inferno' are novels by which author?

5. Which diminutive actor starred alongside Arnold Schwarzenegger in the film comedy 'Twins'?

6. Which actor plays Queen Vic landlord Mick Carter in TV soap 'EastEnders'?

7. Which popular Irish ballad is sung to the tune 'Londonderry Air'?

8. What was the full name of the character played by John Travolta in the musical 'Grease'?

9. 'A Picture of You' was a 2013 album by which Irish singer?

10. Which actor played the bespectacled wizard in the 'Harry Potter' film series?

11. Who won his third Best Actor Oscar in 2013 for his portrayal of US President Abraham Lincoln?

12. Which brand of American whiskey is made in Lynchburg, Tennessee?

13. 'Gotta Get Thru This', 'If You're Not the One' and 'Never Gonna Leave Your Side' were UK number ones for which New Zealand-born singer?

14. Which actor starred alongside Jim Carrey in the 1994 film comedy 'Dumb and Dumber'?

15. 'Going to Sea in a Sieve' is the title of the 2013 autobiography of which radio DJ and broadcaster?

16. Which footballer had spells at Crewe Alexandra, Charlton Athletic, Liverpool, Tottenham Hotspur, Fulham and Blackburn Rovers, as well as winning nine England caps?

17. Which Australian singer played Emma Jackson in 'Home and Away' and later went on to become a judge on TV talent show 'The X Factor'?

18. Which footballer made his England debut in March 2011 against Ghana, the country of birth of both of his parents?

19. On what subject are you most likely to see a programme presented by broadcaster Dan Cruickshank?
    a) architecture
    b) cookery
    c) gardening

20. The classic novel Robinson Crusoe was written by which author?
    a) Daniel Defoe
    b) Daniel Rooney
    c) Daniel Sheringham

EASY

Answers to Quiz 59: Pot Luck

1.	Number 8	11.	The Netherlands
2.	District of Columbia	12.	Cricket
3.	50m	13.	£20.00
4.	Syria	14.	Julius Caesar
5.	True	15.	The North Sea
6.	Three Men and a Baby	16.	Dwight Eisenhower
7.	Robert Pattinson	17.	Jersey
8.	Pacific Ocean	18.	As far as I know
9.	Bishop	19.	Lawyer
10.	Turkey	20.	Belgium

Quiz 61: Pot Luck

EASY

1. EC and WC are postcode districts in which city?

2. Rachel Riley and Susie Dent are regulars on which TV quiz show?

3. In which TV game show did losing contestants go home with their 'BFH'?

4. What is 50 squared?

5. How wide in yards is a football goal?

6. Nurse Gladys Emmanuel was a character in which classic sitcom that was revived in 2014?

7. What is the only US state that is made up entirely of islands?

8. What is sold in a French shop called a 'pâtisserie'?

9. Mount Everest is in which country?

10. King's Acre Pippin and Braeburn are varieties of what type of fruit?

11. What is the world's largest ocean?

12. In the board game Monopoly, how much does a player receive for passing Go?

13. In the Sicilian Mafia, what is the code of honour that demands that members keep silent about any criminal activity?

14. What is the UK's most common road name?

15. Which sporting venue can be found at the postcode M16 0RA?

Answers – page 125

16. During the Second World War, Operation Barbarossa was a Nazi operation to invade which country?

17. What does the acronym 'DINKY' stand for?

18. 'A Cordial Intro Son' is an anagram of which famous footballer?

19. Which room in a house is known in France as 'la salle à manger'?
    a) bathroom
    b) bedroom
    c) dining room

20. What nationality is the teen hearthrob Justin Bieber?
    a) American
    b) Australian
    c) Canadian

EASY

Answers to Quiz 60: Famous Dans

1. Daniel Craig	11. Daniel Day Lewis
2. Paul Daniels	12. Jack Daniel's
3. Danny Boyle	13. Daniel Bedingfield
4. Dan Brown	14. Jeff Daniels
5. Danny DeVito	15. Danny Baker
6. Danny Dyer	16. Danny Murphy
7. Danny Boy	17. Dannii Minogue
8. Danny Zuko	18. Danny Welbeck
9. Daniel O'Donnell	19. Architecture
10. Daniel Radcliffe	20. Daniel Defoe

Quiz 62: Chart-Toppers of the 1980s

EASY

Idenifty the artist or band who topped the charts with the following songs:

1. 'Ashes to Ashes' (1980)

2. 'Woman in Love' (1980)

3. '(Just Like) Starting Over' (1980)

4. 'This Ole House' (1981)

5. 'Prince Charming' (1981)

6. 'Every Little Thing She Does Is Magic' (1981)

7. 'House of Fun' (1982)

8. 'Land of Make Believe' (1982)

9. 'Wherever I Lay My Hat (That's My Home)' (1983)

10. 'I Feel For You' (1984)

11. 'Saving All My Love For You' (1985)

12. 'Chain Reaction' (1986)

13. 'Nothing's Gonna Stop Us Now' (1987)

14. 'It's a Sin' (1987)

15. 'I Just Can't Stop Loving You' (1987)

16. 'Don't Turn Around' (1988)

17. 'A Groovy Kind of Love' (1988)

18. 'Desire' (1988)

19. 'Ride on Time' (1989)

20. 'All Around the World' (1989)

Answers to Quiz 61: Pot Luck

1. London
2. Countdown
3. Bullseye
4. 2500
5. Eight yards
6. Open All Hours
7. Hawaii
8. Cakes and pastries
9. Nepal
10. Apple
11. Pacific Ocean
12. £200.00
13. Omertà
14. High Street
15. Old Trafford football ground
16. Soviet Union
17. Double income, no kids yet
18. Cristiano Ronaldo
19. Dining room
20. Canadian

Quiz 63: Pot Luck

EASY

1. Marvin Humes, co-host of TV talent show 'The Voice', is a member of which band?

2. In the nursery rhyme 'This Little Piggy', where did the first little piggy go?

3. Ken Doherty is the only world snooker champion from which country?

4. By what name is a series of roads called the Gravelly Hill Interchange more commonly known?

5. Which animal features on the badge of the car manufacturer Ferrari?

6. Giovanni Agnelli was the founder of which motor manufacturer?

7. Dave Lanning, Wayne Mardle and Chris Mason are commentators on which sport?

8. An 'Ayrton' is a slang term for which British banknote?

9. The poem 'Daffodils' was written by which English poet?

10. What are the three teams to have won English football's top flight whose name starts with a vowel?

11. 'Just Do It' is the motto of which company?

12. The Great Red Spot is a feature of which planet of the Solar System?

13. Sandra Bullock starred alongside George Clooney in which award-winning 2013 movie?

14. Who was the leader of the Soviet Union during the Second World War?

Answers – page 129

15. What girl's name is also the name given to a female donkey?

16. PTSD are the initials of which medical condition?

17. Which fictional family had a butler called Lurch?

18. In chess, what is the only piece that can jump over other pieces?

19. In the Harry Potter films and books, trains to Hogwarts depart from which London station?
    a) King's Cross
    b) Marylebone
    c) Paddington

20. Complete the title of the long-running radio panel show: 'Just a ...'
    a) Jiffy
    b) Minute
    c) Second

EASY

Answers to Quiz 62: Chart-Toppers of the 1980s

1. David Bowie
2. Barbra Streisand
3. John Lennon
4. Shakin' Stevens
5. Adam and the Ants
6. The Police
7. Madness
8. Bucks Fizz
9. Paul Young
10. Chaka Khan
11. Whitney Houston
12. Diana Ross
13. Starship
14. The Pet Shop Boys
15. Michael Jackson
16. Aswad
17. Phil Collins
18. U2
19. Black Box
20. Lisa Stansfield

Quiz 64: Chart-Toppers of the 1990s

Idenifty the artist or band who topped the charts with the following songs:

1. 'Nothing Compares 2 U' (1990)

2. 'Black or White' (1991)

3. 'Deeply Dippy' (1992)

4. 'I Will Always Love You' (1992)

5. 'Oh Carolina' (1993)

6. 'All That She Wants' (1993)

7. 'Pray' (1993)

8. 'Boom! Shake the Room' (1993)

9. 'Saturday Night' (1994)

10. 'Country House' (1995)

11. 'Fairground' (1995)

12. 'Firestarter' (1996)

13. 'Killing Me Softly' (1996)

14. 'Ooh Aah ... Just a Little Bit' (1996)

15. 'Say You'll Be There' (1996)

16. 'Don't Speak' (1997)

17. 'I Believe I Can Fly' (1997)

18. 'All Around the World' (1998)

19. 'Never Ever' (1998)

20. 'The Millennium Prayer' (1999)

EASY

Answers to Quiz 63: Pot Luck

1. JLS
2. To market
3. Republic of Ireland
4. Spaghetti Junction
5. Horse
6. Fiat
7. Darts
8. £10 note
9. William Wordsworth
10. Arsenal, Aston Villa and Everton
11. Nike
12. Jupiter
13. Gravity
14. Stalin
15. Jenny
16. Post-traumatic stress disorder
17. The Addams Family
18. Knight
19. King's Cross
20. Minute

Quiz 65: Pot Luck

EASY

1. The cuisine sushi orginates from which country?

2. What boy's name is also the capital of the Isle of Man?

3. What is 2014 in Roman numerals?

4. Hass is a variety of which fruit?

5. What is the English equivalent of the Italian name Giuseppe?

6. Christian Grey is the central character in which best-selling 2011 novel?

7. What is the English equivalent of the Spanish name Guillermo?

8. What number comes next: 7, 11, 13, 17?

9. What are the three South American countries whose name starts with a vowel?

10. In slang, which animal is used to describe a sum of £500?

11. True or false – as the crow flies, London is closer to Paris than it is to Edinburgh?

12. In which TV game show could contestants win a chequebook and pen?

13. Which Hollywood starlet is known as K-Stew?

14. A standard bottle of wine contains how many mililitres?

15. In the nursery rhyme, what had Little Bo-Peep lost?

16. What leafy herb is the main ingredient in pesto sauce?

17. The Gobi Desert covers parts of which two countries?

18. Infectious mononucleosis is another name for which disease?

19. The Alsatian is a breed of dog that originated in which country?
    a) Germany
    b) Italy
    c) Sweden

20. What is the most common blood type?
    a) A
    b) B
    c) O

EASY

Answers to Quiz 64: Chart-Toppers of the 1990s

1. Sinead O'Connor
2. Michael Jackson
3. Right Said Fred
4. Whitney Houston
5. Shaggy
6. Ace of Base
7. Take That
8. DJ Jazzy Jeff and the Fresh Prince
9. Whigfield
10. Blur
11. Simply Red
12. The Prodigy
13. The Fugees
14. Gina G
15. The Spice Girls
16. No Doubt
17. R Kelly
18. Oasis
19. All Saints
20. Cliff Richard

Quiz 66: Chart-Toppers of the 2000s

EASY

Idenifty the artist or band who topped the charts with the following songs:

1. 'Ooops! ... I Did it Again' (2000)

2. 'Beautiful Day' (2000)

3. 'Love Don't Cost a Thing' (2001)

4. 'Can't Get You Out of My Head' (2001)

5. 'Dirrty' (2002)

6. 'Freak Like Me' (2002)

7. 'Crazy in Love' (2003)

8. 'Where Is the Love?' (2003)

9. 'Dry Your Eyes' (2004)

10. 'Is This the Way to Amarillo' (2005)

11. 'You're Beautiful' (2005)

12. 'You Raise Me Up' (2005)

13. 'Crazy' (2006)

14. 'Grace Kelly' (2007)

15. 'Ruby' (2007)

EASY

16. 'Merc y' (2008)

17. 'Viva La Vida' (2008)

18. 'Greatest Day' (2008)

19. 'Fight for This Love' (2009)

20. 'Killing in the Name' (2009)

Answers to Quiz 65: Pot Luck

1. Japan
2. Douglas
3. MMXIV
4. Avocado
5. Joseph
6. 50 Shades of Grey
7. William
8. 19 (prime numbers)
9. Argentina, Ecuador and Uruguay
10. Monkey
11. True
12. Blankety Blank
13. Kristen Stewart
14. 750ml
15. Her sheep
16. Basil
17. China and Mongolia
18. Glandular fever
19. Germany
20. O

Quiz 67: Pot Luck

EASY

1. The Canary Islands are situated in which ocean?

2. What is measured using the Beaufort scale?

3. What is the official residence of the president of France?

4. Carnegie Hall is a concert venue in which American city?

5. In which TV soap can characters enjoy a drink in Charlie's Bar?

6. The holy city of Mecca is in which country?

7. What is the fifth planet from the sun?

8. What shape can be equilateral, scalene or isosceles?

9. Which year is represented by the Roman numerals MCMLXVI?

10. What is 4 cubed?

11. Formosa oolong is a variety of which drink?

12. In the 'Winnie the Pooh' books, what type of creature is Eeyore?

13. A nightclub called Rick's Place featured in which classic wartime film?

14. The Tomb of the Unknown Warrior can be found in which British church?

15. The sporting venue Croke Park is in which city?

16. Prior to David Cameron, who was the last British prime minister to be born in England?

17. Which city hosted the Summer Olympics in 1984?

18. The fictional vampire Dracula was created by which author?

19. 1 Canada Square is the official name of which building?
    a) Canary Wharf Tower
    b) London Eye
    c) O_2 Arena

20. Which of the following is an annual literary prize?
    a) The Orange Prize
    b) The Purple Prize
    c) The Yellow Prize

EASY

Answers to Quiz 66: Chart-Toppers of the 2000s

1. Britney Spears
2. U2
3. Jennifer Lopez
4. Kylie Minogue
5. Christina Aguilera
6. Sugababes
7. Beyoncé
8. The Black Eyed Peas
9. The Streets
10. Tony Christie featuring Peter Kay
11. James Blunt
12. Westlife
13. Gnarls Barkley
14. Mika
15. Kaiser Chiefs
16. Duffy
17. Coldplay
18. Take That
19. Cheryl Cole
20. Rage Against the Machine

MEDIUM QUIZZES

Quiz 68: Pot Luck

1. What is the first name of Sherlock Holmes' adversary Professor Moriarty?

2. What vegetable is fermented to make the German food sauerkraut?

3. The Liberty Stadium can be found in which British city?

4. What word can mean both 'to cut' and 'to fasten'?

5. Tom Swift and His Electric Rifle was the original name of which non-lethal, electric-shock weapon?

6. Which film-making brothers directed the 2014 film 'Inside Llewyn Davis'?

7. True or false – Prime Minister David Cameron is a fan of Oxford United Football Club?

8. 'Wrecking Ball' was a 2013 hit for which female singer?

9. Kevin the Gerbil was the best friend of which anarchic puppet character?

10. Which male Christian name is also a unit of measurement for temperature?

11. Which social network celebrated its 10th anniversary in February 2014?

12. True or false – Kaiser Wilhelm II, emperor of Germany during the First World War, was the grandson of Britain's Queen Victoria?

13. The 2014 Winter Olympics were held in which Russian city?

14. Which singer mimed her way through the national anthem at Barack Obama's presidential inauguration in 2013?

15. Acrophobia is the fear of what?

16. 'Connecting people' is a slogan used by which technology company?

17. Which DJ, whose name is slang for 'wrong', was awarded an MBE in 2014?

18. The Royal Pavilion and The Lanes are in which English city?

19. Colin Dexter was the author behind which TV detective?
    a) Frost
    b) Morse
    c) Taggart

20. Complete the title of the play by Shelagh Delaney – 'A Taste of ...'
    a) Bunny
    b) Honey
    c) Money

Answers to Quiz 134: Pot Luck

1. Atlantic
2. Left
3. Inspector Rebus
4. Pele
5. John Major
6. Leeds
7. Violin
8. 1980s
9. True
10. Bizet
11. Des O'Connor (presenters of 'Countdown')
12. Tuberculosis
13. Two
14. 13
15. Virginia
16. Tuesday
17. Johannesburg
18. Boston
19. Manchester
20. Fruit and vegetables

MEDIUM

Quiz 69: Colours

1. 'A Study in Scarlet' was the first story to feature which fictional detective?

2. Played by Katherine Heigl, Izzy Stevens was a character in which long-running American medical drama?

3. What was the title of Prince's first UK top-10 album?

4. In the board game 'Cluedo', what is the name of the unfortunate murder victim?

5. Which sea is an inlet of the Indian Ocean, lying between Africa and Asia?

6. Which American rock group performed alongside Bruno Mars during the half-time show of the 2014 Super Bowl?

7. What colour is the highly alcoholic drink absinthe?

8. Complete the title of the classic album by jazz legend Miles Davis – 'Kind of...'?

9. Stephen Manderson is the real name of which British rapper who topped the charts in 2011 with Emeli Sandé with 'Read All About It'?

10. What is the name of the flag flown by ships in the British Merchant Navy?

11. What type of creature is a red admiral?

12. Which modern-day ITV drama centred on the search for a modern copycat killer replicating the murders of Jack the Ripper?

13. Peter Purves, Sarah Greene and Radzi Chinyanganya have all hosted which TV show?

14. 'Get The Party Started', 'Stupid Girls' and 'So What' were top five UK singles for which American singer?

15. Which female newsreader succeeded James Alexander Gordon in reading the classified football results on BBC Radio 5 Live?

16. What colour jersey is worn by the race leader in the Giro d'Italia cycle race?

17. What name is given to the fire engines used by the British army during times of national emergency?

18. 'Ol' Blue Eyes' was the nickname of which singer and actor?

19. What was the German fighter pilot Manfred Albrecht Freiherr von Richthofen better known as?
    a) The Black Baron
    b) The Red Baron
    c) The White Baron

20. What was the nickname of the eldest son of King Edward III of England?
    a) The Black Prince
    b) The Red Prince
    c) The White Prince

MEDIUM

Answers to Quiz 68: Pot Luck

1. James
2. Cabbage
3. Swansea
4. Clip
5. Taser
6. The Coen brothers
7. False
8. Miley Cyrus
9. Roland Rat
10. Kelvin
11. Facebook
12. True
13. Sochi
14. Beyoncé
15. Heights
16. Nokia
17. Pete Tong
18. Brighton
19. Morse
20. Honey

Quiz 70: Pot Luck

1. Someone suffering from haemophobia has an irrational fear of what?

2. Nancy Sinatra sang the theme song to which James Bond film?

3. Which rank in the Royal Air Force is abbreviated to 'LAC'?

4. In technology, what does the acronym 'wi-fi' stand for?

5. Cape Horn is the southernmost tip of which continent?

6. True or false – the phrase 'Elementary, my dear Watson' never actually appears in any of Arthur Conan Doyle's Sherlock Holmes books?

7. Which British athlete won gold in the 800m and 1500m at the 2004 Olympic Games?

8. Who was the first British prime minister to be born during the reign of Queen Elizabeth II?

9. Which spirit is used to make a mojito cocktail?

10. The ampere is a unit used to measure what?

11. Which country is sometimes referred to as 'the land of the long white cloud'?

12. In the TV comedy 'The Simpsons', what are the names of Ned Flanders' two children?

13. What are the two common English words that end with the letters -shion?

14. SW1A 1AA is the postcode of which famous London landmark?

15. Who is older – George W Bush or Bill Clinton?

16. The fabric mohair is produced by which animal?

17. Which famous football manager was made a UN ambassador against hunger for the World Food Programme in 2014?

18. In 1960, who became the first child to be born to a reigning British monarch for 103 years?

19. Which band topped the charts in 2014 with 'She Looks So Perfect'?
    a) 5 Seconds of Spring
    b) 5 Seconds of Summer
    c) 5 Seconds of Winter

20. Which of the following countries remained neutral during the Second World War?
    a) Canada
    b) Ireland
    c) New Zealand

Answers to Quiz 69: Colours

1. Sherlock Holmes
2. Grey's Anatomy
3. Purple Rain
4. Dr Black
5. Red Sea
6. The Red Hot Chili Peppers
7. Green
8. Blue
9. Professor Green
10. Red Ensign
11. Butterfly
12. Whitechapel
13. Blue Peter
14. Pink
15. Charlotte Green
16. Pink
17. Green Goddess
18. Frank Sinatra
19. The Red Baron
20. The Black Prince

MEDIUM

Quiz 71: World War II

1. Which US president ordered the dropping of atomic bombs on Japan during World War II?

2. In which month of 1939 did the World War II begin?

3. What was the first name of the Italian dictator Mussolini?

4. Which future prime minister was deputy prime minister in Britain's wartime national coalition government?

5. What was the nickname of the German military commander Erwin Rommel?

6. By what name was the Nazi propagandist broadcaster William Joyce also known?

7. Who was the emperor of Japan during World War II?

8. The name of which Norwegian politician, who collaborated with the Nazis during World War II, has become a synonym for a traitor?

9. Churchill, Stalin and Roosevelt met in which Middle-East capital in 1943 to discuss the opening of a second front in western Europe?

10. Which precious metal was used as a codename for one of the beaches used during the Allied Normandy Landings during World War II?

11. In which month of 1944 did the Normandy Landings take place?

12. Which organization was set up in May 1940 as Britain's 'Last Line of Defence' against German invasion?

13. In which year did post-World-War-II rationing end?

14. What was the codename of the operation to invade Normandy in the D-Day landings?

15. Which RAF squadron carried out the 'dambuster' raid during World War II?

16. Which manufacturer produced the famous Hurricane plane, which saw extensive duty in World War II?

17. The Maquis was a group of underground resistance fighters based in which country?

18. What was the first name of the RAF Air Chief Marshal known as 'Bomber' Harris?

19. Which of the following countries was not an 'Axis' power?
a) Italy   b) Japan   c) Turkey

What was the name of the operation that saw Allied forces take control of the Italian island of Sicily in 1943?
a) Operation Husky   b) Operation Grizzly Bear
c) Operation Sea Lion

MEDIUM

Answers to Quiz 70: Pot Luck

1. Blood
2. You Only Live Twice
3. Leading Aircraftman (or Aircraftwoman)
4. Wireless fidelity
5. South America
6. True
7. Kelly Holmes
8. Tony Blair
9. Rum
10. Electrical current
11. New Zealand
12. Rod and Todd
13. Cushion and fashion
14. Buckingham Palace
15. George W Bush
16. Angora goat
17. Jose Mourinho
18. Prince Andrew
19. 5 Seconds of Summer
20. Ireland

Quiz 72: Pot Luck

1. In a One Day International cricket match, each side can bat for a maximum of how many overs?

2. The scene of a major First World War naval battle, Jutland is a peninsula in which country?

3. 'Elementary', the US TV drama featuring Sherlock Holmes, is set in which American city?

4. In 2011, Enda Kenny became the prime minister of which country?

5. Which pop star enjoyed some 'Sexercize' in 2014?

6. What is the second highest mountain in the world?

7. How many stars appear on the flag of New Zealand?

8. Which racehorse owner's colours are purple body with gold braid, scarlet sleeves and black velvet cap with gold fringe?

9. B5 7QU is the postcode of which famous summer sporting venue?

10. True or false – there is a rifle range at the Houses of Parliament?

11. Prior to becoming US president, Barack Obama was a senator for which state?

12. Which classic 1975 film was released in France as 'Les Dents de la Mer'?

13. Roger Taylor was the drummer and John Deacon the bass player with which best-selling British rock band?

14. Al-Shabaab is a militant Islamist organization based in which African country?

15. What name is shared by the home of Middlesbrough FC and Durham County Cricket Club?

16. Which board game takes its name from the Latin for 'I play'?

17. The country known as the USSR ceased to exist in 1991. What did the initials USSR stand for?

18. Cynophobia is the fear of which domestic animal?

19. The 2013 G8 political summit was held in which part of the United Kingdom?
    a) Northern Ireland
    b) Scotland
    c) Wales

20. By what nickname were members of the Nazi paramilitary organization the SA known?
    a) Blueshirts
    b) Brownshirts
    c) Greenshirts

MEDIUM

Answers to Quiz 71: World War II

1.	Harry S Truman	11.	June
2.	September	12.	The Home Guard
3.	Benito	13.	1954
4.	Clement Attlee	14.	Operation Overlord
5.	The Desert Fox	15.	617 Squadron
6.	Lord Haw Haw	16.	Hawker
7.	Hirohito	17.	France
8.	Quisling	18.	Arthur
9.	Tehran	19.	Turkey
10.	Gold	20.	Operation Husky

Quiz 73: Silver and Gold

1. Which film company produced the classic musicals 'Singin' in the Rain', 'The Wizard of Oz' and 'On the Town'?

2. Pierce Brosnan made his debut as James Bond in which film?

3. 'Thank You for Being a Friend' was the theme song to which long-running American sitcom?

4. Which American singer starred alongside Mike Myers in the 2002 film comedy 'Austin Powers in Goldmember'?

5. The 'Goldberg Variations' is a piece of music written by which German composer who was born in 1685?

6. Founded in 1980, which awards are presented at a ceremony just prior to the Oscars to honour the worst films of the year?

7. Which synth duo recorded the hit albums 'Supernature', 'Seventh Tree' and 'Tales of Us'?

8. Ewan McGregor starred alongside Christian Bale in which 1998 film set in the world of 1970s glam rock?

9. Which Hollywood actor appeared alongside Kanye West on the 2005 hit single 'Gold Digger'?

10. Musician Damon Albarn, artist Damien Hirst and fashion designer Mary Quant all spent time at which London educational institution?

11. In which American state is the Golden Gate Bridge situated?

12. Who is the famous mother of actress Kate Hudson?

13. Which racing circuit hosted the British Grand Prix for the first time in 1948?

14. What is the gorilla-inspired nickname of darts champion Tony O'Shea?

15. Which BBC newsreader was born in Chigwell, Essex on 4 August 1970?

16. Which American actress was born Caryn Elaine Johnson on 13 November 1955?

17. Which American actress and comedian provided the voice of Vanellope von Schweetz in the hit 2012 animated movie 'Wreck-It Ralph'?

18. Norrin Radd is the alter ego of which comic-book superhero?

19. In which state of Australia is there a city called Gold Coast?
    a) New South Wales   b) Queensland   c) Victoria

20. Daniel Craig starred alongside Nicole Kidman in which 2007 fantasy-adventure film?
    a) The Golden Compass   b) The Golden Dagger
    c) The Golden Hammer

Answers to Quiz 72: Pot Luck

1. 50
2. Denmark
3. New York
4. Republic of Ireland
5. Kylie Minogue
6. K2
7. Four
8. Queen Elizabeth II
9. Edgbaston cricket ground
10. True
11. Illinois
12. Jaws
13. Queen
14. Somalia
15. The Riverside
16. Ludo
17. Union of Soviet Socialist Republics
18. Dog
19. Northern Ireland
20. Brownshirts

MEDIUM

Quiz 74: Pot Luck

1. Astraphobia is the irrational fear of which weather phenomenon?

2. In the Royal Navy, what rank is abbreviated as 'Cdre'?

3. The name of which Caribbean territory translates into English as 'rich port'?

4. 'Swifter, higher, stronger' is the motto of which organization?

5. Sir Winston Churchill attended which famous public school?

6. The Guggenheim Museum is in which Spanish city?

7. What nationality is the Formula One racing driver Felipe Massa?

8. What is the only Scandinavian country to have hosted football's World Cup?

9. Which actor and comedian is the host of the TV quiz show 'The Guest List'?

10. Who was Muhammad Ali's opponent in the fight known as 'The Rumble in the Jungle'?

11. Which country finished runner-up in the Rugby World Cup in 1987, 1999 and 2011?

12. Which Australian cricketer bowled the delivery known as 'the ball of the century'?

13. Ablutophobia is an irrational fear of what?

14. What is six cubed?

15. Who are the only parent and child to have won the BBC Sports Personality of the Year award?

16. Barcelona striker Neymar plays international football for which country?

17. TKCA 1ZZ is the postcode for which British overseas territory?

18. Clarence House is the official London residence of which member of the Royal Family?

19. A human being takes approximately how many breaths per day?
    a) 3000
    b) 13,000
    c) 23,000

20. Green does not appear on the flag of which of the following countries?
    a) Belarus
    b) Bosnia and Herzegovina
    c) Bulgaria

MEDIUM

Answers to Quiz 73: Silver and Gold

1.	Metro-Goldwyn-Mayer	11.	California
2.	GoldenEye	12.	Goldie Hawn
3.	The Golden Girls	13.	Silverstone
4.	Beyoncé	14.	Silverback
5.	JS Bach	15.	Kate Silverton
6.	The Golden Raspberries	16.	Whoopi Goldberg
7.	Goldfrapp	17.	Sarah Silverman
8.	Velvet Goldmine	18.	Silver Surfer
9.	Jamie Foxx	19.	Queensland
10.	Goldsmiths College	20.	The Golden Compass

Quiz 75: Earth, Wind and Fire

1. What is the biggest-selling single in UK chart history?

2. What is the fourth book in the Harry Potter series?

3. The 2013 film 'Catching Fire' is the second part in which film franchise?

4. On a standard UK plug, what colour is the earth wire?

5. Who was the subject of the 1989 film biopic 'Great Balls of Fire!'?

6. Which multiple Oscar-winning film was based on a 1936 novel by Margaret Mitchell?

7. Author Kenneth Grahame is best known for writing which novel, which was published for the first time in 1908?

8. The 1992 thriller 'Twin Peaks: Fire Walk with Me' was directed by which eccentric film maker?

9. Keanu Reeves played an alien called Klaatu in a 2008 remake of which sci-fi classic?

10. 'Erde' is the word for the earth in which European language?

11. Which Hollywood heart-throb had a UK top 20 hit in 1988 with 'She's Like the Wind'?

12. Which pair performed the 1982 Christmas duet 'Peace On Earth / Little Drummer Boy'?

13. Jarvis Cocker famously mooned at the 1996 Brit Awards while Michael Jackson was singing which song?

14. Which science-fiction film starring John Travolta won seven Golden Raspberry awards in 2001?

15. Which children's television programme is set in the fictional Welsh rural town of Pontypandy?

16. 'Reflektor' was a 2013 album by which critically acclaimed Canadian rock band?

17. Which is the only horse to have won the Aintree Grand National, the Scottish Grand National and the Welsh Grand National?

18. Which German rock group's only UK top-ten single was 1991's 'Wind of Change'?

19. Which band topped the charts in 1996 with 'Firestarter'?
    a) Leftfield
    b) The Prodigy
    c) Underworld

20. Which month provided the title of a 1978 hit for Earth, Wind and Fire?
    a) September
    b) October
    c) November

MEDIUM

Answers to Quiz 74: Pot Luck

1. Thunder and lightning
2. Commodore
3. Puerto Rico
4. The Olympic Games
5. Harrow
6. Bilbao
7. Brazilian
8. Sweden
9. Rob Brydon
10. George Foreman
11. France
12. Shane Warne
13. Washing
14. 216
15. Princess Anne and Zara Phillips
16. Brazil
17. Turks and Caicos
18. The Prince of Wales
19. 23,000
20. Bosnia and Herzegovina

Quiz 76: Pot Luck

MEDIUM

1. Which fictional sleuth had a housekeeper called Mrs Hudson?

2. The tuk-tuk is a type of auto-rickshaw commonly found in which Asian country?

3. 'The Italian Dragon' was the nickname of which British boxer?

4. Who are the two players to have won the men's singles at Wimbledon with the initials BB?

5. In which year did Queen Elizabeth II celebrate her diamond jubilee?

6. In the economic acronym 'BRIC', the letter 'B' represents which country?

7. The warrigal is an alternative name for which antipodean creature?

8. In 'The Wizard of Oz', what is Dorothy's surname?

9. Which flag is flown above Buckingham Palace when the monarch is in residence?

10. A bibliophile is a lover of what type of objects?

11. True or false – prior to finding fame as an actor, David Jason worked as an electrician?

12. A dodecagon is a shape with how many sides?

13. The axilla is the technical name for which part of the human body?

14. In 1951, Kiki Haakonson of Sweden became the first winner of which contest?

15. The Bank of England is based on which London thoroughfare?

Answers – page 157

16. Opened in 1997, what is the name of the reconstructed Elizabethan theatre on the South Bank of the River Thames in London?

17. In which English gaol was Oscar Wilde famously imprisoned?

18. In 2001, who became the first Croat to win the Men's Singles at Wimbledon?

19. Entomophobia is a fear of what type of creatures?
    a) dogs
    b) insects
    c) reptiles

20. Which actress played the title character in the 2011 film 'Bad Teacher'?
    a) Drew Barrymore
    b) Cameron Diaz
    c) Lucy Liu

MEDIUM

Answers to Quiz 75: Earth, Wind and Fire

1. Candle in the Wind 97
2. Harry Potter and the Goblet of Fire
3. The Hunger Games
4. Green and yellow stripes
5. Jerry Lee Lewis
6. Gone with the Wind
7. The Wind in the Willows
8. David Lynch
9. The Day the Earth Stood Still
10. German
11. Patrick Swayze
12. David Bowie and Bing Crosby
13. Earth Song
14. Battlefield Earth
15. Fireman Sam
16. Arcade Fire
17. Earth Summit
18. The Scorpions
19. The Prodigy
20. September

Quiz 77: Light and Dark

1. 'To infinity ... and beyond' is the catchphrase of which film character?

2. 'Out of the Blue', 'Discovery' and 'Time' were albums for which Birmingham rock band?

3. Tunde Baiyewu and Paul Tucker are the members of which pop band who recorded the hit singles 'Lifted', 'Raincloud' and 'High'?

4. Jessica Chastain was nominated for an Oscar in 2013 for her performance as a CIA analyst in which film?

5. Which cult 2001 film starring Jake Gyllenhaal and Drew Barrymore featured a giant rabbit called Frank?

6. A prism refracting white light into a rainbow appears on the cover of which album by English prog rockers Pink Floyd?

7. 'I Believe in a Thing Called Love' was a huge 2003 hit for which Suffolk-based rock band?

8. What was BBC Radio 2 formerly known as?

9. Benedict Cumberbatch played the villainous 'Khan' in which 2013 sci-fi drama?

10. Heath Ledger was posthumously awarded an Oscar in 2009 for his performance in which film?

11. Which British crooner had a top-five hit in 1970 with 'Daughter of Darkness'?

12. Bruce Willis and Cybill Shepherd ran a detective agency in which 1980s TV drama?

13. What is the atmospheric display aurora borealis also known as?

14. Which band recorded the theme song to the 1987 James Bond film 'The Living Daylights'?

15. What astronomical unit of length is equal to just under 9.5 trillion kilometres?

16. Who duetted with Take That on the 1993 number one hit 'Relight My Fire'?

17. In professional boxing, what division allows fighters weighing up to 12 and a half stone to compete?

18. 'We skipped the light fandango, turned cartwheels 'cross the floor' is the opening line of which 1967 number-one single?

19. What is the first book in Philip Pullman's 'His Dark Material's' fantasy series?
    a) Northern Lights   b) Southern Lights   c) Western Lights

20. What is the title of the Texas-set American football TV drama?
    a) Friday Night Lights   b) Saturday Night Lights
    c) Sunday Night Lights

MEDIUM

Answers to Quiz 76: Pot Luck

1. Sherlock Holmes
2. Thailand
3. Joe Calzaghe
4. Boris Becker and Bjorn Borg
5. 2012
6. Brazil
7. Dingo
8. Gale
9. The Royal Standard
10. Books
11. True
12. 12
13. Armpit
14. Miss World
15. Threadneedle Street
16. Shakespeare's Globe
17. Reading
18. Goran Ivanisevic
19. Insects
20. Cameron Diaz

Quiz 78: Pot Luck

1. Which international rugby team plays its home matches at Estadio José Amalfitani?

2. Elsinore Castle in Denmark is the setting for which Shakespeare play?

3. Which vegetable is also the name of a satirical newspaper and website?

4. Italian football giants Juventus are based in which city?

5. Frank Underwood is the central character in which US political drama, which was based on a British TV show?

6. The Pampas is an area of lowlands in which continent?

7. The American leg of the 1985 Live Aid concert was held in which city?

8. In relation to online retailing, what do the initials 'ASOS' stand for?

9. In which film did Clint Eastwood deliver the famous lines, 'You've got to ask yourself one question. Do I feel lucky? Well, do ya, punk?'

10. Prior to Andy Murray, the last British man to win the Men's Singles at Wimbledon did so in which decade?

11. In online slang, what do the initials 'RBTL' stand for?

12. By what name is the medical condition somnambulism more commonly known?

13. Christopher Trace and Leila Williams were the first presenters of which long-running children's television show?

14. In 2010, 33 miners were rescued after spending 69 days trapped underground in a mine in which country?

Answers – page 161

15. 'I Could Be So Good for You' was the theme song to which classic TV drama?

16. 'Marley was dead to begin with' is the opening line from which story by Charles Dickens?

17. What is the only British place-name that appears in the title of a play by Shakespeare?

18. Tracy Draco was the ill-fated wife of which film character?

19. What is the name of the most popular house name in the UK?
    a) The Cottage
    b) The Lodge
    c) Woodlands

20. The UK is made up of approximately how many addresses?
    a) 19 million
    b) 29 million
    c) 39 million

Answers to Quiz 77: Light and Dark

1. Buzz Lightyear
2. Electric Light Orchestra
3. Lighthouse Family
4. Zero Dark Thirty
5. Donnie Darko
6. The Dark Side of the Moon
7. The Darkness
8. The Light Programme
9. Star Trek: Into Darkness
10. The Dark Knight
11. Tom Jones
12. Moonlighting
13. Northern Lights
14. A-ha
15. Light year
16. Lulu
17. Light heavyweight
18. A Whiter Shade of Pale
19. Northern Lights
20. Friday Night Lights

Quiz 79: The Good, the Bad and the Ugly

1. Who wrote the classic fairy tale 'The Ugly Duckling'?

2. Who finished fourth in reality TV show 'Big Brother' in 2002?

3. Buster Bloodvessel was the lead singer with which ska band?

4. 'The Funky Gibbon' was a hit in 1975 for which comedy team?

5. What title was shared by a 1983 single by Wham! and a 1995 film starring Will Smith?

6. Which singer topped the UK album charts in 2007 with 'Good Girl Gone Bad'?

7. Which actor and comedian, best known for a long stint in 'EastEnders', had a top-ten hit in 1975 with a novelty version of 'The Ugly Duckling'?

8. 'Ebenezer Goode' was the only number-one single by which band?

9. Bryan Cranston played crystal-meth dealer Walter White in which acclaimed TV drama?

10. Henry Hill and James Conway are the central characters in which classic crime movie?

11. Margo and Jerry Leadbetter were characters in which classic TV comedy?

12. Robin Williams was nominated for a Best Actor Oscar in 1988 for his performance as DJ Adrian Cronauer in which film?

13. Matt Damon and Ben Affleck won a Best Screenplay Oscar in 1998 for which film?

14. Which American TV drama was set at a fashion magazine called 'Mode'?

15. What is the stage name of Manchester singer-songwriter Damon Gough?

16. What political accord was reached in Northern Ireland on 10 April 1998?

17. Which international sporting event, held for the first time in Moscow in 1986, was created in response to political boycotts of the Olympic Games?

18. What was Adam Ant's only solo UK number-one single?

19. What was the title of a 2009 number one by Lady Gaga?
    a) Bad Company   b) Bad Romance   c) Bad Trip

20. Which British prime minister was once a member of a band called The Ugly Rumours?
    a) Tony Blair   b) Gordon Brown   c) David Cameron

MEDIUM

Answers to Quiz 78: Pot Luck

1. Argentina	11. Read between the lines
2. Hamlet	12. Sleep-walking
3. The Onion	13. Blue Peter
4. Turin	14. Chile
5. House of Cards	15. Minder
6. South America	16. A Christmas Carol
7. Philadelphia	17. Windsor
8. As Seen On Screen	18. James Bond
9. Dirty Harry	19. The Cottage
10. 1930s	20. 29 million

Quiz 80: Pot Luck

1. In late 2013, which American city, home of the Motown record label, entered bankruptcy proceedings?

2. Striker Samuel Eto'o plays international football for which country?

3. What was the Indian city of Mumbai formerly known as?

4. On a standard dartboard, what number lies between 18 and 20?

5. Which former planet was named after the Roman god of the underworld?

6. Actor and comedian Russell Brand is a fan of which English football club?

7. True or false – athlete and Olympic Games organizer Seb Coe was once a Member of Parliament?

8. Merseyside managers Brendan Rodgers and Roberto Martinez both had spells in charge at which football club?

9. In the classic film 'The Jungle Book', what type of animal was Kaa?

10. What does the 'W' in the name of US president George W Bush stand for?

11. In which sport do teams compete for the Fed Cup?

12. The Eagles, Phillies and 76ers are sporting teams in which American city?

13. A USB connection is often used to transfer computer files. What do the initials 'USB' stand for?

14. In May 2014, Narendra Modi became the prime minister of which country?

Answers – page 165

15. Which British sculptor created 'The Angel of the North'?

16. Which artist's mural 'His Flower Girl' was auctioned for almost £130,000 in December 2013?

17. Tea Olive, Pink Dogwood and Flowering Peach are the names of holes at which famous American golf course?

18. In the TV sitcom 'Porridge', what were Fletcher's two Christian names?

19. A lion appears on the flag of which country?
    a) India
    b) Pakistan
    c) Sri Lanka

20. In which field of the arts is Simon Armitage a notable name?
    a) classical music
    b) painting
    c) poetry

MEDIUM

Answers to Quiz 79: The Good, the Bad and the Ugly

1. Hans Christian Andersen
2. Jade Goody
3. Bad Manners
4. The Goodies
5. Bad Boys
6. Rihanna
7. Mike Reid
8. The Shamen
9. Breaking Bad
10. Goodfellas
11. The Good Life
12. Good Morning, Vietnam
13. Good Will Hunting
14. Ugly Betty
15. Badly Drawn Boy
16. Good Friday Agreement
17. The Goodwill Games
18. Goody Two Shoes
19. Bad Romance
20. Tony Blair

Quiz 81: It's Chris

1. In 2013, who became the second British rider to win the Tour de France?

2. Which DJ described himself as 'the saviour of Radio One'?

3. Which broadcaster was the first husband of actress and singer Billie Piper?

4. Who is the lead singer with Coldplay?

5. Which Irish actor played Rhodes in the hit 2011 film comedy 'Bridesmaids' and also stars in the Sky TV comedy 'Moone Boy'?

6. Who won athletics gold for Great Britain in the 400m at the 2008 Olympic Games?

7. Who was the first non-American to play Batman on the big screen?

8. Which Hollywood star appeared in the video to the Fatboy Slim song 'Weapon of Choice'?

9. 'What a Girl Wants', 'Beautiful' and 'Fighter' were hits in the early 2000s for which singer?

10. Which actor played vet James Herriot in the TV drama 'All Creatures Great and Small'?

11. Which rapper received five years' probation and six months' community labour for beating his then girlfriend Rihanna?

12. Which actor and comedian provided the voice of Marty in the 2005 film 'Madagascar' and its subsequent sequels in 2008 and 2012?

13. Footballer Frank Lampard got engaged to which broadcaster in June 2011?

14. Which actor is best known for playing Dr Emmett Brown in the 'Back to the Future' film trilogy?

15. Golfer Greg Norman was the third husband of which American sportswoman?

16. Which American supermodel is credited with popularizing navel piercings?

17. Who played Superman in the 1978 film of the same name?

18. Which British singer took 'The Road To Hell' before 'Driving Home for Christmas'?

19. Christopher Martin-Jenkins was a noted broadcaster on which sport?
    a) cricket
    b) horse racing
    c) tennis

20. In which sport is Chris Foy a match official?
    a) cricket
    b) football
    c) snooker

MEDIUM

Answers to Quiz 80: Pot Luck

1. Detroit
2. Cameroon
3. Bombay
4. 1
5. Pluto
6. West Ham United
7. True
8. Swansea City
9. Snake
10. Walker
11. Tennis
12. Philadelphia
13. Universal Serial Bus
14. India
15. Sir Antony Gormley
16. Banksy
17. Augusta
18. Norman Stanley
19. Sri Lanka
20. Poetry

Quiz 82: Pot Luck

1. The Kumbh Mela is a festival celebrated by followers of which religion?

2. Jazz musician Charlie Parker played which instrument?

3. In which sport might a fortunate player be offered a 'mulligan'?

4. Which is the closest planet to Earth?

5. In which decade was the Eurovision Song Contest held for the first time?

6. In area, which is larger – the Isle of Man or the Isle of Wight?

7. In January 2014, Spaniard Pepe Mel took over as manager of which English football club?

8. Which German-born artist was the court painter for King Henry VIII?

9. Aspiring stand-up comic Rupert Pupkin is the central character in which Martin Scorsese-directed film?

10. What is the largest country in Scandinavia?

11. Sir David Brailsford was a performance director for which Olympic sport?

12. Excluding Greater London, what is Britain's busiest airport?

13. Highgrove House, the country home of the Prince of Wales, is in which English county?

14. In September 2013, who became the prime minister of Australia?

15. 'Mungojerrie and Rumpleteazer', 'Memory' and 'The Awful Battle of The Pekes and the Pollicles' are songs from which musical?

16. Who is the host of the TV comedy quiz show '8 Out of 10 Cats Does Countdown'?

17. What is seven cubed?

18. At the World Indoor Athletics Championships, the shortest race is run over what distance?

19. Which annual festival takes place at Henham Park, Southwold, Suffolk?
    a) Equator Festival
    b) Latitude Festival
    c) Longitude Festival

20. Which of the following is the name of a Welsh rugby player?
    a) Leigh Halfpenny
    b) Leigh Pound
    c) Leigh Shilling

MEDIUM

Answers to Quiz 81: It's Chris

1. Chris Froome
2. Chris Moyles
3. Chris Evans
4. Chris Martin
5. Chris O'Dowd
6. Christine Ohuruogu
7. Christian Bale
8. Christopher Walken
9. Christina Aguilera
10. Christopher Timothy
11. Chris Brown
12. Chris Rock
13. Christine Bleakley
14. Christopher Lloyd
15. Chris Evert
16. Christy Turlington
17. Christopher Reeve
18. Chris Rea
19. Cricket
20. Football

Quiz 83: Television

1. Siegfried and Tristan Farnon were characters in which long-running veterinary drama?

2. Who is the host of the American version of the TV show 'The Apprentice'?

3. The hit detective dramas 'Ashes to Ashes' and 'Life on Mars' took their titles from songs by which musician?

4. 'That's Livin' Alright' by Joe Fagin was the theme song to which classic 1980s drama?

5. Michael Aspel, Liza Tarbuck, Simon Mayo and Bob Holness have all hosted which quiz show?

6. Which famous chef was the star of 'The F Word'?

7. In the sitcom 'Friends', which actor played Monica's on again, off again boyfriend, Dr Richard Burke?

8. The factory canteen at HWD Components is the setting for which TV sitcom?

9. In the sitcom 'Gavin and Stacey', which football team did Gavin support?

10. Who is the host of the daytime TV quiz show 'Perfection'?

11. Which children's TV programme featured a lighthouse keeper called The Captain and characters called Gobo, Wembley, Mokey and Red?

12. An animated character called Mr Chips appears in which TV game show?

13. Michael Brandon and Glynis Barber played which 1980s TV detective duo?

14. The classic comedy 'Fawlty Towers' was set in which English seaside resort?

15. In the TV show 'Countdown', contestants choose how many letters in each round?

16. Which fashion designer was the co-host of the late-night TV show 'Eurotrash'?

17. Which TV soap ran from 2 November 1982 until 4 November 2003?

18. Inspector Edmund Reid, Detective Sergeant Bennet Drake and Captain Homer Jackson are characters in which historical crime drama?

19. What was the setting for the Channel 4 sitcom 'Desmond's?
    a) barber's shop   b) grocer's   c) restaurant

20. Philip and Elizabeth Jennings are the central characters in which espionage drama?
    a) The Americans   b) The Brits   c) The Russians

MEDIUM

Answers to Quiz 82: Pot Luck

1. Hinduism
2. Saxophone
3. Golf
4. Venus
5. 1950s
6. Isle of Man
7. West Bromwich Albion
8. Hans Holbein
9. The King of Comedy
10. Sweden
11. Cycling
12. Manchester
13. Gloucestershire
14. Tony Abbott
15. Cats
16. Jimmy Carr
17. 343
18. 60m
19. Latitude Festival
20. Leigh Halfpenny

Quiz 84: Pot Luck

1. Which renowned comedian, actor and wit said, 'I never forget a face, but in your case I'd be glad to make an exception'?

2. Which planet is named after the Roman ruler of the gods and heavens?

3. In relation to time, what do the initials AM stand for?

4. Which European city is known locally as Den Haag?

5. Which best-selling British band took their name from a South African football team?

6. In 2011, Hosni Mubarak was ousted as president of which country?

7. What were the first names of the motor manufacturers Rolls and Royce?

8. What do the initials 'PVC' stand for?

9. Britain's most prestigious theatre awards are named after which actor?

10. Which American golfer won his second US Masters title in three years in 2014?

11. 'And did those feet in ancient time' is the opening line of which patriotic song?

12. Which gardening organization was founded in 1804 by botanist Joseph Banks?

13. In Olympic athletic events, what is the longest race that takes place solely on the track?

14. In which decade was the voting age in Britain reduced from 21 to 18?

15. 'All the news that's fit to print' is the motto of which international newspaper?

16. In the classic comedy 'Rising Damp', what was the first name of Miss Jones?

17. The Mau Mau Uprising was an armed conflict in which African country?

18. Neil Armstrong was the first man to walk on the moon. Who was the second?

19. Epistaxis is the medical term for what?
    a) ear ache
    b) nose bleed
    c) sprained ankle

20. Which of the following was a code-breaking centre during World War II?
    a) Bletchley Park
    b) Edgeley Park
    c) Sedgeley Park

MEDIUM

Answers to Quiz 83: Television

1. All Creatures Great and Small
2. Donald Trump
3. David Bowie
4. Auf Wiedersehen, Pet
5. Blockbusters
6. Gordon Ramsay
7. Tom Selleck
8. Dinnerladies
9. Tottenham Hotspur
10. Nick Knowles
11. Fraggle Rock
12. Catchphrase
13. Dempsey and Makepeace
14. Torquay
15. Nine
16. Jean-Paul Gaultier
17. Brookside
18. Ripper Street
19. Barber's shop
20. The Americans

Quiz 85: Singing Soap Stars

Identify the soap actor or actress who recorded the following hit songs:

1. 'Too Many Broken Hearts' (1989) – Neighbours

2. 'Anyone Can Fall In Love' (1986) – EastEnders

3. 'Hand on Your Heart' (1989) – Neighbours

4. 'Every Loser Wins' (1986) – EastEnders

5. 'Good Day' (1996) – EastEnders

6. 'Torn' (1997) – Neighbours

7. 'Perfect Moment' (1999) – EastEnders

8. 'One Voice (1993) – Coronation Street

9. 'Kiss Kiss' (2002) – Neighbours

10. 'Baby I Don't Care' (2003) – Brookside

11. 'When I Need You' (1998) – Hollyoaks

12. 'Don't It Make You Feel Good?' (1989) – Neighbours

13. 'Good Thing Going' (2000) – EastEnders

14. 'Born To Try' (2003) – Neighbours

15. 'I Breathe Again' (1999) – Coronation Street

16. 'Sweetness' (1994) – EastEnders

17. 'I Begin to Wonder' (2003) – Home and Away

18. 'Mona' (1990) – Neighbours

19. 'Something Outa Nothing' (1986) – EastEnders

20. 'Just This Side of Love' (1990) – Emmerdale

MEDIUM

Answers to Quiz 84: Pot Luck

1. Groucho Marx
2. Jupiter
3. Ante meridiem
4. The Hague
5. Kaiser Chiefs
6. Egypt
7. Charles and Henry
8. Polyvinyl chloride
9. Sir Laurence Olivier
10. Bubba Watson
11. Jerusalem
12. Royal Horticultural Society
13. 10,000m
14. 1960s
15. New York Times
16. Ruth
17. Kenya
18. Buzz Aldrin
19. Nose bleed
20. Bletchley Park

Quiz 86: Pot Luck

1. Which British actor played George Smiley in the 2011 film 'Tinker, Tailor, Soldier, Spy'?

2. Which board game provided the inspiration for a 2012 film starring Liam Neeson?

3. What name is shared by a member of the band Destiny's Child and the actress nominated for an Oscar in 2012 for her performance in 'My Week with Marilyn'?

4. Which Australian territory is surrounded entirely by the state of New South Wales?

5. True or false – actors Michael and Diane Keaton are brother and sister?

6. Keirin, pursuit and omnium are events in which sport?

7. In 2012, actress, model and singer Jessica Biel married which actor and musician?

8. True or false – rapper, singer and producer Pharrell Williams has a son called Rocket Man Williams?

9. Which city is closer to London as the crow flies – Amsterdam or Dublin?

10. Who was the first man to reach the South Pole?

11. The Tyrrhenian Sea lies on the western coast of which European country?

12. Which British adventurer was the first man to cross both polar ice-caps and climb Mount Everest?

13. Which actress married Prince Rainier, Monaco's head of state, in 1956?

14. In radio, what do the initials 'FM' stand for?

15. Starring Mel Gibson, the 1979 apocalyptic movie 'Mad Max' was set in which country?

Answers – page 177

16. The site of a famous siege in the Boer War, Mafeking is in which modern-day country?

17. Which occupation is shared by Patrick Grant, Richard Anderson and Ozwald Boateng?

18. Home to an American military base, Guantanamo Bay is on which Caribbean island?

19. The Royal Opera House is in which part of London?
    a) Chelsea
    b) Covent Garden
    c) Kensington

20. Which of the following events is not part of an Olympic decathlon?
    a) discus
    b) hammer
    c) javelin

MEDIUM

Answers to Quiz 85: Singing Soap Stars

1. Jason Donovan
2. Anita Dobson
3. Kylie Minogue
4. Nick Berry
5. Sean Maguire
6. Natalie Imbruglia
7. Martine McCutcheon
8. Bill Tarmey
9. Holly Vallance
10. Jennifer Ellison
11. Will Mellor
12. Stefan Dennis
13. Sid Owen
14. Delta Goodrem
15. Adam Rickitt
16. Michelle Gayle
17. Dannii Minogue
18. Craig McLachlan (and Check 1-2)
19. Letitia Dean and Paul Medford
20. Malandra Burrows

Quiz 87: History

1. Jawaharlal Nehru was the first prime minister of which country?

2. What was the name of the archbishop who was murdered by followers of King Henry II at Canterbury Cathedral in 1170?

3. Eva Peron, the subject of the hit musical 'Evita', was the first lady of which country?

4. Who is Britain's longest-reigning monarch?

5. Who was Britain's longest serving 20th-century prime minister?

6. The Battle of Waterloo was fought in which year?

7. Which country underwent a 'Cultural Revolution' between 1966 and 1976?

8. Which king led the English to victory in the Battle of Agincourt?

9. What famous document, first sealed in 1215, translates into English as 'Great Charter'?

10. In 1314, Robert the Bruce led the Scottish forces to victory over the English in which famous battle?

11. Who was the leader of the Soviet Union during the Cuban Missile Crisis?

12. In 1783, who became Britain's youngest prime minister at the age of just 24?

13. Who was Britain's first Welsh-speaking prime minister?

14. The United Kingdom joined the European Community in which year?

15. In which year did the Channel Tunnel open?

16. Which British prime minister was assassinated in 1812?

17. General Augusto Pinochet was the leader of which South American country?

18. Which American city was devastated by a massive earthquake and fire in 1906?

19. In which year did Queen Victoria die?
    a) 1891
    b) 1901
    c) 1911

20. 2014 marks which anniversary of the birth of Shakespeare?
    a) 400th
    b) 450th
    c) 500th

MEDIUM

Answers to Quiz 86: Pot Luck

1. Gary Oldman
2. Battleships
3. Michelle Williams
4. Australian Capital Territory
5. False
6. Cycling
7. Justin Timberlake
8. True
9. Amsterdam
10. Roald Amundsen
11. Italy
12. Sir Ranulph Fiennes
13. Grace Kelly
14. Frequency modulation
15. Australia
16. South Africa
17. Tailor
18. Cuba
19. Covent Garden
20. Hammer

Quiz 88: Pot Luck

1. A wheel-like symbol known as the 'Ashoka Chakra' appears on the flag of which Asian country?

2. In relation to dates, what do the initials 'BCE' stand for?

3. The Little Mermaid statue can be found in which European capital?

4. Which former pirate radio station celebrated its 50th anniversary in 2014?

5. Standing 170m high, the Spinnaker Tower is a feature of which English coastal city?

6. An instrumental piece of music called 'Yakety Sax' was the theme tune for which comedian?

7. Which American TV series featured a night spot called the Bada Bing?

8. In which year did the first gay weddings in England take place?

9. In terms of personnel, which country has the largest army in the world?

10. MacLaren's pub is one of the main settings for which long-running American sitcom?

11. Birmingham solicitor's clerk Anthony E Pratt was the inventor of which popular board came?

12. Wat Tyler was the leader of which famous 14th-century rebellion?

13. In 'The Simpsons', what is the nickname of Springfield's baseball team?

14. Which wartime heroine did Justin Bieber describe as 'a great girl. Hopefully she would have been a Belieber.'?

15. Which team were the first winners of the Cricket World Cup?

16. The song 'Always Look on the Bright Side of Life' first appeared in which film comedy?

17. Which Page 3 model co-hosted the 1989 BRIT Awards alongside Fleetwood Mac's Mick Fleetwood?

18. Football club Internazionale is based in which Italian city?

19. Author Martina Cole is associated with which genre of fiction?
    a) crime
    b) romance
    c) science fiction

20. Which of the following is a London music festival?
    a) Dancebox
    b) Groovebox
    c) Lovebox

MEDIUM

Answers to Quiz 87: History

1. India	11. Nikita Khrushchev
2. Thomas Becket	12. William Pitt the Younger
3. Argentina	13. David Lloyd George
4. Queen Victoria	14. 1973
5. Margaret Thatcher	15. 1994
6. 1815	16. Spencer Perceval
7. China	17. Chile
8. Henry V	18. San Francisco
9. Magna Carta	19. 1901
10. Bannockburn	20. 450th

Quiz 89: Famous Jacks

1. Which footballer made his full England debut against Hungary on 11 August 2010?

2. What is the name of the captain in the 'Pirates of the Caribbean' film franchise?

3. What was the name of the character played by Kiefer Sutherland in the hit TV drama '24'?

4. Which actor received his first Oscar nomination in 1970 for his performance in the cult classic 'Easy Rider'?

5. Which British racing driver received a knighthood in 2001?

6. Between 2006 and 2013, Scott Maslen played which character in TV soap 'EastEnders'?

7. Which actor starred as Jerry alongside Marilyn Monroe and Tony Curtis in the classic comedy 'Some Like It Hot'?

8. Which golfer won 18 major championships between 1962 and 1986?

9. What number-one hit by the Rolling Stones was also the title of a 1986 spy comedy starring Whoopi Goldberg?

10. In which sport was Australia's Jack Brabham a notable name?

11. Which English football manager led Ireland to the World Cup Finals in 1990 and 1994?

12. Which actor, whose credits include 'Shallow Hal' and 'School of Rock', is one half of the rock band Tenacious D?

13. Who was the first black heavyweight boxing champion of the world?

14. 'Chances', 'Lucky' and 'The World is Full of Married Men' are novels by which Anglo-American author?

15. Played by John Barrowman, Captain Jack Harkness is the central character in which 'Dr Who' spin-off?

16. According to the proverb, what 'makes Jack a dull boy'?

17. Which world champion athlete was runner-up in TV show 'Strictly Come Dancing' in 2005?

18. Which eccentric wicketkeeper won 54 Test caps for England between 1988 and 1998?

19. Based on a novel by Lee Child, what was the title of a 2012 film starring Tom Cruise?
a) Jack Leader   b) Jack Reacher   c) Jack Striver

20. Jackson is the capital city of which US state?
a) Alabama   b) Mississippi   c) Missouri

MEDIUM

Answers to Quiz 88: Pot Luck

1. India
2. Before Common Era
3. Copenhagen
4. Radio Caroline
5. Portsmouth
6. Benny Hill
7. The Sopranos
8. 2014
9. China
10. How I Met Your Mother
11. Cluedo
12. The Peasants' Revolt
13. Springfield Isotopes
14. Anne Frank
15. West Indies
16. Monty Python's Life of Brian
17. Samantha Fox
18. Milan
19. Crime
20. Lovebox

Quiz 90: Pot Luck

1. The musical 'I Can't Sing' was a spoof of which TV show?

2. In which month do Americans mark 'Veterans Day'?

3. True or false – the late Hollywood star Heath Ledger first found fame in TV soap 'Neighbours'?

4. Nollywood is the name of the film industry of which African country?

5. Film-maker Woody Allen is an accomplished player of which musical instrument?

6. According to former prime minister Harold Wilson, what 'is a long time in politics'?

7. Minnie Higginbottom was the real name of which actress, best known for playing Northern battleaxes?

8. Which of the footballing Charlton brothers is older – Bobby or Jack?

9. Who is the patron saint of children, seamen, scholars, brides and the hungry?

10. Ricky Wilson is the lead singer with which band?

11. In which decade was VAT introduced in the UK?

12. 2014 marked the 100th anniversary of which poet and playwright, best known for 'Under Milk Wood'?

13. Who is the only British prime minister to be a science graduate?

14. Who is the leading run-scorer in the history of Test cricket?

15. What is the final event of a women's Olympic heptathlon?

Answers – page 185

16. True or false – Queen Elizabeth II was born in Buckingham Palace?

17. Which long-running TV drama was set in the fictional London borough of Canley?

18. Which 20th-century US president was a peanut farmer prior to entering politics?

19. On which subject is Robert Peston a noted journalist?
    a) economics
    b) horse racing
    c) football

20. Which of the following American states does not share a land border with Canada?
    a) Minnesota
    b) Oregon
    c) Washington

MEDIUM

Answers to Quiz 89: Famous Jacks

1. Jack Wilshere
2. Jack Sparrow
3. Jack Bauer
4. Jack Nicholson
5. Sir Jackie Stewart
6. Jack Branning
7. Jack Lemmon
8. Jack Nicklaus
9. Jumpin' Jack Flash
10. Motor racing
11. Jack Charlton
12. Jack Black
13. Jack Johnson
14. Jackie Collins
15. Torchwood
16. All work and no play
17. Colin Jackson
18. Jack Russell
19. Jack Reacher
20. Mississippi

Quiz 91: North, South, East and West

MEDIUM

1. Charlotte is the largest city in which American state?

2. Which country knocked England out of the 1990 World Cup?

3. The 2010 album 'Gravity' was the last to be released by which band?

4. Which country hosted football's World Cup in 2010?

5. Which football team plays its home games at a ground that is also the name of a wife of Henry VIII?

6. Who won his second best-director Oscar in 2005 for 'Million Dollar Baby'?

7. Based on a novel by John Updike, which 1987 film starred Cher, Michelle Pfeiffer and Susan Sarandon as a trio of single women who saw their wishes granted?

8. UEA are the initials of which English higher-education establishment?

9. 'Northern Star' was a top-five hit in 1999 for which former Spice Girl?

10. 'Maria', 'America' and 'Tonight' are songs from which Leonard Bernstein musical?

11. The Cobblers is the nickname of which English football team?

12. The 1985 hit 'We Close Our Eyes' was the only top-ten single for which band?

13. Which was the first English football club to complete the League and Cup double?

14. 'There Is Nothing Like a Dame', 'Some Enchanted Evening' and 'Happy Talk' are songs from which Rodgers and Hammerstein musical?

15. Which crime drama from the 1990s featured a Canadian mounted policeman who worked with the Chicago police?

16. By what name is the constellation Crux also known?

17. James Dean received the first ever posthumous Oscar nomination in 1955 for his performance in which film?

18. South Central is a district of which American city?

19. Daniel Craig, Christopher Eccleston and Mark Strong all starred in which 1996 TV drama? 'Our Friends in the ...'
    a) North   b) South   c) West

20. Eastville is a district of which English city?
    a) Birmingham   b) Bristol   c) Liverpool

MEDIUM

Answers to Quiz 90: Pot Luck

1. The X Factor
2. November
3. False – he was in 'Home and Away'
4. Nigeria
5. Clarinet
6. A week
7. Kathy Staff
8. Jack
9. St Nicholas
10. Kaiser Chiefs
11. 1970s
12. Dylan Thomas
13. Margaret Thatcher
14. Sachin Tendulkar
15. 800m
16. False
17. The Bill
18. Jimmy Carter
19. Economics
20. Oregon

Quiz 92: Pot Luck

1. Which combat sport has the initials MMA?

2. As a teenager, which technology entrepreneur created Traf-O-Data, a company that sold traffic-counting systems to local governments?

3. What type of creature is a flying fox?

4. Which film by the Coen Brothers was turned into a 2014 TV series starring Martin Freeman?

5. 'Some boys kiss me, some boys hug me, I think they're ok' are the opening words to which hit song?

6. The detective drama 'Endeavour' is based on a character created by which author?

7. In the Metropolitan Police, which rank comes above Chief Inspector?

8. Which Spice Girl celebrated her 40th birthday on 17 April 2014?

9. Dominic Toretto is the central character in which film franchise?

10. Prior to taking the throne, which English monarch was known as Prince Hal?

11. Wisteria Lane in the fictional town of Fairview was the setting for which American TV drama?

12. Which children's TV character was described as 'An old, saggy cloth cat. Baggy and a bit loose at the seams, but Emily loved him'?

13. On which day of the week does the annual Royal Maundy Service take place?

14. Which four American states share a land border with Mexico?

15. True or false – Boy Scouts can earn a badge in circus skills?

16. Which fictional TV detective has had assistants called Maddie, Carla, Joey and Polly?

17. Which French fashion designer and broadcaster created Madonna's famous 'cone bra'?

18. Which girl group provided the Motown record label with its first UK number one hit single?

19. Thor is the Norse god of what?
    a) Sunshine   b) Thunder   c) Wine

20. What nationality is the tennis champion Caroline Wozniacki?
    a) Danish   b) Polish   c) Ukrainian

MEDIUM

Answers to Quiz 91: North, South, East and West

1. North Carolina
2. West Germany
3. Westlife
4. South Africa
5. West Ham United (Boleyn Ground)
6. Clint Eastwood
7. The Witches of Eastwick
8. University of East Anglia
9. Mel C
10. West Side Story
11. Northampton Town
12. Go West
13. Preston North End
14. South Pacific
15. Due South
16. Southern Cross
17. East of Eden
18. Los Angeles
19. North
20. Bristol

Quiz 93: Smith and Jones

1. 'Me and Mrs Jones' was the only UK top 20 single for which American soul singer?

2. Played by Hugo Weaving, 'Agent Smith' is the principal baddie in which sci-fi film franchise?

3. Which American musician produced Michael Jackson's hit albums 'Off The Wall', 'Thriller' and 'Bad'?

4. CIA agent Stan Smith, his wife Francine, and their children Hayley and Steve are the central characters in which US animated comedy?

5. Who was Britain's first female Home Secretary?

6. 'Real Real Real', 'Right Here Right Now' and 'International Bright Young Thing' were hits in the 1990s for which indie rock band?

7. The Smithsonian American Art Museum is located in which US city?

8. Which Nottingham-born fashion designer was the subject of an exhibition at the Design Museum in late 2013 and early 2014?

9. Which former 'Blue Peter' presenter finished third in the 2007 series of 'Strictly Come Dancing'?

10. During the University Boat Race, the crews pass under two bridges. Barnes Bridge is one, what is the other?

11. Which actress plays Betty Draper in American TV drama 'Mad Men'?

12. Which religious movement was founded by American Joseph Smith in 1830?

13. Which brewery produces beverages called Yorkshire Stingo and Taddy Lager?

14. 'The Bald Eagle' was the nickname of which English football manager who had spells in charge at Blackburn, Birmingham, Oxford, QPR, Newcastle, Portsmouth and Derby?

15. Which singer had top-ten hits in the 1980s with 'New Song', 'What Is Love?' and 'Pearl in the Shell'?

16. Which Trinidadian footballer has played for Southampton, Sheffield Wednesday (on loan), Sunderland, Stoke City and Cardiff City?

17. Which controversial female journalist appeared in the 2014 season of 'Celebrity Big Brother'?

18. Kelly Jones is the lead singer with which rock band?

19. TV sitcom 'Citizen Smith' was set in which area of London?
a) Teddington   b) Tooting   c) Tottenham

20. Danny Jones is a guitarist and singer with which band?
a) Busted   b) McFly   c) One Direction

MEDIUM

Answers to Quiz 92: Pot Luck

1. Mixed martial arts
2. Bill Gates
3. Bat
4. Fargo
5. Material Girl by Madonna
6. Colin Dexter
7. Superintendent
8. Victoria Beckham
9. The Fast and the Furious
10. Henry V
11. Desperate Housewives
12. Bagpuss
13. Thursday
14. California, New Mexico, Arizona and Texas
15. True
16. Jonathan Creek
17. Jean-Paul Gaultier
18. The Supremes
19. Thunder
20. Danish

Quiz 94: Pot Luck

1. Daft Punk collaborated with which hip-hop star on the hit 2013 single 'Get Lucky'?

2. 'Retches' is an anagram of which English city?

3. Guadaloupe and Martinique are overseas territories of which European country?

4. England cricketer Eoin Morgan was born and brought up in which country?

5. Which Hollywood actress is the mother of Melanie Griffith?

6. Washington DC lies on which river?

7. Which Rolling Stone wrote the children's book 'Gus and Me: The Story of My Granddad and My First Guitar'?

8. What is the 'Only Fools and Horses'-inspired nickname of footballer Peter Crouch?

9. DS Siobhan Clarke is the sidekick of which fictional detective?

10. Tashkent is the capital city of which country?

11. The fastest goal ever scored in a World Cup qualifier came against England in 1993. Which unlikely team scored it?

12. In Olympic diving competitions, how high is the platform from which the competitors perform?

13. The spice saffron comes from which flower?

14. True or false – the revolutionary leader Ernesto 'Che' Guevara was a qualified doctor?

15. A stamp of which animal appears on eggs to show that they are from Britain?

16. Which former prime minister was appointed a special guardian to Princes William and Harry following the death of Diana, Princess of Wales?

17. Hampshire, Gloucestershire Old Spots, and Oxford Sandy and Black are breeds of which farmyard animal?

18. William White was the real name of which camp comedian who died in 1995?

19. In the Harry Potter books and films, which word describes a person without any magical powers?
a) buggle   b) huggle   c) muggle

20. Which of the following British politicians is the youngest?
a) David Cameron   b) Nick Clegg   c) Ed Miliband

MEDIUM

Answers to Quiz 93: Smith and Jones

1. Billy Paul
2. The Matrix
3. Quincy Jones
4. American Dad!
5. Jacqui Smith
6. Jesus Jones
7. Washington DC
8. Paul Smith
9. Gethin Jones
10. Hammersmith Bridge
11. January Jones
12. Church of Jesus Christ of Latter-day Saints (Mormon Church)
13. Samuel Smith
14. Jim Smith
15. Howard Jones
16. Kenwyne Jones
17. Liz Jones
18. Stereophonics
19. Tooting
20. McFly

Quiz 95: Sports Movies

Identify the sports and games that feature in the films listed below:

1. 'Rush' (2013)

2. 'Moneyball' (2011)

3. 'Seabiscuit' (2003)

4. 'Cinderella Man' (2005)

5. 'Cool Runnings' (1993)

6. 'Kingpin' (1996)

7. 'The Legend of Bagger Vance' (2000)

8. 'Invictus' (2009)

9. 'Slap Shot' (1977)

10. 'The Color of Money' (1986)

11. 'Pumping Iron' (1977)

12. 'Any Given Sunday' (1999)

13. 'Match Point' (2005)

14. 'Rounders' (1998)

15. 'Fire in Babylon' (2010)

16. 'Big Wednesday' (1978)

17. 'The Luzhin Defence' (2000)

18. 'Dogtown and Z Boys' (2001)

19. 'Breaking Away' (1979)

20. 'This Sporting Life' (1963)

MEDIUM

Answers to Quiz 94: Pot Luck

1. Pharrell Williams
2. Chester
3. France
4. Ireland
5. Tippi Hedren
6. Potomac River
7. Keith Richards
8. Rodney
9. Rebus
10. Uzbekistan
11. San Marino
12. 10m
13. Crocus
14. True
15. Lion
16. John Major
17. Pig
18. Larry Grayson
19. Muggle
20. Ed Miliband

Quiz 96: Pot Luck

1. Ofwat is the body responsible for economic regulation of which privatized industry?

2. The film and musical 'The Commitments' was based on a novel by which Irish author?

3. @rustyrockets is the Twitter handle of which controversial actor and comedian?

4. Which word can mean 'a devotional painting of Jesus Christ or another holy figure' or 'a symbol on a computer screen'?

5. Colt Seavers was the central character in which American drama?

6. Which Irish county was also the name of a TV detective played by George Baker?

7. The football club Partick Thistle is based in which city?

8. Which British actor won his first Oscar for his performance in the 1986 film 'Hannah and Her Sisters'?

9. 'Hitsville USA' was the nickname of the headquarters of which American record label, founded by Berry Gordy in 1959?

10. Port Vale Football Club is based in which English city?

11. Which item of footwear is known in Australia as a thong?

12. Which fish is the main ingredient in the Scandinavian dish 'gravlax'?

13. Which name is shared by a band formed by a former Beatle and the first film to win the Best Picture Oscar?

14. Which nationality is the fashion designer Karl Lagerfeld?

15. The Daredevils are an Indian Premier League cricket team based in which city?

16. Which of the Spice Girls has a daughter called Bluebell Madonna?

17. Owais Shah, Ravi Bopara and Moeen Ali have all played international cricket for which country?

18. As the crow flies, which city is nearer to London – Athens or Moscow?

19. Complete the title of the 2005 number-one single by Oasis: 'The Importance of Being...'
a) Earnest
b) Idle
c) Rich

20. Which author created the fictional detective Wallander?
a) Stieg Larsson
b) Henning Mankell
c) Jo Nesbo

MEDIUM

Answers to Quiz 95: Sports Movies

1. Motor racing
2. Baseball
3. Horse racing
4. Boxing
5. Bobsleigh
6. Ten-pin bowling
7. Golf
8. Rugby union
9. Ice hockey
10. Pool
11. Bodybuilding
12. American football
13. Tennis
14. Poker
15. Cricket
16. Surfing
17. Chess
18. Skateboarding
19. Cycling
20. Rugby league

Quiz 97: Sporting Nicknames

Identify these sports stars from their nicknames:

1. Darth Maple (darts)

2. Psycho (football)

3. The Manx Missile (cycling)

4. The Big Easy (golf)

5. Chef (cricket)

6. The Special One (football)

7. The Rocket (snooker)

8. The Wally with the Brolly (football)

9. Bangers (cricket)

10. Chariots (rugby league)

11. Calamity (football)

12. The Cannibal (cycling)

13. Tugga (cricket)

14. King of Clay (tennis)

15. The Atomic Flea (football)

16. Kun (football)

17. Whispering Death (cricket)

18. Jackpot (darts)

19. The Raging Potato (rugby union)

20. El Niño (golf)

Answers to Quiz 96: Pot Luck

1. The water industry
2. Roddy Doyle
3. Russell Brand
4. Icon
5. The Fall Guy
6. Wexford
7. Glasgow
8. Michael Caine
9. Motown
10. Stoke-on-Trent
11. A flip-flop
12. Salmon
13. Wings
14. German
15. Delhi
16. Geri Halliwell
17. England
18. Athens
19. Idle
20. Henning Mankell

Quiz 98: Pot Luck

1. After ten years of marriage, which celebrity couple announced that they were 'consciously uncoupling' in March 2014?

2. Red Square is in which European capital city?

3. The maple leaf is a symbol associated with which country?

4. Ofgem is the name of the government regulator for which markets?

5. Reblochon cheese originates in which country?

6. Who won his first World Snooker Championship in 2014?

7. Which former manager of the England football team was nicknamed 'Turnip' after a loss to Sweden?

8. Martin and Ann Bryce, Howard and Hilda Hughes, and Paul Ryman were characters in which 1980s sitcom?

9. True or false – tennis star Laura Robson is the daughter of former England football captain Bryan Robson?

10. On a pencil, what do the initials 'HB' stand for?

11. Which British politician once insulted a rival by saying 'He has all the virtues I dislike and none of the vices I admire'?

12. True or false – gorillas are meat eaters?

13. A standard London 'Monopoly' board contains how many Community Chest squares?

14. The Sphinx has a human head and the body of which animal?

15. Who played the title character in the 2014 biblical epic 'Noah'?

16. Which sport is divided into periods of play called chukkas?

17. Wendi Deng is the former wife of which businessman?

18. Margaret Thatcher died in 2013 while staying at which famous hotel?

19. Complete the title of a famous piece of music by the Russian composer Stravinsky: 'The Rite of...'
    a) Spring
    b) Summer
    c) Autumn

20. Which of the following was a 2011 thriller starring Jason Statham?
    a) The Electrician
    b) The Mechanic
    c) The Plumber

MEDIUM

Answers to Quiz 97: Sporting Nicknames

1. John Part	11. David James
2. Stuart Pearce	12. Eddy Merckx
3. Mark Cavendish	13. Steve Waugh
4. Ernie Els	14. Rafa Nadal
5. Alastair Cook	15. Lionel Messi
6. Jose Mourinho	16. Sergio Aguero
7. Ronnie O'Sullivan	17. Michael Holding
8. Steve McClaren	18. Adrian Lewis
9. Marcus Trescothick	19. Keith Wood
10. Martin Offiah	20. Sergio Garcia

Quiz 99: Famous Eds

1. Which Northern Irish racing driver won four races during a Formula One career that ran from 1993 to 2002?

2. What was the name of the character played by Jennifer Saunders in the sitcom 'Absolutely Fabulous'?

3. 'Auld Reekie' is the nickname of which city?

4. Edo is the former name of which Asian capital city?

5. Which American rocker was voted the 'Greatest Guitarist of All Time' by readers of 'Guitar World' magazine in 2012?

6. Which actor and comedian hopes to stand in the London mayoral elections in 2020?

7. Guitarist Richey Edwards, who went missing in 1995, was a member of which rock band?

8. Bjorn Borg is one of two Swedes to have won the Men's Singles at Wimbledon. Who is the other?

9. Which comic actor won 'Celebrity Masterchef' in 2013?

10. Who captained the England women's cricket team to victory in the 2013/14 Ashes series?

11. Which British actor, who died in 2009, played the title character in the TV drama 'The Equalizer'?

12. Chris Penn played 'Nice Guy' Eddie Cabot in which Quentin Tarantino film?

13. 'Three Steps To Heaven' was the only UK number one single for which rock 'n' roller?

14. What name is shared by a district in North London and the capital city in the Canadian province of Alberta?

15. Which actress played mob wife Carmela in 'The Sopranos' and the title character in medical drama 'Nurse Jackie'?

16. Which English surgeon, who died in 1829, discovered a vaccine for smallpox?

17. Which American actor was nominated for acting Oscars in 1997 for 'Primal Fear' and in 1999 for 'American History X'?

18. Edwards Airforce Base is located in which American state?

19. 'Knock On Wood' was a hit single for which soul singer?
    a) Eddie Boyd
    b) Eddie Floyd
    c) Eddie Lloyd

20. In which sport is Fidel Edwards a notable performer?
    a) basketball
    b) cricket
    c) football

MEDIUM

Answers to Quiz 98: Pot Luck

1. Gwyneth Paltrow and Chris Martin
2. Moscow
3. Canada
4. Gas and electricity
5. France
6. Mark Selby
7. Graham Taylor
8. Ever Decreasing Circles
9. False
10. Hard and black
11. Sir Winston Churchill
12. False
13. Three
14. Lion
15. Russell Crowe
16. Polo
17. Rupert Murdoch
18. The Ritz
19. Spring
20. The Mechanic

Quiz 100: Pot Luck

1. Who were the two English players to score at the 2014 World Cup?

2. 'Why, she wouldn't even harm a fly' is the last line of which film chiller?

3. Which British actress and one time 'Bond girl' was born Joyce Penelope Wilhelmina Frankenberg?

4. Which Oscar-winning actor is older – Sean Penn or Kevin Spacey?

5. Which footballer holds the record for the most Premier League appearances at a single club?

6. In which century was the composer Mozart born?

7. 'Once a jolly swagman camped by a billabong / Under the shade of a coolibah tree' are the opening lines to which song?

8. True or false – broadcaster Noel Edmonds is a former presenter of motoring TV show 'Top Gear'?

9. General Wojciech Jaruzelski was the last Communist leader of which East European country?

10. The world championship in which sport was hosted at Jollee's Nightclub in Stoke between 1979 and 1985?

11. Who is older – Stephen Fry or Hugh Laurie?

12. 'Before the Year Dot' was the title of the autobiography of which veteran British actress?

13. The volcano Eyjafjallajökull, which let out a gigantic ash cloud in 2010, is in which country?

14. Who was the first Scotsman to win golf's US Masters?

15. In which year did the Trafalgar Square poll-tax riots take place?

16. Which South American country is home to the largest population of Roman Catholics in the world?

17. Sir Alec Guinness won his only acting Oscar for his performance in which film?

18. What are the four American states whose names start and end with the same letter?

19. What was the title of the dancing-inspired 2014 film starring Nick Frost?
    a) Argentine Fury
    b) Brazilian Fury
    c) Cuban Fury

20. The name of which Asian city translates into English as 'Fragrant Harbour'?
    a) Hong Kong
    b) Kuala Lumpur
    c) Shanghai

MEDIUM

Answers to Quiz 99: Famous Eds

1. Eddie Irvine
2. Edina Monsoon
3. Edinburgh
4. Tokyo
5. Eddie Van Halen
6. Eddie Izzard
7. Manic Street Preachers
8. Stefan Edberg
9. Ade Edmondson
10. Charlotte Edwards
11. Edward Woodward
12. Reservoir Dogs
13. Eddie Cochran
14. Edmonton
15. Edie Falco
16. Edward Jenner
17. Edward Norton
18. California
19. Eddie Floyd
20. Cricket

Quiz 101: Places

1. Which scripted reality TV show is set in Brentwood?

2. The alcoholic drink cognac is named after a town in which country?

3. Mount Elbert is the highest peak in which North American mountain range?

4. Which Australian city was named after the consort of the British king William IV?

5. The Dolomite Mountains are located in which European country?

6. Which sea is bordered by Ukraine, Georgia, Russia, Turkey, Bulgaria and Romania?

7. The home of Yorkshire County Cricket Club is named after which Leeds suburb?

8. Which town in the Dordogne department of France was also the title of a popular 1980s TV drama?

9. The Andes mountain range is in which continent?

10. Abruzzo, Basilicata and Liguria are regions of which European country?

11. Tynecastle and Easter Road are football grounds in which British city?

12. The seaport of Agadir is in which North African country?

13. What is America's third largest city by population?

14. Which girl's name is also the name of a town in East Yorkshire that is the home to a racecourse and a famous 13th-century minster?

15. Which American state is home to the highest proportion of people over the age of 65?

16. The River Fleet flows under which UK city?

17. What name is shared by a small port on the south shore of Belfast Lough in Northern Ireland and a Welsh port on the south shore of the Menai Strait?

18. Which town in Yorkshire is also the name of the capital of the Canadian state of Nova Scotia?

19. Mount Logan is the highest mountain in which country?
    a) Australia
    b) Canada
    c) USA

20. The area of Patagonia is in which South American country?
    a) Argentina
    b) Brazil
    c) Colombia

Answers to Quiz 100: Pot Luck

1. Wayne Rooney and Daniel Sturridge
2. Psycho
3. Jane Seymour
4. Kevin Spacey
5. Ryan Giggs
6. 18th century
7. Waltzing Matilda
8. True
9. Poland
10. Darts
11. Stephen Fry
12. June Brown
13. Iceland
14. Sandy Lyle
15. 1990
16. Brazil
17. The Bridge on the River Kwai
18. Alaska, Arizona, Alabama, Ohio
19. Cuban Fury
20. Hong Kong

MEDIUM

Quiz 102: Pot Luck

1. What high street shop was also the name of an ancient Greek city ruled by King Pheidon?

2. What is the name of the official country residence of the British prime minister?

3. In Greek mythology, Hercules slayed which snakelike, nine-headed monster?

4. The ghost of Banquo appears in which play by Shakespeare?

5. Which word, which means a sequence of rulers from the same family, was the title of a popular 1980s American drama?

6. Which royal was played on film in 2013 by Naomi Watts?

7. Which actor, writer, broadcaster and TV panel-show host presented the BAFTA film awards in 2013 and 2014?

8. In relation to fashion, what does the phrase 'prêt-à-porter' mean?

9. True or false – only male wasps can sting?

10. The San Andreas Fault lies in which American state?

11. Who was the governor of Texas from 1995 until 2000?

12. Phil Knight is the co-founder of which global company?

13. 'Mr Mojo Risin' was the nickname of which short-lived rock star?

14. Alex Murphy is the central character in which crime-fighting movie franchise, which was rebooted in 2014?

15. What is albumen more commonly known as?

16. True or false – England goalkeeper Joe Hart's real first name is Rupert?

17. Which two American states include the letter X in their name?

18. In terms of population, what is the smallest country to have won football's World Cup?

19. Which of the following is a derogatory term for the police?
    a) Babylon
    b) Gomorrah
    c) Sodom

20. Which of the following is largest?
    a) golf ball
    b) squash ball
    c) table tennis ball

MEDIUM

Answers to Quiz 101: Places

1. The Only Way Is Essex
2. France
3. The Rocky Mountains
4. Adelaide
5. Italy
6. Black Sea
7. Headingley
8. Bergerac
9. South America
10. Italy
11. Edinburgh
12. Morocco
13. Chicago
14. Beverley
15. Florida
16. London
17. Bangor
18. Halifax
19. Canada
20. Argentina

Quiz 103: Famous Phils

MEDIUM

1. Tom Hanks won his first Best Actor Oscar for which film?

2. 'The Cat' was the nickname of which England cricketer, now a TV presenter and broadcaster?

3. Bespectacled wizard Harry Potter made his debut in which book?

4. What name is shared by an ancient Aegean people and a boorish, narrow-minded person who is hostile to the arts?

5. 'In the Air Tonight' was the debut solo single by which singer?

6. What 2013 film starring Tom Hanks told the story of the hijacking of the US ship MV Maersk Alabama by Somali pirates?

7. Steve Coogan was nominated for a Best Adapted Screenplay Oscar in 2014 for which film?

8. Philip Pirrip is the central character in which novel by Charles Dickens?

9. Which American music producer created the recording technique known as the 'wall of sound'?

10. Who is the only English footballer to win the European Golden Shoe Award as the continent's top goal scorer?

11. Phil Oakey is the frontman of which synth pop band?

12. Dart player Phil Taylor is from which English city?

13. Which actor, broadcaster and panel-show regular plays Councillor Cowdrey in the children's TV show 'Bottom Knocker Street'?

14. 'EastEnders' hard man Phil Mitchell is played by which actor?

15. Philipp Lahm plays international football for which country?

16. Which golfer won the 2013 Open Golf Championship?

17. Which Dutch football team plays its home matches at the Philips Stadion?

18. Who won his only Oscar for his portrayal of the author Truman Capote?

19. Philology is the study of the history of what?
    a) flags
    b) language
    c) reptiles

20. In which game are Phil Hellmuth and Phil Ivey notable names?
    a) bowls
    b) poker
    c) pool

MEDIUM

Answers to Quiz 102: Pot Luck

1. Argos
2. Chequers
3. Hydra
4. Macbeth
5. Dynasty
6. Diana, Princess of Wales
7. Stephen Fry
8. Ready to wear
9. False
10. California
11. George W Bush
12. Nike
13. Jim Morrison
14. Robocop
15. Egg white
16. False – it's Charles
17. New Mexico and Texas
18. Uruguay
19. Babylon
20. Golf ball

Quiz 104: Pot Luck

1. The name of which pantomime character can also mean 'lacking character, principles or strength'?

2. Gruyère cheese is named after a town in which country?

3. Which 1992 film starring Al Pacino was a remake of an Italian film called 'Profumo di donna'?

4. How many seconds are there in a week?

5. The American flag features how many stripes?

6. Who was Britain's longest-serving deputy prime minister?

7. Which comic actor hosted the Brit Awards in 2011, 2012, 2013 and 2014?

8. What are the four Asian countries whose names contain four letters?

9. Who are the three Welshmen to have won the World Snooker Championship?

10. What breed of dog appears of the front cover of the Blur album 'Parklife'?

11. Oakwell is the home ground of which English football team?

12. The dance known as the 'cha-cha-cha' originated in which country?

13. What type of bird can be bearded, penduline or long-tailed?

14. In 2013, which boy band released a brand of perfume called 'That Moment'?

15. Which film franchise featured a baddie called Biff Tannen?

16. During the 2013/14 football season Martin Jol, Rene Meulensteen and Felix Magath all managed which club?

17. 'I must be cruel only to be kind' is a line from which Shakespeare play?

18. In the Harry Potter series of books and films, what are the names of the fours houses at Hogwarts?

19. Football matches in the Europa League are usually held on which night of the week?
    a) Wednesday
    b) Thursday
    c) Friday

20. Sanjeev Bhaskar stars in which BBC drama?
    a) The Indian Chef
    b) The Indian Dentist
    c) The Indian Doctor

MEDIUM

Answers to Quiz 103: Famous Phils

1. Philadelphia
2. Phil Tufnell
3. Harry Potter and the Philosopher's Stone
4. Philistine
5. Phil Collins
6. Captain Phillips
7. Philomena
8. Great Expectations
9. Phil Spector
10. Kevin Phillips
11. The Human League
12. Stoke-on-Trent
13. Phill Jupitus
14. Steve McFadden
15. Germany
16. Phil Mickelson
17. PSV Eindhoven
18. Philip Seymour Hoffman
19. Language
20. Poker

Quiz 105: Music

1. Which female singer and 'Strictly Come Dancing' contestant released the 2014 album 'Wanderlust'?

2. One Direction was one of only two acts to have two albums amongst the top 40 best-selling albums of 2013. Which male singer was the other?

3. Which Australian heavy metal band hold the record for the most UK Top 40 singles without ever reaching the top 10?

4. 'Anything Is Possible' and 'Evergreen' was a million-selling double A-side in 2002 from which former TV talent-show winner?

5. Which rock legend kept 'Anarchy in The UK' off the UK number one spot in 1977 with 'I Don't Want to Talk About It'?

6. What is the biggest-selling band in the history of the UK singles chart that is not from Britain or America?

7. FGTH are the initials of which massive band from the 1980s?

8. Which Canadian-born Eurovision winner had to 'Think Twice' in 1994?

9. What is the biggest-selling football song in the history of the UK Singles Chart?

10. Which veteran rockers were the opening act at the 1985 Live Aid concert?

11. The 2014 Brit-award-winning single 'Waiting All Night' is by which band?

12. Which former Beatle topped the charts in 1971 and 2002 with 'My Sweet Lord'?

13. Which Irish band recorded the massive 1997 hit album 'Talk On Corners'?

14. Which girl group became 'Whole Again' in 2001?

15. Which band, whose hits included 'Lessons In Love' and 'Something About You', took their name from the book 'The Hitchhiker's Guide to the Galaxy'?

16. What sort of 'Lines' provided Blondie with the title of a hit 1978 album?

17. Bill Medley and Bobby Hatfield were the members of which vocal duo?

18. Which band was 'Hungry Like the Wolf' in 1982?

19. Which veteran band are known for their lips and tongue symbol?
    a) The Beatles   b) The Rolling Stones   c) The Who

20. Which band topped the charts for the first time in 2014 with the album 'So Long, See You Tomorrow'?
    a) Beijing Bicycle Club   b) Birmingham Bicycle Club
    c) Bombay Bicycle Club

MEDIUM

Answers to Quiz 104: Pot Luck

1. Wishy-washy
2. Switzerland
3. Scent of a Woman
4. 604,800
5. 13
6. John Prescott
7. James Corden
8. Iran, Iraq, Laos and Oman
9. Ray Reardon, Terry Griffiths and Mark Williams
10. Greyhound
11. Barnsley
12. Cuba
13. Tit
14. One Direction
15. Back to the Future
16. Fulham
17. Hamlet
18. Gryffindor, Hufflepuff, Ravenclaw and Slytherin
19. Thursday
20. The Indian Doctor

Quiz 106: Pot Luck

1. Which American city is the home to a statue of the fictional crime-fighter Robocop?

2. 'Change we can believe in' was a slogan associated with which US president?

3. Disgraced cyclist Lance Armstrong admitted to drug-taking in an interview with which American talk show host?

4. Whom did Barack Obama defeat to win the 2012 US Presidential Election?

5. Which England spin bowler retired from cricket midway through England's disastrous 2013/14 Ashes series Down Under?

6. What was the name of the teletext service operated by the BBC?

7. Celine Dion's huge hit 'My Heart Will Go On' appeared on which movie soundtrack?

8. Striker Luis Suarez plays international football for which country?

9. Jarlsberg cheese comes from which country?

10. Who was the last British prime minister whose surname started with a vowel?

11. Which English city is situated at the confluence of the rivers Eden, Caldew and Petteril, just south of the Scottish border?

12. Which two popes were canonized in a ceremony in Rome in April 2014?

13. With a population of 1.1 million Dublin is the largest city in the Republic of Ireland. What is the second largest?

14. The 'Enigma Variations' and 'Pomp and Circumstance' are works by which classical composer?

15. The majority of Italian professional football matches are played on which day of the week?

16. Étienne is the French equivalent of which English name?

17. Who was the deputy prime minister during John Major's premiership?

18. By what name is the spice haldi more commonly known?

19. Where would a stevedore work?
    a) dockyard
    b) farm
    c) mine

20. 'If You Wait' was the title of the 2013 debut from which English band?
    a) London Academy
    b) London Comprehensive
    c) London Grammar

Answers to Quiz 105: Music

1. Sophie Ellis-Bextor
2. Michael Bublé
3. AC/DC
4. Will Young
5. Rod Stewart
6. Abba
7. Frankie Goes to Hollywood
8. Celine Dion
9. 'Three Lions' by Baddiel and Skinner and The Lightning Seeds
10. Status Quo
11. Rudimental
12. George Harrison
13. The Corrs
14. Atomic Kitten
15. Level 42
16. Parallel Lines
17. The Righteous Brothers
18. Duran Duran
19. The Rolling Stones
20. Bombay Bicycle Club

Quiz 107: Steves

1. Which American film maker won Best Director Oscars for 'Saving Private Ryan' and 'Schindler's List'?

2. Paul and Pauline Calf are alter egos of which comedian and actor?

3. Which snooker player appeared on reality TV show 'I'm a Celebrity ... Get Me Out of Here' in 2013?

4. Which British film-maker, who shares his name with a Hollywood icon, was nominated for a Best Director Oscar in 2014 for '12 Years a Slave'?

5. Who is the front man for American rock band Aerosmith?

6. FC Twente won the Dutch first division in 2010 under the stewardship of which English manager?

7. Who played Jeeves alongside Hugh Laurie's Bertie Wooster in the TV comedy drama 'Jeeves and Wooster'?

8. Michael Barrett is the real name of which British singer who has had over 30 UK top 40 singles?

9. Kehinde is the middle name of which London comedian and broadcaster?

10. Who was the first English footballer to win the Champions League with a non-English club?

11. The classic pirate adventure 'Treasure Island' was written by which novelist?

12. Which actor played weatherman Brick Tamland in the 2004 hit comedy 'Anchorman: The Legend of Ron Burgundy' and its 2013 sequel?

13. Who was the only England footballer to be named in the Team of the Tournament at the 2012 European Championships?

14. Which musician-turned-actor played Steve Owen in TV soap 'EastEnders'?

15. Broadhall Way is the home ground of which English football club?

16. Which British actor plays the title character in the police drama 'DCI Banks'?

17. By what name is the British magician Steven Frayne more commonly known?

18. Who presented the BBC sport's show 'Grandstand' from 1991 until 2005 and later worked for ITV and Sky covering motor sports?

19. Cricketer Stephen Fleming was the long-time captain of which country?
    a) Australia   b) New Zealand   c) West Indies

20. In which sport is 'Stone Cold' Steve Austin a notable name?
    a) boxing   b) football   c) wrestling

MEDIUM

Answers to Quiz 106: Pot Luck

1. Detroit
2. Barack Obama
3. Oprah Winfrey
4. Mitt Romney
5. Graeme Swann
6. Ceefax
7. Titanic
8. Uruguay
9. Norway
10. Anthony Eden
11. Carlisle
12. John XXIII and John Paul II
13. Cork
14. Edward Elgar
15. Sunday
16. Stephen
17. Michael Heseltine
18. Turmeric
19. Dockyard
20. London Grammar

Quiz 108: Pot Luck

1. 'Ike' was the nickname of which 20th-century American president?

2. Which Canadian city hosted the 2010 Winter Olympics?

3. Which covers a larger area – a basketball court or a tennis court?

4. The River Rhine flows into which European sea?

5. 'I do wish we could chat longer but I'm having an old friend for dinner' is a line from which 1991 film chiller?

6. 'Poirot and Me' was the title of which actor's 2013 autobiography?

7. Which pair of movie characters went on an 'Excellent Adventure' and a 'Bogus Journey'?

8. What nationality is the former Formula One world champion Niki Lauda?

9. Joel and Ethan are the first names of which film-making siblings?

10. Fill in the blank – Blue, Engelbert Humperdinck, ____, Molly

11. A tercentenary marks an anniversary of how many years?

12. Which British politician delivered the controversial 'Rivers of Blood' speech?

13. Which Dutch city is Europe's largest seaport?

14. Who was the mother of Queen Elizabeth I?

15. Robin Hood and Maid Marian appear in which pantomime?

16. Jeera powder is an alternative name for which spice?

Answers – page 221

17. A white cross on a black background is the flag of which English county?

18. The initials CH are used as an abbreviation for which European country?

19. Redruth in Cornwall was once a major centre of the mining of what?
a) coal
b) diamonds
c) tin

20. In games of Australian Rules Football, what shape is the pitch?
a) oval
b) rectangular
c) square

MEDIUM

Answers to Quiz 107: Steves

1. Steven Spielberg
2. Steve Coogan
3. Steve Davis
4. Steve McQueen
5. Steve Tyler
6. Steve McClaren
7. Stephen Fry
8. Shakin' Stevens
9. Stephen K Amos
10. Steve McManaman
11. Robert Louis Stevenson
12. Steve Carell
13. Steven Gerrard
14. Martin Kemp
15. Stevenage
16. Stephen Tompkinson
17. Dynamo
18. Steve Rider
19. New Zealand
20. Wrestling

Quiz 109: Famous Nicks

1. Who was first elected to Parliament in 2005 after winning the Sheffield Hallam seat?

2. Which golfer won the first of his three Open Championship titles in 1987?

3. Jacques Chirac was succeeded as president of France by which politician?

4. In the BBC crime drama 'New Tricks', who plays Dan Griffin?

5. 'The Incredible Sulk' is the nickname of which much-travelled footballer?

6. Who won the Oscar for Best Actress in 2003 for her performance in 'The Hours'?

7. In 2012, who became the first British woman to win an Olympic boxing gold medal?

8. Which broadcaster succeeded Andrew Marr as the BBC's political editor?

9. The Bad Seeds are the backing band for which Antipodean singer?

10. Who was the original host of the UK version of the game show 'Wheel of Fortune'?

11. Which German Formula One driver started 183 races between 2000 and 2011 but failed to win a race?

12. Which animator created the characters 'Wallace and Gromit' and 'Shaun the Sheep'?

13. Who was the keyboard player with new romantics Duran Duran?

14. Which footballer scored Premier League goals for Spurs, Middlesbrough, Everton, Liverpool, Leeds and Hull?

15. 'You Remind Me', 'Someday' and 'Rockstar' were UK top 10 hits for which Canadian band?

16. The novels 'High Fidelity', 'How to Be Good' and 'Juliet, Naked' are by which best-selling British author?

17. Which actor received Best Actor Oscar nominations in 1992 for 'Prince of Tides' and in 1999 for 'Affliction'?

18. Which former cricketer hosted the culinary TV show 'Britain's Best Dish'?

19. Which British actor first found fame playing Mike Watt in the cult TV comedy 'Spaced'?

20. 'Don't Hold Your Breath' was a UK number one single in 2011 for which American female singer?

MEDIUM

Answers to Quiz 108: Pot Luck

1. Dwight Eisenhower
2. Vancouver
3. Basketball court
4. North Sea
5. The Silence of the Lambs
6. David Suchet
7. Bill and Ted
8. Austrian
9. The Coen brothers
10. Bonnie Tyler (UK Eurovision entrants 2011 to 2014)
11. 300
12. Enoch Powell
13. Rotterdam
14. Anne Boleyn
15. Babes in the Wood
16. Cumin
17. Cornwall
18. Switzerland
19. Tin
20. Oval

Quiz 110: Pot Luck

1. Which legendary Olympic athlete's Twitter biography reads 'Anything is possible I don't think limits'?

2. Hobart is the capital of which Australian state?

3. What is the smallest denomination of note in the euro currency?

4. Who is the famous father of the film director Duncan Jones?

5. The tiny state of Lesotho is entirely surrounded by which other country?

6. Which British Olympic gold-medal-winning sailor helped the US team to victory in the 2013 America's Cup?

7. What is the only city in the world to span two continents?

8. True or false – Benjamin Franklin is a former president of the USA?

9. Wallonia is a region of which European country?

10. What nationality is the record-breaking distance runner Haile Gebrselassie?

11. What is 25 squared?

12. 'Lunes' is the Spanish word for which day of the week?

13. The Bantams is the nickname of which Yorkshire football club?

14. Brothers Kolo and Yaya Touré play international football for which country?

15. What is the only sign of the zodiac that is represented by an inanimate object?

16. 'Take things as they are. Punch when you have to punch. Kick when you have to kick' is a quote from which martial artist?

17. A geiger counter is an instrument used to detect what?

18. Which TV presenter ran, swam and cycled her way from Edinburgh to London in 2014 to raise funds for Sport Relief?

19. What would you do with a brisket?
    a) eat it
    b) play it
    c) wear it

20. Which of the following is not an Olympic sport?
    a) judo
    b) karate
    c) taekwondo

MEDIUM

Answers to Quiz 109: Famous Nicks

1. Nick Clegg
2. Nick Faldo
3. Nicolas Sarkozy
4. Nicholas Lyndhurst
5. Nicolas Anelka
6. Nicole Kidman
7. Nicola Adams
8. Nick Robinson
9. Nick Cave
10. Nicky Campbell
11. Nick Heidfeld
12. Nick Park
13. Nick Rhodes
14. Nick Barmby
15. Nickelback
16. Nick Hornby
17. Nick Nolte
18. Mark Nicholas
19. Nick Frost
20. Nicole Scherzinger

Quiz 111: Connections part 1

1. Which actor played the title character in the TV drama 'Kavanagh QC'?

2. The play 'Toad of Toad Hall' is an adaptation of which classic children's book?

3. What was the nickname of snooker star Jimmy White?

4. Robert 'Bobby' Drake is the alter ego of which comic-book superhero?

5. Which plane accounted for around 60% of enemy kills during the Battle of Britain?

6. What is the official presidential anthem of the United States?

7. Inventor Flint Lockwood, Steve the Monkey and Sam Sparks are characters in which 2009 film animation and its 2013 sequel?

8. If a clothes label shows a circle in a square covered by a cross what mustn't you do?

9. Marti Pellow was the lead singer with which Scottish band?

10. What was the last UK number one by The Kinks?

11. Errol Brown was the lead singer with which band that topped the charts in 1977 with 'So You Win Again'?

12. Who was the original host of TV panel show 'Through the Keyhole'?

13. What was the name of the dog owned by cartoon character Tintin?

14. 'Since You've Been Gone' and 'I Surrender' were top-ten hits for which British rock band?

15. Tom Jones sang the theme song to which James Bond film?

16. Which classic TV comedy was based on a play called 'The Banana Box'?

17. Artis Leon Ivey Jr is the real name of which hip-hop star who topped the charts with 'Gangsta's Paradise'?

18. Dustin Hoffman won an Oscar in 1989 for his performance in which film?

19. 'Mylo Xyloto' was a 2011 album by which British band?

20. What is the connection between the answers?

MEDIUM

Answers to Quiz 110: Pot Luck

1. Usain Bolt
2. Tasmania
3. €5
4. David Bowie
5. South Africa
6. Sir Ben Ainslie
7. Istanbul
8. False
9. Belgium
10. Ethiopian
11. 625
12. Monday
13. Bradford City
14. Ivory Coast
15. Libra
16. Bruce Lee
17. Radioactivity
18. Davina McCall
19. Eat it
20. Karate

Quiz 112: Pot Luck

1. Which river flows through the city of Gloucester?

2. According to Karl Marx, what 'is the opium of the people'?

3. Soul singer Gladys Knight performed the theme song to which James Bond film?

4. True or false – 'Sex and the City' star Kim Cattrall was born in Manchester?

5. In relation to motoring, what do the initials 'DVLA' stand for?

6. The Battle of Monte Cassino was fought in which war?

7. In the cartoon 'Wacky Races', which pair drove a car called the Mean Machine?

8. Which soap actor is the host of TV game show 'Reflex'?

9. In which year did Sir Steve Redgrave win his first Olympic gold medal?

10. Which star of the cult film 'Withnail and I' joined the cast of Downton Abbey in 2014?

11. Fill in the missing name – ____, David Tenant, Matt Smith, Peter Capaldi

12. Aviophobia is the fear of what?

13. In the pantomime 'Jack and the Beanstalk', Jack swapped what animal for some magic beans?

14. The American drama 'Knots Landing' was a spin-off from which TV soap?

15. Which Hollywood star received his first Oscar nomination in 1989 for his performance in 'Big'?

16.   Marsala wine comes from which Mediterranean island?

17.   The Cape of Good Hope is in which country?

18.   In astrology, what is the first sign of the zodiac?

19.   Sale is a suburb of which English city?
      a) Birmingham
      b) Manchester
      c) Sheffield

20.   Which of the following is a place in Yorkshire?
      a) Idle
      b) Lazy
      c) Slothful

MEDIUM

Answers to Quiz 111: Connections part 1

1.   John Thaw
2.   The Wind in the Willows
3.   The Whirlwind
4.   Iceman
5.   Hawker Hurricane
6.   Hail to the Chief
7.   Cloudy with a Chance of Meatballs
8.   Do not tumble dry
9.   Wet Wet Wet
10. Sunny Afternoon
11. Hot Chocolate
12. Sir David Frost
13. Snowy
14. Rainbow
15. Thunderball
16. Rising Damp
17. Coolio
18. Rain Man
19. Coldplay
20. They all relate to the weather

Quiz 113: Reality TV

1. What is the name of the trophy awarded to the winners of 'Strictly Come Dancing'?

2. Girls Aloud were formed after winning which short-lived talent contest?

3. Who were the only two professional dancers to take part in all of the first ten series of 'Strictly Come Dancing'?

4. Who was the original host of 'The X Factor'?

5. Emma Willis is the female host of which TV talent show?

6. Alesha Dixon replaced which choreographer on the 'Strictly Come Dancing' judging panel?

7. Which cricketer won 'I'm a Celebrity ... Get Me Out of Here' in 2003?

8. Who were the first group to win 'The X Factor'?

9. Which 'Loose Woman' won 'Celebrity Big Brother' in 2012?

10. Which fashion designer appeared on the 2013 series of 'Strictly Come Dancing'?

11. Which actress provides the voice-over commentary on 'The Only Way Is Essex'?

12. What is the name of the band leader on 'Strictly Come Dancing'?

13. Vicky Pattison, Holly Hagan and Charlotte Crosby appear in which scripted reality show?

14. Which star of 'The X Factor' won 'I'm a Celebrity ... Get Me Out of Here' in 2010?

15. Ashley Banjo is the leader of which dance troupe, which won 'Britain's Got Talent' in 2009?

16. Which actor and comedian was the first winner of 'Celebrity Big Brother'?

17. Which band who found fame in 'The X Factor' launched their own range of condoms?

18. Which former newspaper editor was a member of the original judging panel on 'Britain's Got Talent'?

19. Who was not a head chef in the celebrity cooking show 'Hell's Kitchen'?
    a) Gordon Ramsay
    b) Michel Roux
    c) Marco-Pierre White

20. Which 'EastEnders' actress won 'The X Factor – Battle of the Stars'?
    a) Lucy Benjamin
    b) Letitia Dean
    c) Tamzin Outhwaite

MEDIUM

Answers to Quiz 112: Pot Luck

1. Severn
2. Religion
3. Licence to Kill
4. False – she was born in Liverpool
5. Driver and Vehicle Licensing Agency
6. World War II
7. Dick Dastardly and Muttley
8. Shane Richie
9. 1984
10. Richard E Grant
11. Christopher Eccleston (Dr Who actors)
12. Flying
13. Cow
14. Dallas
15. Tom Hanks
16. Sicily
17. South Africa
18. Aries
19. Manchester
20. Idle

Quiz 114: Pot Luck

1. Actor Richard Thorp, who died in May 2013, appeared in which TV soap for over 30 years?

2. Which country was formerly known as East Pakistan?

3. In February 2014, Viktor Yanukovych was ousted as president of which European country?

4. Finn, laser and 49er are classes in which Olympic sport?

5. Which TV property expert is the daughter of the sixth Baron Hindlip?

6. In which sport must players roll a stone into a house?

7. Which British athlete won heptathlon gold at the 2000 Olympics?

8. The controversial 2014 TV documentary series 'Benefits Street' was filmed in which English city?

9. True or false – post boxes in France are green?

10. What are the four American states whose names end with the letter O?

11. True or false – actor Joaquin Phoenix was born Joaquin Bottom?

12. The Mekong River is in which continent?

13. Europe's eastern border is formed by which Russian mountain range?

14. In which century was the composer Beethoven born?

15. Roger Lloyd Pack, who died in January 2014, played which character in 'Only Fools and Horses'?

16. Which Berkshire town is home to the Royal Military Academy, which trains officers in the British Army?

17. Which modern-day city was formerly known as Constantinople?

18. Kenny Ball was associated with which genre of music?

19. Which pop star helped design a brand of beer called 'Gold'?
    a) Tony Hadley
    b) Simon Le Bon
    c) Boy George

20. Which of the following is a mountain range in Slovenia and Italy?
    a) The Graham Alps
    b) The Jonathan Alps
    c) The Julian Alps

MEDIUM

Answers to Quiz 113: Reality TV

1. The Glitterball Trophy
2. Popstars: The Rivals
3. Anton Du Beke and Brendon Cole
4. Kate Thornton
5. The Voice
6. Arlene Phillips
7. Phil Tufnell
8. Little Mix
9. Denise Welch
10. Julien McDonald
11. Denise Van Outen
12. Dave Arch
13. Geordie Shore
14. Stacey Solomon
15. Diversity
16. Jack Dee
17. JLS
18. Piers Morgan
19. Michel Roux
20. Lucy Benjamin

Quiz 115: Sport

MEDIUM

1. In which sporting event is the winner awarded a green jacket?

2. Who was the first athlete to successfully defend the men's 1,500m title at the Summer Olympics?

3. Field goal, extra point and safety are ways of scoring points in which sport?

4. In judo, which belt signifies a higher rank – blue or brown?

5. In 2013, Britain's Tai Woffinden became world champion in which sport?

6. Which city is home to Britain's most northerly racecourse?

7. Prior to becoming manager of the England team, Roy Hodgson was boss at which club?

8. The opening race of the 2014 Formula One season took place in which country?

9. In relation to the business of football regulations, what do the initials 'FFP' stand for?

10. Which British golfer won his first major tournament in 2013 after claiming the US Open?

11. In yards, how long is an American football field from goal line to goal line?

12. Who was the first midfielder to score 150 goals in football's Premier League?

13. What is bigger – a full-size football or a full-size volleyball?

14. What nationality is the golfer Vijay Singh?

15. Which number lies between 4 and 6 on a standard tournament dartboard?

16. What is the maximum number of clubs a player can carry in his or her bag during a round of golf?

17. Home Park is the home ground of which English football team?

18. The Real Deal was the nickname of which world heavyweight boxing champion?

19. Uttoxeter racecourse is in which English county?
    a) Leicestershire
    b) Staffordshire
    c) Warwickshire

20. Which South American country was in England's group at the 2014 World Cup?
    a) Argentina
    b) Colombia
    c) Uruguay

MEDIUM

Answers to Quiz 114: Pot Luck

1. Emmerdale
2. Bangladesh
3. Ukraine
4. Yachting
5. Kirstie Allsopp
6. Curling
7. Denise Lewis
8. Birmingham
9. False
10. Colorado, Idaho, New Mexico and Ohio
11. True
12. Asia
13. The Urals
14. 18th century
15. Trigger
16. Sandhurst
17. Istanbul
18. Jazz
19. Tony Hadley
20. The Julian Alps

Quiz 116: Pot Luck

1. Moselle wine comes from which European country?

2. Which European principality has a coastline of just 3.5 miles?

3. The Kruger National Park is a nature reserve in which Commonwealth country?

4. Katrina Amy Alexandria Alexis Infield is the real name of which celebrity and tabloid favourite?

5. The cartoon characters Danny, 'Erbert, Fatty, Plug, Toots, Wilfred and Spotty attend which fictional school?

6. Thames Ironworks FC is the former name of which London football club?

7. True or false – TV presenter Tess Daly appeared in a couple of music videos for the band Duran Duran?

8. The IRB is the global governing body for which sport?

9. In which James Bond film did 007 get married?

10. The series of comic fantasy novels known as 'Discworld' was created by which author?

11. HBO is a popular American TV channel. What do the initials 'HBO' stand for?

12. 'Jueves' is the Spanish word for which day of the week?

13. The Maghreb is a region of which continent?

14. Helvetia is the female personification of which European country?

15. What is the second largest of the Channel Islands?

16. Which social network was launched on 21 March 2006?

Answers – page 237

17. Devon shares borders with which three English counties?

18. What is the last sign of the zodiac?

19. What is a shillelagh?
    a) food
    b) a musical instrument
    c) a weapon

20. Billy Bowden, Aleem Dar and Asad Rauf are match officials in which team sport?
    a) cricket
    b) football
    c) rugby union

MEDIUM

Answers to Quiz 115: Sport

1. The Masters
2. Sebastian Coe
3. American football
4. Brown
5. Speedway
6. Perth
7. West Bromwich Albion
8. Australia
9. Financial Fair Play
10. Justin Rose
11. 100 yards
12. Frank Lampard
13. A football
14. Fijian
15. 13
16. 14
17. Plymouth Argyle
18. Evander Holyfield
19. Staffordshire
20. Uruguay

Quiz 117: Red, White and Blue

1. Which soul singer was nicknamed 'The Walrus of Love'?

2. What is the name of Tottenham Hotspur's ground?

3. Which organization was founded in 1863 in Geneva, Switzerland, by Henry Dunant and Gustave Moynier?

4. Model and TV presenter Lisa Butcher was formely married to which celebrity chef?

5. Which sport is played by a team called the Cardiff Blues?

6. Which Spanish artist went through a 'blue period' between 1900 and 1904?

7. 1600 Pennsylvania Avenue is the address of which famous building?

8. Which charity event was held for the first time on 5 February 1988?

9. Which flag is flown on a ship when everyone is aboard and the vessel is about to proceed to sea?

10. What is the nickname of the Belgian national football team?

11. The Blue House is the official residence of the president of which Asian country?

12. Based on a novel by Tom Clancy, which 1990 naval thriller starred Sean Connery as a rogue Russian submarine commander wanting to defect?

13. 'Vaccinium corymbosum' is the scientific name for which popular fruit?

14. 'Is This Love' and 'Here I Go Again' were the only top-ten singles by which English hard-rock band?

15. Blue Note is a record label associated with which genre of music?

16. 'Seven Nation Army' and 'Hotel Yorba' were hits for which American indie rock band?

17. What name is shared by a hit single for singer Bobby Vinton and a 1986 film directed by David Lynch?

18. 'Pick Up the Pieces' was the only UK top 10 single for which Scottish funk band?

19. Which American author wrote the children's books 'Charlotte's Web', 'Stuart Little' and 'The Trumpet of the Swan'?
    a) AB White
    b) EB White
    c) OB White

20. In which sport is Australian Cameron White a notable performer?
    a) cricket
    b) rugby union
    c) tennis

MEDIUM

Answers to Quiz 116: Pot Luck

1. Germany
2. Monaco
3. South Africa
4. Katie Price (Jordan)
5. Bash Street School
6. West Ham United
7. True
8. Rugby union
9. On Her Majesty's Secret Service
10. Terry Pratchett
11. Home Box Office
12. Thursday
13. Africa
14. Switzerland
15. Guernsey
16. Twitter
17. Cornwall, Dorset and Somerset
18. Pisces
19. A weapon
20. Cricket

Quiz 118: Pot Luck

MEDIUM

1. 'Roads? Where we're going we don't need roads!' is the last line of which classic 1980s film?

2. Which organ is inflamed in a person suffering from hepatitis?

3. In a game of backgammon, each player starts with how many checkers?

4. 'Ha' is an abbreviation to denote which unit of measurement?

5. What fruit is the main ingredient in the popular liqueur crème de cassis?

6. 'Mes que un club' is the famous motto of which European football club?

7. Which South American country takes its name from the Latin word for silver?

8. Gobi is a popular ingredient in Indian cuisine. What does it mean in English?

9. Which are wider – football posts or rugby posts?

10. Which TV personality drives a car with the registration plate AMS1?

11. True or false – in his spare time TV presenter Vernon Kay plays American football for the London Warriors?

12. The name of which area of east London, home to a famous market, derives from 'hospital of St Mary'?

13. Who is Radio One's longest-serving breakfast show DJ?

14. True or false – Jordan once represented the United Kingdom at the Eurovision Song Contest?

15. Peter Pascoe was the sidekick of which grumpy TV detective?

16. 'You're gonna need a bigger boat' is a line from which 1975 blockbuster?

17. Which former 'page-three girl' went on to play Carrie Nicholls in TV soap 'Emmerdale'?

18. Which alcoholic drink is sometimes known as the 'green fairy'?

19. Which of the following was a hit for the Arctic Monkeys?
    a) Lardy Bum
    b) Mardy Bum
    c) Tardy Bum

20. Gene Hackman played Detective Popeye Doyle in which classic crime movie?
    a) The French Connection
    b) The Italian Connection
    c) The Sicilian Connection

MEDIUM

Answers to Quiz 117: Red, White and Blue

1. Barry White
2. White Hart Lane
3. The Red Cross
4. Marco Pierre White
5. Rugby union
6. Pablo Picasso
7. The White House
8. Red Nose Day
9. The Blue Peter
10. The Red Devils
11. South Korea
12. The Hunt for Red October
13. Blueberry
14. Whitesnake
15. Jazz
16. The White Stripes
17. Blue Velvet
18. The Average White Band
19. EB White
20. Cricket

Quiz 119: Science

1. Which bone of the body is also known as the clavicle?

2. What are the names of the blood vessels that carry oxygen-rich blood away from the heart?

3. Which event occurs when the moon passes in front of the sun, casting a shadow on the earth?

4. Which part of the human body is abbreviated to CNS?

5. What is the name of the process by which plants use the energy from sunlight to make their own food?

6. Phobos and Deimos are the names of the moons of which planet?

7. What is the name of the tissue that connects muscles to bones?

8. What is the only element of the periodic table that starts with the letter X?

9. What is the longest bone in the human body?

10. Hertz is a unit used to measure what?

11. Approximately 73% of the human brain is made up of what?

12. In relation to electricity, what do the initials 'AC' stand for?

13. And what do the initials 'DC' stand for?

14. In relation to broadband technology, what do the initials 'ISDN' stand for?

15. Which element of the Periodic Table has the chemical symbol Mn and the atomic number 25?

16. Which of the senses is also known as olfaction?

17. What is measured using an ammeter?

18. What is nitrous oxide more commonly known as?

19. By what collective name are helium, neon, argon, krypton, xenon and radon known?
    a) the noble gases
    b) the profound gases
    c) the worthy gases

20. The human foot is made up of how many bones?
    a) 16
    b) 26
    c) 36

Answers to Quiz 118: Pot Luck

1. Back to the Future
2. Liver
3. 15
4. Hectare
5. Blackcurrant
6. Barcelona
7. Argentina
8. Cauliflower
9. Football posts
10. Alan Sugar
11. True
12. Spitalfields
13. Chris Moyles
14. False
15. Andy Dalziel
16. Jaws
17. Linda Lusardi
18. Absinthe
19. Mardy Bum
20. The French Connection

Quiz 120: Pot Luck

1. Prior to embarking on a solo career, Justin Timberlake was a member of which boy band?

2. Which fruit is sometimes known in America as an alligator pear?

3. The multiple Olympic and World Champion distance runner Tirunesh Dibaba is from which African country?

4. Who is the host of the TV quiz show 'Ejector Seat'?

5. The Browns are an NFL franchise based in which American city?

6. In the TV series 'The Lone Ranger', what was the name of Tonto's horse?

7. Which actor who starred in the classic western 'The Magnificent Seven' later appeared in the British drama 'Hustle'?

8. What was the first name of the TV private detective 'Magnum'?

9. Which Shakespeare play contains the line 'A rose by any other name would smell as sweet'?

10. In which game can players check-raise, semi-bluff and continuation-bet?

11. Which word, meaning a small drink of whisky, is also the currency of Armenia?

12. 'Queso' is the Spanish word for what food?

13. Dart player Simon Whitlock is from which country?

14. Which English university plays its home cricket matches at a ground called Fenner's?

15. Who was the puppet sidekick of children's TV presenter Phillip Schofield?

Answers – page 245

16. Who was the famous grandfather of the painter Lucian Freud?

17. Which member of boy band Boyzone played barman Ciaran McCarthy in TV soap 'Coronation Street'?

18. Which West Indian holds the record for scoring a Test century in the fewest number of balls?

19. Which comedy duo starred in the TV sitcom 'House of Fools'?
    a) Ant and Dec
    b) Armstrong and Miller
    c) Reeves and Mortimer

20. Who is the host of the TV talent show 'The Great British Sewing Bee'?
    a) Zoe Ball
    b) Tess Daly
    c) Claudia Winkleman

Answers to Quiz 119: Science

1. Collar bone
2. Arteries
3. Solar eclipse
4. Central Nervous System
5. Photosynthesis
6. Mars
7. Tendon
8. Xenon
9. Femur (thigh bone)
10. Frequency
11. Water
12. Alternating current
13. Direct current
14. Integrated Services Digital Network
15. Manganese
16. Smell
17. Electrical current
18. Laughing gas
19. The noble gases
20. 26

MEDIUM

Quiz 121: Italy

MEDIUM

1. What is the capital city of Italy?

2. What are the two independent states that lie within Italy?

3. Neapolitan is the name used to describe people from which Italian city?

4. Which artist painted the ceiling of the Sistine Chapel?

5. Firenze is the Italian name for which city?

6. In which century did Italy become a unified country?

7. What is the Italian word for a motorway?

8. True or false – Italy shares a land border with Slovenia?

9. Leonardo Da Vinci's 'Last Supper' fresco is located in a former monastery in which Italian city?

10. On what part of the body would someone wear an item of clothing known in Italy as 'il cappello'?

11. Which two Italian cities appear in the titles of plays by Shakespeare?

12. England manager Roy Hodgson had brief spells in charge of which two Italian football clubs?

13. What is the name of the major river that flows through the city of Rome?

14. In which year did Italy last host football's World Cup?

15. Shakespeare's play 'Romeo and Juliet' is set in which Italian city?

16. Which Italian city is home to the world's oldest film festival?

17. Linate and Malpensa are the names of the airports that serve which major Italian city?

18. The controversial horse race known as the 'palio' takes place in which Italian city?

19. In which year did Italy not win football World Cup?
    a) 1982
    b) 1990
    c) 2006

20. The Fiat motor company is based in which Italian city?
    a) Milan
    b) Naples
    c) Turin

MEDIUM

Answers to Quiz 120: Pot Luck

1. N Sync
2. Avocado
3. Ethiopia
4. Andi Peters
5. Cleveland
6. Scout
7. Robert Vaughn
8. Thomas
9. Romeo and Juliet
10. Poker
11. Dram
12. Cheese
13. Australia
14. Cambridge
15. Gordon the Gopher
16. Sigmund Freud
17. Keith Duffy
18. Sir Viv Richards
19. Reeves and Mortimer
20. Claudia Winkleman

Quiz 122: Pot Luck

1. Which town in the north east of England was also the title of a comedy drama starring Vic Reeves and Gina McKee?

2. What does 'Dieu et mon droit', the motto of the British monarch, translate to in English?

3. A candle wrapped in barbed wire is the logo of which human rights organization?

4. 'Love' and 'Kiss' are fragrances created by which reality TV-created boy band?

5. In the nursery rhyme 'Polly Put the Kettle On', who took it off again?

6. Who was the original host of the charades-based TV panel show 'Give Us a Clue'?

7. Which actor, best known for appearing in 'The Fast Show' and 'Father Brown' shares his name with a World Snooker Champion?

8. 'Once more unto the breach, dear friends, once more' is a line from which Shakespeare play?

9. What type of building provided Sam Bailey with the title of the 2013 Christmas number one?

10. True or false – a cello has six strings?

11. A character called the Soup Dragon appeared in which children's TV animation?

12. According to the Shakespearean quote, what 'is the soul of wit'?

13. The World Snooker Championship starts each year in which month?

14. Hodges and Peacock are the surnames of which veteran British musical duo?

15. What country is the largest apple producer in the world?

16. Thomas Plant, James Lewis and Jonty Hernden regularly appear on TV talking about what subject?

17. Sakura cheese comes from which country?

18. What day of the week is known in Spanish as 'sábado'?

19. If something is cooked 'a la Crecy' it is garnished with what vegetable?
    a) carrot
    b) lettuce
    c) cucumber

20. 'Rather Be' was a 2014 chart topper for which band?
    a) Clean Bandit
    b) Dirty Bandit
    c) Grubby Bandit

MEDIUM

Answers to Quiz 121: Italy

1. Rome
2. San Marino and Vatican City
3. Naples
4. Michelangelo
5. Florence
6. 19th century
7. Autostrada
8. True
9. Milan
10. On their head (it's a hat)
11. (The Merchant of) Venice and (The Two Gentlemen of) Verona
12. Inter Milan and Udinese
13. River Tiber
14. 1990
15. Verona
16. Venice
17. Milan
18. Siena
19. 1990
20. Turin

Quiz 123: Name the Decade

In which decade of the 20th century did the following events take place?

1. Neil Armstrong became the first man to walk on the Moon.

2. The first mobile phone call was made.

3. Football's World Cup took place for the first time.

4. Alfred Hitchcock's classic chiller 'Psycho' was released.

5. Bill Clinton was elected President of the USA for the first time.

6. TV programmes in Britain were broadcast in colour for the first time.

7. Decimal currency was introduced in the UK.

8. The first UK motorway opened.

9. The Berlin Wall was erected.

10. Harold Wilson became British prime minister for the first time.

11. The first Harry Potter novel was published.

12. Britain abolished the death penalty.

13. The hit film 'The Godfather' was released.

14. Elvis Presley died.

15. Concorde made its maiden flight.

16. The first text message was sent.

17. Prince Philip was born.

18. The UK driving test became compulsory.

19. The first Rugby World Cup was held.

20. Penicillin was discovered.

MEDIUM

Answers to Quiz 122: Pot Luck

1. Hebburn
2. God and my right
3. Amnesty International
4. JLS
5. Sukey
6. Michael Aspel
7. Mark Williams
8. Henry V
9. Skyscraper
10. False
11. The Clangers
12. Brevity
13. April
14. Chas and Dave
15. China
16. Antiques
17. Japan
18. Saturday
19. Carrot
20. Clean Bandit

Quiz 124: Pot Luck

1. 'Always On My Mind' was a Christmas number one in 1987 for which band?

2. The Battle of Naseby was fought in which war?

3. Which international football team plays its home games at Windsor Park?

4. How many balls are used in a game of billiards?

5. Marshall Mathers is the real name of which American hip-hop star?

6. Which actor starred in the classic comedy 'Rising Damp' and the Caribbean crime drama 'Death In Paradise'?

7. The Trevi Fountain is situated in which European city?

8. 'Alas poor Yorick! I knew him Horatio' is a line from which Shakespeare play?

9. What is the square root of 1600?

10. What type of animal is a Bolognese?

11. The Jurassic Coast stretches into which two English counties?

12. 'Omnia Omnibus Ubique—All Things for All People, Everywhere' is the motto of which London department store?

13. In 2014, which multi-millionaire businessman bought the Open golf championship venue, Turnberry?

14. Julia Roberts won her first Oscar for which 2000 film?

15. One of the driest places on earth, the Atacama Desert is in which continent?

16. Which member of pop band Take That made his acting debut in 2009, playing Micky Shannon in 'Heartbeat'?

17. Which of the McGann brothers stars in the BBC drama 'Call The Midwife'?

18. Which Belgian author created the fictional detective Maigret?

19. Which famous London building can be found at 32 London Bridge St, London SE1 9SG?
    a) The Cheese Grater
    b) The Gherkin
    c) The Shard

20. What was the title of a classic 1926 silent film starring Buster Keaton?
    a) The Colonel
    b) The General
    c) The Sergeant

MEDIUM

Answers to Quiz 123: Name the Decade

1.	1960s	11.	1990s
2.	1970s	12.	1960s
3.	1930s	13.	1970s
4.	1960s	14.	1970s
5.	1990s	15.	1960s
6.	1960s	16.	1990s
7.	1970s	17.	1920s
8.	1950s	18.	1930s
9.	1960s	19.	1980s
10.	1960s	20.	1920s

Quiz 125: Husbands and Wives

Identify the celebrity who has been married to each of the following people:

1. Linda Eastman, Heather Mills, Nancy Shevell

2. Alana Hamilton, Rachel Hunter, Penny Lancaster

3. Freddy Moore, Bruce Willis, Ashton Kutcher

4. Tommy Lee, Kid Rock, Rick Salomon

5. Melissa Lee Gatlin, Toni Lawrence, Cynda Williams, Pietra Dawn Cherniak, Angelina Jolie

6. Jim Threapleton, Sam Mendes, Ned Rocknroll

7. James Dougherty, Joe DiMaggio, Arthur Miller

8. Ronnie Knight, Stephen Hollings, Scott Mitchell

9. Peter Andre, Alex Reid, Kieran Hayler

10. Nancy Barbato, Ava Gardner, Mia Farrow, Barbara Marx

11. Dan Donovan, Jim Kerr, Liam Gallagher, Jeremy Healy

12. Maxwell Reid, Anthony Newley, Ronald S Kass, Peter Holm, Percy Gibson

13. Peter Allen, Jack Haley Jr, Mark Gero, David Gest

14. Danny Keough, Michael Jackson, Nicolas Cage, Michael Lockwood

15. Mimi Rogers, Nicole Kidman, Katie Holmes

16. Ojani Noa, Chris Judd, Marc Anthony

17. Sue Walpole, Julie Gullick, Alison Holloway, Tracy Hilton, Michelle Cotton

18. David Justice, Eric Benet, Olivier Martinez

19. Don Johnson, Steven Bauer, Don Johnson, Antonio Banderas

20. John Turnbull, Lance Gerrard-Wright, Brian Monet

MEDIUM

Answers to Quiz 124: Pot Luck

1.	The Pet Shop Boys	11.	Devon and Dorset
2.	The English Civil War	12.	Harrods
3.	Northern Ireland	13.	Donald Trump
4.	Three	14.	Erin Brokovich
5.	Eminem	15.	South America
6.	Don Warrington	16.	Gary Barlow
7.	Rome	17.	Stephen McGann
8.	Hamlet	18.	Georges Simenon
9.	40	19.	The Shard
10.	Dog	20.	The General

Quiz 126: Pot Luck

1. SW1A 2AA is the postcode for which famous London address?

2. The name of what Chinese city is used to describe a finish in darts where the player must hit a single, treble and double of the same number?

3. Who is older – UKIP politician Nigel Farage or actor Nicolas Cage?

4. The Miracles was the name of the backing band of which singer?

5. 'Going Straight' was the sequel to which TV comedy?

6. 'Humble Pie' was the title of the autobiography of which TV chef?

7. True or false – the brother of Dec (of Ant and Dec fame) is a Catholic priest?

8. In the TV sitcom 'Friends', which actor played Ross and Monica's father, Jack?

9. What sporting event was televised on Channel 4 for the first time on Saturday 6 April 2013?

10. In which year did Gordon Brown become the British prime minister?

11. What are the four African countries whose name ends with the letter I?

12. Patrick Chukwuemeka Okogwu is the real name of which alliterative British rap star?

13. In the TV programme 'Teletubbies', which Teletubby was red?

14. SJP NYC is a brand of perfume created by which actress?

15. In 2014, who became the leading scorer in a single UEFA Champions League season?

16. Who played eccentric billionaire Howard Hughes in the 2004 film biopic 'The Aviator'?

17. For which film did Sandra Bullock win her first Best Actress Oscar?

18. In which sport do teams compete for the Copa Libertadores?

19. What is the nickname of the veteran American boxing world champion, Bernard Hopkins?
    a) The Assassin
    b) The Executioner
    c) The Undertaker

20. In which Commonwealth country is Waitangi Day a national holiday?
    a) Australia
    b) New Zealand
    c) South Africa

MEDIUM

Answers to Quiz 125: Husbands and Wives

1. Paul McCartney
2. Rod Stewart
3. Demi Moore
4. Pamela Anderson
5. Billy Bob Thornton
6. Kate Winslet
7. Marilyn Monroe
8. Barbara Windsor
9. Katie Price (Jordan)
10. Frank Sinatra
11. Patsy Kensit
12. Joan Collins
13. Liza Minnelli
14. Lisa Marie Presley
15. Tom Cruise
16. Jennifer Lopez
17. Jim Davidson
18. Halle Berry
19. Melanie Griffith
20. Ulrika Jonsson

Quiz 127: Football

1. Which club reached the FA Cup final for the first time in 2014?

2. The Brewers is the nickname of which English football club?

3. In 2005, which team became the first winners of an FA Cup final decided by a penalty shoot-out?

4. The headquarters of football's governing body, FIFA, are in which city?

5. England's biggest ever defeat in international football came at the hands of which country?

6. Which was the first country to win the World Cup final following a penalty shoot-out?

7. Two seahorses features on the badge of which Premier League club?

8. Who was the first black player to captain the England national football team?

9. What are the two English clubs to have an unbeaten record in the final of the European Cup?

10. 'Nil satis nisi optimum' is the Latin motto of which English club?

11. The first ever FA Cup final was held at which cricket ground?

12. Which country will host the 2016 European Championships?

13. True or false – the first Africa Cup of Nations was held before the first European Championships?

14. Which are the two English clubs that have lost in the final of the European Cup or Champions League and never won the trophy?

15. Who was the first, and so far only, player to win 100 international caps for Scotland?

16. TV soap Coronation Street featured a dog named after which goalkeeper?

17. Which were the first two countries to co-host the European Championships?

18. Which was the only country that made its World Cup finals debut in the 2014 tournament?

19. Which ground holds the record for hosting the most FA Cup semi-finals (including replays)?
    a) Hillsborough
    b) Old Trafford
    c) Villa Park

20. 'Los Merengues' is a nickname of which European club?
    a) Barcelona
    b) Juventus
    c) Real Madrid

Answers to Quiz 126: Pot Luck

1. 10 Downing Street
2. Shanghai
3. Nicolas Cage
4. Smokey Robinson
5. Porridge
6. Gordon Ramsay
7. True
8. Elliott Gould
9. The Grand National
10. 2007
11. Burundi, Djibouti, Malawi and Mali
12. Tinie Tempah
13. Po
14. Sarah Jessica Parker
15. Cristiano Ronaldo
16. Leonardo DiCaprio
17. The Blind Side
18. Football
19. The Executioner
20. New Zealand

MEDIUM

Quiz 128: Pot Luck

MEDIUM

1. In 1984, Malcolm Morley became the first winner of which art award?

2. The Prado Museum is in which European capital city?

3. What connects a name for an unofficial detective and a magazine edited by Ian Hislop?

4. Former Italian prime minister Silvio Berlusconi is the owner of which football club?

5. In UK law, for what do the initials 'CPS' stand?

6. What animal features on the badge of the motor manufacturer Alfa Romeo?

7. Which politician said that 'democracy is the worst form of government, except for all those other forms that have been tried from time to time'?

8. As the crow flies, is London closer to Barcelona or Prague?

9. True or false – playboy Formula One driver James Hunt bred budgies in his spare time?

10. Which prime minister had a longer spell in 10 Downing Street – Tony Blair or Margaret Thatcher?

11. Which bespectacled TV cook wrote the autobiography 'Toast: The Story of a Boy's Hunger'?

12. Which classic 1972 film was released in Spain as 'El Padrino'?

13. Actor Nigel Pivaro played which 'Coronation Street' rogue?

14. What were the surnames of the American outlaws Bonnie and Clyde?

15. Ernest Hemingway's memoir 'A Moveable Feast' is set in which city?

16. Which infamous prison was nicknamed 'The Rock'?

17. David Stirling was the founder of which regiment of the British Army?

18. Which businessman and 'dragon' on the TV show 'Dragons' Den' is the owner of the car registration plate RYM4N?

19. The KGB spies Kim Philby, Guy Burgess, Anthony Blunt and Donald McLean attended which British university?
    a) Oxford
    b) Cambridge
    c) Hull

20. In astronomy, what name is given to a region of space where conditions are favourable for life?
    a) Cinderella zone
    b) Goldilocks zone
    c) Rapunzel zone

MEDIUM

Answers to Quiz 127: Football

1. Hull City
2. Burton Albion
3. Arsenal
4. Zurich
5. Hungary
6. Brazil
7. Newcastle United
8. Paul Ince
9. Aston Villa and Nottingham Forest
10. Everton
11. The Oval
12. France
13. True
14. Arsenal and Leeds United
15. Kenny Dalglish
16. Peter Schmeichel
17. Belgium and the Netherlands
18. Bosnia and Herzegovina
19. Villa Park
20. Real Madrid

Quiz 129: Postcodes

Identify the town or city that has the following postcode prefixes (for example, B = Birmingham):

1. AB

2. BH

3. BN

4. BS

5. CM

6. CT

7. DH

8. DN

9. DY

10. GL

11. IV

12. LS

13. NR

14. PL

15. PO

MEDIUM

16. SY

17. TA

18. TQ

19. WN

20. WV

Answers to Quiz 128: Pot Luck

1. The Turner Prize
2. Madrid
3. Private Eye
4. AC Milan
5. Crown Prosecution Service
6. Snake
7. Winston Churchill
8. Prague
9. True
10. Margaret Thatcher
11. Nigel Slater
12. The Godfather
13. Terry Duckworth
14. Parker and Barrow
15. Paris
16. Alcatraz
17. The SAS
18. Theo Paphitis
19. Cambridge
20. Goldilocks zone

Quiz 130: Pot Luck

1. Maastricht, the venue for the signing of a major international treaty, is in which country?

2. FCA are the initials of which City financial body?

3. What shape are the wax cells that make up a honeycomb?

4. 'Viernes' is the Spanish word for which day of the week?

5. What are the four US states whose names end with the letter N?

6. 'Help me escape this feelin' of insecurity / I need you so much but I don't think you really need me' are the opening lines to which 1993 number one?

7. The profile of which British monarch appeared on the Penny Black postage stamp?

8. Who served as the British prime minister for just 363 days between 1963 and 1964?

9. Which smoothie played Lewis Archer in TV soap 'Coronation Street'?

10. Who is older – Robert De Niro or Al Pacino?

11. Which of TV's 'Teletubbies' has a triangular antenna on his head?

12. True or false – Hollywood star Drew Barrymore is a cousin of British broadcaster Michael Barrymore?

13. Which sportsman is the owner of the award-winning Cromlix House Hotel in Kinbuck, Perthshire?

14. 'The Key', 'Girlfriend' and 'Someday' are perfumes created by which male teen heartthrob?

MEDIUM

Answers – page 265

15. The boxing match known as the 'Rumble in the Jungle' took place in which African capital city?

16. What was introduced in London on 17 February 2003?

17. Which Spanish name provided the title of a UK top 10 hit for Lady Gaga in 2010?

18. The hormone insulin is produced by which organ of the body?

19. In which game was Britain's Nigel Short a world-class performer?
    a) chess
    b) poker
    c) squash

20. Which sporting organization was founded first?
    a) The FA
    b) The MCC
    c) The RFU

MEDIUM

Answers to Quiz 129: Postcodes

1. Aberdeen
2. Bournemouth
3. Brighton
4. Bristol
5. Chelmsford
6. Canterbury
7. Durham
8. Doncaster
9. Dudley
10. Gloucester
11. Inverness
12. Leeds
13. Norwich
14. Plymouth
15. Portsmouth
16. Shrewsbury
17. Taunton
18. Torquay
19. Wigan
20. Wolverhampton

Quiz 131: Connections part 2

1. What is the name of the ceremony where a king or queen is crowned?

2. Cockney Rebel were the backing band for which singer who topped the charts with 'Make Me Smile (Come Up and See Me)'?

3. What is the highest rank in the Royal Navy?

4. What name is given to a person who rules a kingdom if the king or queen is too young or ill to take charge?

5. Which American state is nicknamed 'The Garden State'?

6. Which DJ presents the Absolute Radio Breakfast Show as well as the Radio 5 panel show 'Fighting Talk'?

7. In modern slang, what do the initials 'FWB' stand for?

8. Complete the title of a 1962 novel by John Le Carre – 'A Murder of ...'?

9. In the story of 'Ali Baba and the 40 Thieves', which phrase opens the mouth of a cave where the thieves have hidden their treasure?

10. Which England footballer started his career at Middlesbrough, had a loan spell at Sunderland, then played for Aston Villa, Liverpool and West Ham United?

11. The Ashmolean Museum is in which English city?

12. Zac Efron played Troy Bolton in which hit 2006 film?

13. Walton, Wavertree and West Derby are parliamentary constituencies in which English city?

14. What was Michael Jackson's first UK top 10 album?

15. '00-147' is the nickname of which snooker player?

16. Which Eurovision Song Contest winner later went on to co-host the TV show 'Record Breakers'?

17. Which fruit is used in a mojito cocktail?

18. What was the only UK top-five single from The Spin Doctors?
    a) Two Kings
    c) Two Princes
    c) Two Queens

19. Which number US president was Bill Clinton?
    a) 41st
    b) 42nd
    c) 43rd

20. What is the connection between the answers?

Answers to Quiz 130: Pot Luck

1. Netherlands
2. Financial Conduct Authority
3. Hexagonal
4. Friday
5. Michigan, Oregon, Washington and Wisconsin
6. Relight My Fire by Take That
7. Queen Victoria
8. Sir Alec Douglas-Home
9. Nigel Havers
10. Al Pacino
11. Tinky Winky
12. False
13. Andy Murray
14. Justin Bieber
15. Kinshasa
16. The Congestion Charge
17. Alejandro
18. Pancreas
19. Chess
20. The MCC

Quiz 132: Pot Luck

1. Which actor was Madonna's first husband?

2. What nationality is the racing driver Mark Webber?

3. British actor Stephen Graham plays which gangster in the TV drama 'Boardwalk Empire'?

4. What is the name of the tube station that features in TV soap 'EastEnders'?

5. Which alcoholic drink is made by fermenting honey?

6. Detective drama 'Endeavour' is set in which city?

7. True or false – politician Tony Blair is the nephew of dancer and entertainer Lionel Blair?

8. In 2013 it was announced that which female author would feature on the new £10 note?

9. Which popular British TV drama is known in Denmark as 'Kriminalkommisær Barnaby'?

10. Who was the first Arsenal player to score 30 goals in a Premier League season?

11. What major British organization was privatized in October 2013?

12. True or false – Liverpool footballer Martin Skrtel is a qualified tattoo artist?

13. Which actress gained her first Best Actress Oscar nomination for the 2010 film 'Winter's Bone'?

14. How many middle names does Prince George of Cambridge have?

15. Who was awarded a Bafta in 2013 after being hailed the 'most memorable Bond girl yet'?

16. What is the lowest three-figure prime number?

17. In June 2013, which celebrity couple had a baby daughter called North?

18. Which US TV sitcom from the 1990s featured a butler called Jeffrey?

19. Kimchi is the national dish of which country?
    a) Indonesia
    b) Japan
    c) Korea

20. Russian Caravan is a variety of which drink?
    a) coffee
    b) cola
    c) tea

Answers to Quiz 131: Connections part 2

1. Coronation
2. Steve Harley
3. Admiral of the Fleet
4. Regent
5. New Jersey
6. Christian O'Connell
7. Friends with benefits
8. Quality
9. Open, sesame
10. Stewart Downing
11. Oxford
12. High School Musical
13. Liverpool
14. Off the Wall
15. Nigel Bond
16. Cheryl Baker
17. Lime
18. Two Princes
19. 42nd
20. They all contain the name of a famous street

MEDIUM

Quiz 133: Anagrams

Rearrange the letters to make the name of a city in the UK:

1. Lads For

2. Bye Currant

3. Thump Roots

4. Tech Riches

5. Red Ref Ho

6. Canal Rest

7. Chilli Fed

8. Or Pin

9. Busy Liars

10. Rec Towers

11. Never Sins

12. Pat Sash

13. Nee Beard

14. Revamp Not Howl

15. Snot Rep

16. Rings Lit

17. Cheers Twin

18. Phantoms Out

19. Tougher Probe

20. Closet Urge

Answers to Quiz 132: Pot Luck

1. Sean Penn
2. Australian
3. Al Capone
4. Walford East
5. Mead
6. Oxford
7. False
8. Jane Austen
9. Midsomer Murders
10. Thierry Henry
11. Royal Mail
12. True
13. Jennifer Lawrence
14. Two
15. The Queen
16. 101
17. Kim Kardashian and Kanye West
18. The Fresh Prince of Bel Air
19. Korea
20. Tea

Quiz 134: Pot Luck

1. The British overseas territory of St Helena is an island in which ocean?

2. Cars in Australia are driven on which side of the road?

3. The 1987 novel 'Knots and Crosses' was the first book to feature which fictional detective?

4. In 2014, which footballing legend launched a diamond collection made from the carbon contained in his hair?

5. Which 20th-century British prime minister was the son of a former trapeze artist?

6. Loiner is a nickname given to people from which English city?

7. Yehudi Menuhin was a virtuoso on which musical instrument?

8. In which decade did wearing a seat belt in the front seat of a car become compulsory?

9. True or false – former world heavyweight boxing champion Mike Tyson is a pigeon fancier?

10. The opera 'Carmen' was written by which composer?

11. Which name is missing from the following list – Richard Whiteley, Des Lynam, _____, Jeff Stelling, Nick Hewer

12. The BCG vaccine is used to inoculate people against which disease?

13. In how many James Bond films did Timothy Dalton play 007?

14. In a game of contract bridge, each player is dealt how many cards?

15. Langley, home to the CIA headquarters, is in which American state?

16. 'Dienstag' is the German word for which day of the week?

17. As the crow flies, which city is closer to London – Buenos Aires or Johannesburg?

18. The American sitcom 'Cheers' was set in which city?

19. The Bridgewater Hall is a concert venue in which city?
    a) Birmingham
    b) Glasgow
    c) Manchester

20. What type of produce is sold at New Covent Garden Market?
    a) fish
    b) fruit and vegetables
    c) meat

Answers to Quiz 133: Anagrams

1. Salford
2. Canterbury
3. Portsmouth
4. Chichester
5. Hereford
6. Lancaster
7. Lichfield
8. Ripon
9. Salisbury
10. Worcester
11. Inverness
12. St Asaph
13. Aberdeen
14. Wolverhampton
15. Preston
16. Stirling
17. Winchester
18. Southampton
19. Peterborough
20. Gloucester

MEDIUM

DIFFICULT
QUIZZES

Quiz 135: Pot Luck

1. Which TV and film awards are voted on by members of the Hollywood Foreign Press Association?

2. Who were the two Dutch footballers to win the European Footballer of the Year award three times?

3. American sitcom 'Happy Days' was set in which city?

4. Which Manchester-born singer also produces a series of fine wines under the label 'Il Cantante' (the Singer)?

5. The Stephen Joseph Theatre is located in which English seaside resort?

6. Inspector Chester Campbell appeared in which BBC crime drama that aired for the first time in 2013?

7. Which British broadcaster made his TV debut in 1970 in an advert for Rice Krispies?

8. In 2013, which city became the UK's first City of Culture?

9. Which snooker player is nicknamed 'The Jester from Leicester'?

10. Which actress, comedian and writer created the clothing label 'Sixteen47'?

11. In which year were the Olympic Games hosted in Asia for the first time?

12. Iraklion is the capital city of which popular Greek holiday island?

13. Which major American city takes its name from the French word for 'strait'?

14. Which British actress played Winnie Mandela in the 2014 film 'Mandela: Long Walk to Freedom'?

15. Which 'X Factor' winner was the champion on the maiden series of the winter sports reality TV show 'The Jump'?

Answers – page 277

16. Which fictional dog was originally going to be called 'Too Much'?

17. In which year did China regain sovereignty of Hong Kong from Great Britain?

18. Dr Who's time-travelling craft the TARDIS is an acronym. What does the R stand for?

19. Which of the following TV presenters is the oldest?
    a) Zoe Ball
    b) Tess Daly
    c) Claudia Winkleman

20. Vanessa Selbst, Erik Seidel and Tony G are notable performers in which game?
    a) chess
    b) poker
    c) pool

Answers to Quiz 200: New and Old

1. Gary Oldman
2. The Old Curiosity Shop
3. Newport County
4. Old Kent Road
5. New Kids on the Block
6. New Hampshire
7. Harry Enfield and Paul Whitehouse
8. Shrewsbury Town
9. Sir Isaac Newton
10. Oldham Athletic
11. New Musical Express
12. Olivia Newton-John
13. Argentina
14. Newbury
15. Old Street
16. The 40-Year-Old Virgin
17. New Brunswick
18. Paul Newman
19. Old Harry
20. Harvard

DIFFICULT

Quiz 136: Music part 1

1. Tim Bergling is the real name of which Swedish DJ and producer, who topped the charts in 2013 with 'Wake Me Up'?

2. Which female singer topped the charts in late 2013 with a cover of Keane's 'Somewhere Only We Know'?

3. What are the first names of the songwriting partnership Bacharach and David?

4. 'I took her to a supermarket / I don't know why but I had to start it somewhere' are lines from which number-two hit from 1995?

5. Which Irish singer first rose to prominence in the 1960s as the lead vocalist with R&B band Them?

6. Which symbol of the French revolution is also the name of a British rock band who recorded the 2013 album 'Bad Blood'?

7. 'Something to Remember', 'Confessions on a Dance Floor' and 'Hard Candy' are albums by which legendary solo artist?

8. 'Dear Darlin'' was a top five single for which former 'X Factor' star?

9. The 2013 Comic Relief single by One Direction, 'One Way or Another (Teenage Kicks)', was a medley of songs by which two bands?

10. Appearing for 66 consecutive weeks since its release in 2012, which debut album has featured in the Official Albums Chart Top 10 for the longest amount of time?

11. Released in November 2013, whose 'Swings Both Ways' became the 1000th album to reach Number 1 on the UK's Official Albums Chart?

12. The soundtrack to which film was the 12th-biggest-selling album in the UK in 2013?

13. Which market town in North Yorkshire was also the title of a Mercury-Prize-nominated album from dance music duo Disclosure?

14. Which European port provided the Beautiful South with the title of a top-five single?

15. Darts player Phil 'The Power' Taylor takes his nickname from a song by which German dance act?

16. 'I Knew You Were Trouble' was a number two hit single in 2013 for which American singer-songwriter?

17. Lesane Parish Crooks was the real name of which hip-hop star who was killed in 1996?

18. What is the biggest-selling album in UK chart history that is not a greatest hits collection?

19. What sort of jukebox provided Bruno Mars with the title of a 2013 album?
a) Unorthodox Jukebox   b) Unusual Jukebox
c) Unplayable Jukebox

20. Between 1984 and 1994, pop princess Madonna had how many consecutive Top 40 singles?
a) 25   b) 30   c) 35

Answers to Quiz 135: Pot Luck

1. The Golden Globes
2. Johan Cruyff and Marco Van Basten
3. Milwaukee
4. Mick Hucknall
5. Scarborough
6. Peaky Blinders
7. Jonathan Ross
8. Derry / Londonderry
9. Mark Selby
10. Dawn French
11. 1964
12. Crete
13. Detroit
14. Naomie Harris
15. Joe McElderry
16. Scooby Doo
17. 1997
18. Relative
19. Tess Daly
20. Poker

DIFFICULT

Quiz 137: Pot Luck

1. In 1956, which Englishman became the first winner of the European Footballer of the Year award?

2. Cillian Murphy plays gang leader Tommy Shelby in which British crime drama?

3. In 1985, which capital city was named the first ever European Capital of Culture?

4. In the TV sitcom 'Frasier', what was the name of the broadcaster's man-eating producer?

5. Which singer won 'The X Factor' in the year that One Direction finished third?

6. Which Italian astronomer, philosopher and mathematician said, 'I have never met a man so ignorant that I couldn't learn something from him'?

7. In September 2013, American Marin Alsop became the first woman to take charge of which event?

8. Which 1989 film was the first general release to be awarded a 12 certificate in the UK?

9. With 22 awards, which European band holds the record for the most Grammys won by a group?

10. Despite not wishing to be 'the subject of any monument', a statue of which author was unveiled in Portsmouth in 2014 on what would have been his 202nd birthday?

11. The 2013 film 'Saving Mr Banks' was about the making of which movie?

12. Mimas, Enceladus and Tethys are moons of which planet of the Solar System?

13. Which actress plays Lady Mary Crawley in TV drama 'Downton Abbey'?

14. In which year did Winston Churchil become British prime minister for the first time?

DIFFICULT

Answers – page 281

15. Published in 2014, 'The Body Book' is by which Hollywood actress, who appeared in the film 'Charlie's Angels'?

16. American cop drama 'Blue Bloods' is set in which city?

17. Which prolific crime writer created the fictional detective Alex Cross?

18. The name of which English city is also the name of the capital of the US state of Nebraska?

19. In which field is Sir David Chipperfield a notable name?
    a) architecture
    b) classical music
    c) physics

20. Radio One DJ Zane Lowe is from which country?
    a) Australia
    b) New Zealand
    c) South Africa

Answers to Quiz 136: Music part 1

1. Avicii
2. Lily Allen
3. Burt and Hal
4. Common People' by Pulp
5. Van Morrison
6. Bastille
7. Madonna
8. Olly Murs
9. Blondie and The Undertones
10. 'Our Version of Events' by Emeli Sandé
11. Robbie Williams
12. Les Miserables
13. Settle
14. Rotterdam
15. Snap
16. Taylor Swift
17. Tupac Shakur
18. Sgt Pepper's Lonely Hearts Club Band
19. Unorthodox Jukebox
20. 35

DIFFICULT

Quiz 138: Football

1. Dave Beasant was the first goalkeeper to save an FA Cup final penalty at Wembley. Who was the second?

2. Which team returned to the Football League after a five-year absence after winning the Conference in 2014?

3. Who was the first foreign manager to win the FA Cup in England?

4. Which alliteratively named striker is the only Scot to score in three World Cups?

5. Which was the last team to win the FA Cup that was comprised entirely of English players?

6. Up to 2014, four English players had won the European Footballer of the Year award. Name them.

7. Which European team plays its home matches at the Donbas Arena?

8. What is the capacity of Wembley Stadium?

9. Which two teams took part in the first all-Spanish Champions League final?

10. In 1991, who became the first African team to play an international match at Wembley?

11. Who was the first footballer to score for seven different Premier League clubs?

12. Which club holds the record for being relegated from England's top flight the most times?

13. In terms of population, which is the smallest nation to have reached the quarter-final of the World Cup?

14. In 1998, who became the first player to lose in the FA Cup final at Wembley with three different clubs?

15. Aged 42 years and 39 days, who is the oldest player to appear in a World Cup match?

16. What is the smallest city to host a World Cup final?

17. Queen Elizabeth II has handed out two trophies at Wembley. The first was to Bobby Moore. Who received the second?

18. Which two teams took part in the FA Cup match known as the 'White Horse Final'?

19. Which Italian goalkeeper holds the record for the most consecutive minutes without conceding a World Cup goal?
a) Gianluigi Buffon   b) Walter Zenga   c) Dino Zoff

20. Just Fontaine holds the record for the most goals in a single World Cup tournament. How many did he score in 1958?
a) 11   b) 12   c) 13

Answers to Quiz 137: Pot Luck

1. Sir Stanley Matthews
2. Peaky Blinders
3. Athens
4. Roz Doyle
5. Matt Cardle
6. Galileo
7. The Last Night of the Proms
8. Batman
9. U2
10. Charles Dickens
11. Mary Poppins
12. Saturn
13. Michelle Dockery
14. 1940
15. Cameron Diaz
16. New York
17. James Patterson
18. Lincoln
19. Architecture
20. New Zealand

DIFFICULT

Quiz 139: Pot Luck

1. The first Winter Olympic Games were hosted in which French resort?

2. @S_C_ is the Twitter handle of which famous rapper and businessman?

3. 'Starry Night' is a work by which Dutch painter?

4. Britain's multiple gold-medal-winning athlete Mo Farah was born in which African country?

5. Two films that won Best Picture at the Oscars in the 1990s feature animals in their title. Which two?

6. In 2014, Jose Mourinho's first home Premier League defeat in 78 games as Chelsea manager came at the hands of which club?

7. In which sport can a player score a behind?

8. In which month does the annual Cheltenham horse-racing festival take place?

9. In which decade were the Oscars awarded for the first time?

10. Which British politician appeared alongside Catherine Tate's grumpy teenager character Lauren, in a 2007 Comic Relief sketch?

11. The Khmer Republic is a former name of which Asian country?

12. Which Radio 1 DJ was rushed to hospital in the middle of his Breakfast Show in March 2014 after accidentally swallowing a shard of glass?

13. The phrase 'patriotism is not enough' is attributed to which British nurse, who was executed by a German firing squad during the First World War?

14. In which state was US president George W Bush born?

DIFFICULT

15. True or false – there is an island in Thailand that is named after James Bond?

16. Which European capital city was also the name of a band that had a UK number-one hit single in 1986?

17. Which two Lauras were nominated for the Best British Female award at the 2014 Brits?

18. The words 'algebra', 'alcohol' and 'alkali' derive from which language?

19. Approximately how many records have appeared in the UK Top 40 since the charts began in 1952?
    a) 27,000   b) 30,000   c) 33,000

20. What is the nickname of the building located at 122 Leadenhall Street, London?
    a) The Cheese Grater   b) The Gherkin   c) The Tooth Pick

Answers to Quiz 138: Football

1. Mark Crossley
2. Luton Town
3. Ruud Gullit
4. Joe Jordan
5. West Ham United (in 1975)
6. Stanley Matthews, Bobby Charlton, Kevin Keegan, Michael Owen
7. Shakhtar Donetsk
8. 90,000
9. Real Madrid and Valencia
10. Cameroon
11. Craig Bellamy
12. Birmingham City
13. Northern Ireland
14. John Barnes
15. Roger Milla
16. Berne
17. Jurgen Klinsmann (at Euro 96)
18. Bolton Wanderers and West Ham United
19. Walter Zenga
20. 13

DIFFICULT

Quiz 140: Light and Dark

1. 'Racing Through the Dark' is the title of the autobiography of which British cyclist who has won multiple stages of the Tour de France?

2. Who is the lead singer with the rock band Snow Patrol?

3. 'The Life of Riley', 'Change' and 'Lucky You' were hits in the 1990s for which band?

4. What type of insect is a darkling?

5. Daniel Day-Lewis and Juliette Binoche starred in which 1988 film that was adapted from a novel by Czech writer Milan Kundera?

6. The Charge of the Light Brigade took place during which battle of the Crimean War?

7. 'White Lightning' was the nickname of which South African fast bowler who took 330 wickets in 72 Test match appearances?

8. Which 2010 film features a teenager who discovers he is the descendant of a Greek god and sets out on an adventure to settle an ongoing battle between the gods?

9. Which Hindu festival is also known as the festival of lights?

10. Which electro band recorded the 2008 top-five album 'Made in the Dark'?

11. Which Irish actor played the title character in the cult 1990 superhero film 'Darkman'?

12. 'Enola Gay', 'Sailing on the Seven Seas' and 'Souvenir' were hits for which synth-pop band?

13. 'In the darkness there must come out to light' is a line from which song by reggae legend Bob Marley?

14. What was the title of Madonna's 1998 UK number one album?

15. Which 2010 film starring Mel Gibson was a remake of a BBC political thriller from the 1980s?

16. Released in 1986, 'There Is a Light That Never Goes Out' is a song by which iconic Manchester band?

17. Which veteran singer topped the charts in 2008 with an album called 'Home Before Dark'?

18. 'Lights' was a number one album in 2010 for which female singer?

19. Which Jewish festival is also known as the Feast of Lights?
    a) Hanukkah
    b) Purim
    c) Yom Kippur

20. Which superhero featured in the 2013 film 'The Dark World'?
    a) Batman
    b) Spiderman
    c) Thor

Answers to Quiz 139: Pot Luck

1. Chamonix
2. Jay Z
3. Vincent van Gogh
4. Somalia
5. 'Dances with Wolves' and 'The Silence of the Lambs'
6. Sunderland
7. Australian Rules Football
8. March
9. 1920s
10. Tony Blair
11. Cambodia
12. Nick Grimshaw
13. Edith Cavell
14. Connecticut
15. True
16. Berlin
17. Laura Marling and Laura Mvula
18. Arabic
19. 33,000
20. The Cheese Grater

DIFFICULT

Quiz 141: Pot Luck

1. The Big Bash is a competition held in Australia in which sport?

2. Gavrilo Princip was the assassin of which historical figure?

3. What is the southernmost borough of New York City?

4. Which female hip-hop star carried out 30 wedding ceremonies during the 2014 Grammy Awards?

5. Which three-time European Footballer of the Year became president of football's governing body UEFA in 2007?

6. Which Tory MP donned her swimsuit for the 2014 series of TV talent show 'Splash!'?

7. Madam Professor Minerva McGonagall was a teacher at which fictional school?

8. What are the middle names of Prince William's son George?

9. David Cameron and Barack Obama caused controversy after posing for a 'selfie' at Nelson Mandela's memorial service with the prime minister of which European country?

10. The House of Doreon was a fashion label founded by which singer and actress?

11. Three people were killed in April 2013 after a bomb went off near the closing stages of a marathon in which American city?

12. In a tug of war, each team is made up of how many members?

13. The 2014 film 'A Long Way Down' was based on a 2005 novel by which British author?

14. Which saint, who was stoned to death in 36AD, is celebrated as the first Christian martyr?

15. Which two Asian countries are linked by the Khyber Pass?

16. What sport takes place at stadiums in Hall Green, Crayford and Brough Park?

17. What was the first Nordic country to host the Summer Olympic Games?

18. In July 2013, president Mohamed Morsi was ousted from power in which African country?

19. Prior to Benedict XVI, who was the last pope to resign from office?
    a) Gregory XII   b) John XXIII   c) John Paul I

20. Bjørn Dæhlie, the most successful Winter Olympian of all time, represented which country?
    a) Denmark   b) Norway   c) Sweden

Answers to Quiz 140: Light and Dark

1. David Millar
2. Gary Lightbody
3. The Lightning Seeds
4. Beetle
5. The Unbearable Lightness of Being
6. The Battle of Balaclava
7. Allan Donald
8. Percy Jackson and the Lightning Thief
9. Diwali
10. Hot Chip
11. Liam Neeson
12. Orchestral Manoeuvres In The Dark
13. Could You Be Loved
14. Ray of Light
15. Edge of Darkness
16. The Smiths
17. Neil Diamond
18. Ellie Goulding
19. Hanukkah
20. Thor

DIFFICULT

Quiz 142: Crime and Punishment

1. 1963's 'Great Train Robbery' was carried out on a train travelling to London from which city?

2. The so-called 'mastermind' behind the 'Great Train Robbery' died in 2013 at the age of 81. What was his name?

3. Which fashion designer was shot dead on the steps of his Miami Beach home in 1997?

4. Who was assassinated by a killer called Sirhan Sirhan?

5. Timothy McVeigh was executed in 2001 after planting a bomb in 1995 that killed 168 people in which American city?

6. By what name is Richard John Bingham more commonly known?

7. Who was the last woman to be executed in the UK?

8. On 13 May 1981, Mehmet Ali Agca unsuccessfully attempted to assassinate which high-profile public figure?

9. By what nickname was the American serial killer Albert DeSalvo known?

10. The classic novel 'Crime and Punishment' is by which Russian author?

11. What was the name of the Norwegian murderer who killed 77 people in Oslo and on the island of Utoya in July 2011?

12. Where in the UK were there prisons called Albany and Parkhurst?

13. The crime organization known as the Camorra is based in which Italian city?

14. What was the name of the bank that collapsed in 1995 following huge losses caused by 'rogue trader' Nick Leeson?

15. What position was held by Albert Pierrepoint and Harry Allen?

16. In UK law enforcement, what did the initials SOCA stand for?

17. In which decade was the last execution by guillotine carried out in France?

18. Convicted fraudster Allen Stanford was based on which Caribbean island?

19. In July 1982, cat burglar Michael Fagan broke into which supposedly impregnable place?
    a) Buckingham Palace
    b) 10 Downing Street
    c) The White House

20. Serial killers Fred and Rose West lived in which street?
    a) Brooklyn Street
    b) Cromwell Street
    c) Suffolk Street

Answers to Quiz 141: Pot Luck

1. Cricket
2. Archduke Franz Ferdinand of Austria
3. Staten Island
4. Queen Latifah
5. Michel Platini
6. Penny Mordaunt
7. Hogwarts (in the Harry Potter series)
8. Alexander Louis
9. Denmark
10. Beyoncé
11. Boston
12. Eight
13. Nick Hornby
14. St Stephen
15. Afghanistan and Pakistan
16. Greyhound racing
17. Sweden
18. Egypt
19. Gregory XII
20. Norway

DIFFICULT

Quiz 143: Pot Luck

1. 'It's Up to You New York' was the title of a 2013 novel by which TV presenter?

2. Who was the first, and up to 2014 is the only, US President to have been born in the state of Illinois?

3. What form of transport is an Italian 'vaporetto'?

4. Who is older – Christian Bale or Ewan McGregor?

5. Which footballer is the owner of the Southport restaurant The Warehouse Kitchen and Bar?

6. Which English town is home to a rugby league team nicknamed the Vikings?

7. The only royal palace in America is in which state?

8. Which 1982 song by the Weather Girls re-entered the charts in 2014 in response to a UKIP councillor who blamed heavy flooding on gay marriage being legalized?

9. Which European capital city featured in the title of a 2014 film directed by Wes Anderson and starring Ralph Fiennes and Bill Murray?

10. What is the name of the Queen Elizabeth II's first great-grandchild?

11. In January 2014, which American state became the first to legalize cannabis?

12. 68 people were killed by extremists from Islamist group Al-Shabaab in an attack on a shopping centre in which African capital?

13. In which decade were the Olympic Games held in Antwerp, Paris and Amsterdam?

14. 'Rockferry' was a best-selling 2008 album by which Welsh singer?

15. 'Qomolangma' is the Chinese name for which mountain?

Answers – page 293

16. Which business magnate was the mayor of New York from 2002 until 2013?

17. Which town in the US state of Nebraska gives its name to a version of poker?

18. Which actor plays Moriarty in the contemporary BBC drama 'Sherlock'?

19. What was the name of the massive storm that battered Britain in October 2013?
    a) Storm St George
    b) Storm St Jude
    c) Storm St Patrick

20. Which veteran rocker now plays with a band called The Sensational Space Shifters?
    a) Noddy Holder
    b) Robert Plant
    c) Ronnie Wood

Answers to Quiz 142: Crime and Punishment

1. Glasgow
2. Bruce Reynolds
3. Gianni Versace
4. Bobby Kennedy
5. Oklahoma City
6. Lord Lucan
7. Ruth Ellis
8. Pope John Paul II
9. The Boston Strangler
10. Dostoevsky
11. Anders Breivik
12. Isle of Wight
13. Naples
14. Barings Bank
15. Executioner
16. Serious Organised Crime Agency
17. 1970s
18. Antigua
19. Buckingham Palace
20. Cromwell Street

DIFFICULT

Quiz 144: Transport

1. In which country will you find a style of rickshaw called the Cocotaxi?

2. The Shinkansen is a high-speed rail network in which country?

3. The first ever commercial airline flight took place in which American state?

4. Queen Street is a railway station in which Scottish city?

5. What is the only London railway terminus that is not on the London Underground?

6. What was Vanessa Paradis' first UK hit single?

7. Which city is served by McCarran International Airport?

8. What is the busiest railway station in London?

9. Which group had a top-ten hit in 2006 with 'Chasing Cars'?

10. What was banned on London Transport on 1 June 2008?

11. 'Motion & Emotion' is a slogan associated with which car manufacturer?

12. Which is the only London Underground line that connects with all other lines?

13. Southern Cross Station is the major railway station of which city?

14. Which form of transport provided Lily Allen with the title of a 2014 top-ten single?

15. BHX is the international code for which airport?

16. Which motor manufacturer brands itself as the 'Ultimate Driving Machine'?

17. Arlanda, Barkaby and Bromma airports serve which European capital city?

18. In which decade was the Automobile Association founded?

19. The London Underground is made up of how many stations?
    a) 270
    b) 280
    c) 290

20. What is Britain's busiest railway station outside of London?
    a) Birmingham New Street
    b) Glasgow Central
    c) Manchester Piccadilly

DIFFICULT

Quiz 145: Pot Luck

1. Which Britpop star-turned-farmer wrote the 2012 memoir 'All Cheeses Great and Small: A Life Less Blurry'?

2. Bodie and Doyle were the central characters in which TV drama that ran from 1977 until 1983?

3. What is the maximum allowable height for a NASA astronaut?

4. Full forward, ruck rover and forward pocket are positions in which sport?

5. Anna Wing, who died in July 2013 at the age of 98, played which East End soap matriarch?

6. Excluding the in-goal areas, what is the maximum length in metres of a rugby union pitch?

7. Sergey Bubka was the long-time world record holder in which athletics event?

8. In 2010, who became the Green Party's first Westminster MP?

9. Named after a 1972 album, which British rock band created their own beer called 'Piledriver'?

10. In which language is Father Christmas known as Daidí na Nollag?

11. Margaret Mary Emily Anne Hyra is the real name of which Hollywood actress?

12. Dandini is a character that appears in which pantomime?

13. Which country is the largest producer of coffee in the world?

14. In a Formula One Grand Prix race, what colour flag is flown to indicate danger?

15. On a standard dartboard, what number lies between 12 and 14?

16. In the 'Toy Story' film trilogy, what is the name of the boy who owns the toys?

17. Which martial art takes its name from the Japanese words for 'gentleness' and 'art'?

18. What is the only number whose letters are in alphabetical order?

19. In 2013, 13-year-old Jack Durand became a British champion in which game?
    a) chess
    b) pool
    c) Scrabble

20. At an auction in Geneva in 2013, a diamond was sold for £52m. What colour was the precious stone?
    a) blue
    b) pink
    c) white

Answers to Quiz 144: Transport

1. Cuba
2. Japan
3. Florida
4. Glasgow
5. Fenchurch Street
6. Joe Le Taxi
7. Las Vegas
8. Waterloo
9. Snow Patrol
10. Alcohol
11. Peugeot
12. Jubilee
13. Melbourne
14. Air Balloon
15. Birmingham
16. BMW
17. Stockholm
18. 1900s
19. 270
20. Birmingham New Street

DIFFICULT

Quiz 146: Alliterative Answers

1. Who played Norman Bates in Gus Van Sant's 1998 remake of the Hitchcock classic 'Psycho'?

2. Bruce Willis played a cat burglar forced to steal a work by Leonardo Da Vinci in which 1991 action comedy?

3. Which actor played Hank Moody in the US TV drama 'Californication'?

4. What was the name of the cruise ship that sank off the coast of Isola del Giglio in Italy on 13 January 2012?

5. Which actor was nominated for a Golden Globe award in 2014 for playing a resourceful sailor in 'All Is Lost'?

6. Which aptly named horse won the 1992 Grand National, just five days before the general election?

7. Nick Dunne is the central character in which best-selling 2012 thriller by American author Gillian Flynn?

8. In 1988, who became the first female prime minister of a Muslim country after winning the election in Pakistan?

9. 'Ulysses' and 'The Portrait of the Artist as a Young Man' are novels by which Irish author who died in 1941?

10. In 'The Simpsons', who is the principal of Springfield Elementary School?

11. Which TV policeman was created by author Alan Hunter?

12. Actor Paul Walker, who died in a car crash in November 2013, played Brian O'Conner in which film franchise?

13. By what name is the Stadio Giuseppe Meazza more commonly known?

14. The Spanish football league club Real Sociedad are based in which city?

Answers – page 299

15. Skyler White, Jesse Pinkman and Saul Goodman were characters in which US TV drama?

16. Which American actress said, 'How come when Kanye acts like an idiot he gets a gold record, but when I act like an idiot, I get a police record?'

17. Which male vocalist won the Critics' Choice Award at the 2014 Brits?

18. Who picks the letters and solves the number puzzles on TV quiz show 'Countdown'?

19. Which actor, comedian and quiz show host also provides the voice of the alien supercomputer Mr Smith in the TV show 'The Sarah Jane Adventures'?

20. Which actress, best known for starring in a long-running sitcom, plays Jules Lobb in US drama 'Cougar Town'?

Answers to Quiz 145: Pot Luck

1. Alex James
2. The Professionals
3. 6ft 4in (193cm)
4. Australian Rules Football
5. Lou Beale
6. 100m
7. Pole vault
8. Caroline Lucas
9. Status Quo
10. Irish
11. Meg Ryan
12. Cinderella
13. Brazil
14. Yellow
15. 9
16. Andy
17. Ju-Jitsu
18. Forty
19. Scrabble
20. Pink

DIFFICULT

Quiz 147: Pot Luck

1. Where is the annual Ironman World Championship held?

2. The name of which Hollywood actor, born in July 1942, is made up of the surnames of two former US presidents?

3. Which German footballer, who had spells in England with Aston Villa and West Ham, came out as gay in January 2014?

4. Steve Arnott, Kate Fleming, Ted Hastings and Matt 'Dot' Cottan are characters in which British police drama?

5. Which musician's Best Male nomination at the 2014 Brit Awards came 30 years after he was last nominated for the same award?

6. A women's lacrosse team is made up of how many players?

7. Which veteran British rock band won a Grammy in 2014 for their album 'God Is Dead?'?

8. Which pantomime appears in the title of a 1973 album by David Bowie?

9. True or false – the Vatican has its own cricket club?

10. Filbert Street is the former home ground of which English football club?

11. Aneto is the highest peak in which European mountain range?

12. Which winner of TV talent show 'The Apprentice' opened her first cosmetic skin clinic in 2014?

13. The Manzanares is a river which flows through which European capital city?

14. Groningen and Limburg are provinces of which European country?

15. Controversial Canadian politician Rob Ford served as the mayor of which city?

16. 'The Racketeer' was a 2013 novel by which best-selling thriller writer?

17. Ladysmith is a town in which Commonwealth country?

18. Which gemstone provided the title of a 1969 thriller directed by Alfred Hitchcock?

19. Which pop star wrote the best-selling children's book 'The English Roses'?
    a) Madonna
    b) Kylie Minogue
    c) Britney Spears

20. Which veteran British broadcaster had a tattoo of a scorpion inked on his back in 2013?
    a) David Attenborough
    b) David Dimbleby
    c) Jeremy Paxman

Answers to Quiz 146: Alliterative Answers

1.	Vince Vaughn	11.	George Gently
2.	Hudson Hawk	12.	Fast & Furious
3.	David Duchovny	13.	San Siro Stadium
4.	Costa Concordia	14.	San Sebastian
5.	Robert Redford	15.	Breaking Bad
6.	Party Politics	16.	Lindsay Lohan
7.	Gone Girl	17.	Sam Smith
8.	Benazir Bhutto	18.	Rachel Riley
9.	James Joyce	19.	Alexander Armstrong
10.	Seymour Skinner	20.	Courtney Cox

DIFFICULT

Quiz 148: The Good, the Bad and the Ugly

1. Lee Brilleaux and Wilko Johnson were members of which band, who had a top-ten hit in 1979 with 'Milk and Alcohol'?

2. 'Bad Education' is a film written and directed by which Spanish film-maker?

3. In the TV comedy 'Roseanne', who played the title character's husband, Dan?

4. A mischievous character called Robin Goodfellow appears in which Shakespeare comedy?

5. According to the proverb, 'no good deed goes ...'?

6. Which actor won a Best Supporting Actor Oscar in 1997 for his performance in the film 'Jerry Maguire'?

7. Gerard Butler starred alongside Katherine Heigl in which 2009 romantic comedy?

8. In 2010, Goodluck Jonathan became the president of which African country?

9. Billy Bob Thornton starred in which 2005 film about a hard-living coach who tries to change the fortunes of a little-league baseball team?

10. Nicholas Lyndhurst played time-traveller Gary Sparrow in which 1990s TV comedy?

11. 'Cats in the Cradle' and 'Everything About You' were hits in the 1990s for which American rock band?

12. Which hip-hop star founded the record label Bad Boy Records?

13. The fictional Abbey Grove School is the setting for which BBC sitcom?

14. Which broadcaster and composer wrote the theme music to TV shows 'The Vicar of Dibley' and 'The Black Adder'?

15. 'The Good Ol' Boys' by Waylon Jennings was the theme tune to which popular 1980s TV drama?

16. Gloria Gaynor had two top-five UK singles. 'I Will Survive' was one but what was the other?

17. Bob Hoskins starred alongside Helen Mirren in which 1980 British gangster film?

18. Which 1952 film about the movie business starring Kirk Douglas holds the record for the most Oscars won without being nominated for Best Picture?

19. Which band's biggest hits were 'Lifestyles of the Rich and Famous' and 'I Just Wanna Live'?
    a) Good Calvin   b) Good Charlene   c) Good Charlotte

20. Which was the title of the 2003 film comedy?
    a) Good Bye Lenin   b) Good Bye Stalin   c) Good Bye Trotsky

Answers to Quiz 147: Pot Luck

1. Hawaii
2. Harrison Ford
3. Thomas Hitzlsperger
4. Line of Duty
5. David Bowie
6. 12
7. Black Sabbath
8. Aladdin (Aladdin Sane)
9. True
10. Leicester City
11. The Pyrenees
12. Leah Totton
13. Madrid
14. The Netherlands
15. Toronto
16. John Grisham
17. South Africa
18. Topaz
19. Madonna
20. David Dimbleby

DIFFICULT

Quiz 149: Pot Luck

1. 2002's 'Confessions of a Dangerous Mind' was the first film directed by which A-list Hollywood actor?

2. Which English city was also the title of a film nominated for Best Picture at the 2012 Oscars?

3. In which sport can a player be penalized for pass interference, holding or a neutral-zone infraction?

4. Which English city is also the surname of a singer who topped the UK singles charts in 1988?

5. Which town in Essex is home to the longest leisure pier in the world?

6. The Dart is a railway network in which European city?

7. Which Hollywood actress said, 'I played a lawyer in a movie so many times I think I am a lawyer. And clearly I'm not a lawyer, because I got arrested' after running foul of the law in 2013?

8. TV comedy 'The Office' was set in which southern English town?

9. The Goroka Mudmen are a group of people living in which country?

10. Which Yorkshire seaside town is also the name of a city in Ontario, Canada?

11. Which footballer appeared on the front cover of the classic video game 'FIFA14'?

12. Which famous American building has the ZIP code 20500?

13. A blue plaque commemorating which 'Carry On' star was unveiled in Marylebone on 22 February 2014, which would have been the actor's 88th birthday?

14. A PGCE is a qualification that allows successful candidates to join which profession?

15. Which English actress and model appeared as a DJ in the 2013 video game 'Grand Theft Auto V'?

16. Which state, bordered by Connecticut and Massachusetts, is the smallest in America by area?

17. Which club's run of 94 seasons in the Football League ended in 2014 when it was relegated to the Conference?

18. Oliver 'Daddy' Warbucks is a character in which musical, which was turned into a hit film in 1982?

19. Which thriller writer, who died in 2013, was an insurance broker before finding success as an author?
    a) Tom Clancy   b) Len Deighton   c) Frederick Forsyth

20. Jack Donaghy is one of the central characters in which American TV comedy?
    a) '30 Rock'   b) 'How I Met Your Mother'
    c) 'The Big Bang Theory'

Answers to Quiz 148: The Good, the Bad and the Ugly

1. Dr Feelgood
2. Pedro Almodovar
3. John Goodman
4. A Midsummer Night's Dream
5. Unpunished
6. Cuba Gooding Jr
7. The Ugly Truth
8. Nigeria
9. The Bad News Bears
10. Goodnight Sweetheart
11. Ugly Kid Joe
12. Sean 'Diddy' Combs (aka Puff Daddy)
13. Bad Education
14. Howard Goodall
15. The Dukes of Hazzard
16. Never Can Say Goodbye
17. The Long Good Friday
18. The Bad and the Beautiful
19. Good Charlotte
20. Good Bye Lenin

DIFFICULT

Quiz 150: Famous Jacks

1. Who played Jack Regan in the 2013 film 'The Sweeney'?

2. By what name is the Scottish artist Jack Hogan more commonly known?

3. Who was the first rider to win the Tour de France five times?

4. The Jaguars are an American football team based in which city?

5. Adam Sandler won Razzies in both the Worst Actor and Worst Actress categories for his performance in which 2011 film comedy?

6. Which actor played the medical examiner Quincy in the TV drama of the same name?

7. 'Old Hickory' was the nickname of which president of the USA?

8. Which British actor played James Norrington in the 'Pirates of the Caribbean' film series?

9. Which Scottish singer won TV talent show 'The X Factor' in 2007?

10. Who won an Oscar in 1997 for his performance as misanthropic author Melvin Udall in 'As Good As It Gets'?

11. 'The Master' was the nickname of which English cricketer, who scored 61,760 runs and 199 centuries during a 29-year career?

12. Which actor hosted the Oscars ceremony for the first time in 2009?

13. Yacov Moshe Maza is the real name of which Jewish American actor and comedian?

14. 'Reet Petite (The Sweetest Girl in Town)' was the only UK number-one single for which American soul man?

Answers – page 307

15. 'Full Fathom Five', 'Autumn Rhythm' and 'Number Thirty-two' are works by which abstract impressionist painter who died in 1956?

16. Which former Labour Party cabinet minister is an honorary president of Blackburn Rovers FC?

17. Which American athlete won gold in the heptathlon at the 1988 and 1992 Olympic Games?

18. Which 1997 film, directed by Quentin Tarantino, was an adaptation of Elmore Leonard's novel 'Rum Punch'?

19. Jackie Lomax was lead singer with which 1960s band?
a) The Grave Diggers   b) The Pall Bearers
c) The Undertakers

20. Simon Rouse played Jack Meadows in which British police drama?
a) The Bill   b) Cracker   c) Inspector Morse

Answers to Quiz 149: Pot Luck

1. George Clooney
2. Lincoln
3. American football
4. (Belinda) Carlisle
5. Southend-on-Sea
6. Dublin
7. Reese Witherspoon
8. Slough
9. Papua New Guinea
10. Scarborough
11. Lionel Messi
12. The White House
13. Kenneth Williams
14. Teaching
15. Cara Delevingne
16. Rhode Island
17. Bristol Rovers
18. Annie
19. Tom Clancy
20. 30 Rock

DIFFICULT

Quiz 151: Pot Luck

1. What is the first name of the fictional Scandinavian detective Wallander?

2. In 2014, Bill de Blasio became the mayor of which city?

3. True or false – Australian fast bowler Peter Siddle, former US President Bill Clinton and comedian Russell Brand all follow a vegan diet?

4. Home to an annual meeting of the World Economic Forum, the resort of Davos is in which country?

5. The Eredivisie is the name of the top-flight football league in which European country?

6. 'Spreading love with every invention, forever devoted to the kingdom of monsters' is the Twitter bio of which pop star?

7. With a capacity of 98,787, what is the largest football ground in Europe?

8. 'Brighton Rock', 'Our Man in Havana' and 'The Third Man' were written by which English novelist?

9. Prior to becoming governor of the Bank of England, Mark Carney was the governor of the which country's central bank?

10. Ophidiphobia is the fear of what type of creatures?

11. Which London department store shares its name with a human-rights pressure group?

12. What is the second largest city in Portugal?

13. What is the name of the disgraced banker nicknamed 'Fred the Shred'?

14. The one-armed drummer Rick Allen is a member of which British heavy rock band?

15. 'Fanfare for the Common Man' is a piece of music by which American composer?

16. Which indie rockers won five awards at the 2014 NME awards?

17. Which fashion designer said, "I never said that [Adele] was fat. I said that she was a little roundish; a little roundish is not fat... But after that she lost eight kilos so I think the message was not that bad'?

18. In 2012, which Radio 1 DJ mistakenly read out the Top 40 that was four weeks out of date and totally wrong?

19. The Wanderers is a cricket ground located in which city?
    a) Johannesburg   b) Mumbai   c) Sydney

20. The football match known as the 'Derby della Madonnina' takes place in which city?
    a) Milan   b) Rome   c) Turin

Answers to Quiz 150: Famous Jacks

1. Ray Winstone
2. Jack Vettriano
3. Jacques Anquetil
4. Jacksonville
5. Jack and Jill
6. Jack Klugman
7. Andrew Jackson
8. Jack Davenport
9. Leon Jackson
10. Jack Nicholson
11. Jack Hobbs
12. Hugh Jackman
13. Jackie Mason
14. Jackie Wilson
15. Jackson Pollock
16. Jack Straw
17. Jackie Joyner-Kersee
18. Jackie Brown
19. The Undertakers
20. The Bill

DIFFICULT

Quiz 152: Places

1. In which country is the Adirondack mountain range located?

2. Beograd is the local name for which central European capital city?

3. Wilford, Mapperley Park and Lenton are areas of which English city?

4. Dar al-Beida is the local name for which Arab city?

5. Which American state contains no land that is below 1000m above sea level?

6. In 1995, Astana succeeded Almaty as the capital city of which central Asian republic?

7. Which English racecourse is located in Esher in Surrey?

8. Al-Qahirah is the local name for which North African capital city?

9. Dhaka is the capital city of which country?

10. Ajaccio is the largest city on which Mediterranean island?

11. Belo Horizonte, the scene of one of English football's greatest humiliations, is a city in which country?

12. Chernobyl, the scene of a major nuclear accident in 1986, is in which modern-day country?

13. Mount Aconcagua, the highest point in the Western Hemisphere, is in which South American country?

14. Which European capital city was once known as the 'Little Paris of the East'?

Answers – page 311

15. The volcanic Mount Teide is on which popular holiday island?

16. Which Australian city is situated at the base of the Mount Lofty Ranges?

17. Motor-racing circuit Donington Park is located in which English county?

18. The ruins of the ancient city of Babylon are in which modern-day country?

19. Which of the following is the name of a Ukrainian river?
    a) River Bug
    b) River Drug
    c) River Slug

20. Achill Island lies off the coast of which country?
    a) Ireland
    b) Scotland
    c) Wales

Answers to Quiz 151: Pot Luck

1. Kurt
2. New York
3. True
4. Switzerland
5. The Netherlands
6. Lady Gaga
7. Camp Nou in Barcelona
8. Graham Greene
9. Canada
10. Snakes
11. Liberty
12. Porto
13. Fred Goodwin
14. Def Leppard
15. Aaron Copland
16. Arctic Monkeys
17. Karl Lagerfeld
18. Greg James
19. Johannesburg
20. Milan

DIFFICULT

Quiz 153: Pot Luck

1. 'In Arduis Fidelis' is the motto of which corps of the British Army?

2. Social networking site Facebook was founded while Mark Zuckerberg was studying at which university?

3. MoMA is a famous museum in New York City. What do the initials MoMA stand for?

4. Which fictional detective said, 'When you have excluded the impossible, whatever remains, however improbable, must be the truth'?

5. A coffee shop called Cafe Nervosa often featured in which American sitcom?

6. In which decade did the first officially recognized cricket Test match take place?

7. The musical 'Love Never Dies' was based on a novel by which English thriller writer?

8. Which major Italian city hosted the 2006 Winter Olympics?

9. In which year did the Battle of Agincourt take place?

10. US president John F Kennedy is buried in which American cemetery?

11. Max Bialystock and Leo Bloom are the central characters in which musical?

12. The only flag in the world that isn't quadrilateral belongs to which Asian country?

13. What is the longest river in Europe?

14. Which American hip-hop star said, 'I'm totally weird, and I'm totally honest, and I'm totally inappropriate sometimes. But for me to say I wasn't a genius, I'd be totally lying to you and to myself'?

15. The Luzhniki Stadium can be found in which European capital?

16. True or false – action star Jackie Chan trained at an opera school as a youngster?

17. Which brand of chocolate bar is also the name of a mobile phone operating system?

18. Gauteng is a landlocked province in which Commonwealth country?

19. Stade Velodrome is a sporting arena in which French city?
    a) Lyon
    b) Marseille
    c) Nice

20. What was the name of the Serbian secret society that plotted the assassination of Archduke Franz Ferdinand in 1914?
    a) Black Hand
    b) Red Hand
    c) White Hand

Answers to Quiz 152: Places

1. USA
2. Belgrade
3. Nottingham
4. Casablanca
5. Colorado
6. Kazakhstan
7. Sandown Park
8. Cairo
9. Bangladesh
10. Corsica
11. Brazil
12. Ukraine
13. Argentina
14. Bucharest
15. Tenerife
16. Adelaide
17. Leicestershire
18. Iraq
19. River Bug
20. Ireland

DIFFICULT

Quiz 154: Television part 1

1. Tim Campbell was the first winner of which reality TV show?

2. Which song, most notably used in the film 'Casablanca', was also the title of a sitcom starring Dame Judi Dench and Geoffrey Palmer?

3. Student comedy drama 'Fresh Meat' is set in which city?

4. In the TV quiz 'Pointless', by how much is the prize pool boosted for giving a pointless answer?

5. Complete the title of the BBC3 makeover show – 'Snog, Marry, ...'?

6. The 1990s series 'Grace & Favour' was a spin-off from which classic 1970s comedy?

7. Coronation Street landlord Duggie Ferguson was formerly a professional in which sport?

8. Which classic comedy character made his TV debut as a sports reporter on the spoof current-affairs show 'The Day Today'?

9. What was the name of the ill-fated ITV breakfast TV show hosted by Adrian Chiles and Christine Bleakley?

10. Which comedy was the only American show to be nominated at Britain's National Television Awards in 2014?

11. In TV game show 'The Cube', each contestant starts with how many lives?

12. Based on a popular board game, which TV game show was hosted by Richard Madeley and set in the fictional Arlington Grange?

13. Which comedian hosted the TV game show 'Celebrity Ding Dong'?

14. In which year was Channel 4 launched?

15. 'Because of You' by Dexys Midnight Runners was the theme song to which 1980s sitcom?

16. Which comedy won the Best Sitcom award at the National Television Awards in both 2013 and 2014?

17. 'Overkill' was the title of the theme tune to which long-running British police drama?

18. In which decade did the BBC broadcast television for the first time?

19. In the TV sitcom 'Allo, Allo!', what was the name of Rene's tone-deaf wife?
    a) Edith
    b) Michelle
    c) Yvette

20. Gillian Anderson starred in which detective drama?
    a) The Fall
    b) The Return
    c) The Rise

Answers to Quiz 153: Pot Luck

1.	Royal Army Medical Corps	11.	The Producers
2.	Harvard	12.	Nepal
3.	Museum of Modern Art	13.	Volga
4.	Sherlock Holmes	14.	Kanye West
5.	Frasier	15.	Moscow
6.	1870s	16.	True
7.	Frederick Forsyth	17.	Kit Kat
8.	Turin	18.	South Africa
9.	1415	19.	Marseille
10.	Arlington	20.	Black Hand

DIFFICULT

Quiz 155: Pot Luck

1. Whose birthday, 2 October, is commemorated around the world as an International Day of Nonviolence?

2. Which veteran broadcaster was the winner of 'Country Life' magazine's Gentleman of the Year award in 2014?'

3. Which award-winning actor is the husband of Penelope Cruz?

4. What is the name of the top prize awarded at the annual dog show Crufts?

5. Between 2009 and 2014, Denmark's Anders Rasmussen was the Secretary General of which organization?

6. Which civilian and military medal is awarded for 'acts of the greatest heroism or of the most conspicuous courage in circumstances of extreme danger'?

7. An agency called Sterling Cooper & Partners was the setting for which American TV drama?

8. By what name was a Polish man called Karol Józef Wojtyła better known?

9. What title of a song by the Sugababes was also the name of a game show hosted by Ant and Dec?

10. In metres, how high off the ground is the rim of a basketball net?

11. Which football manager was fined £100,000 after head-butting Hull City's David Meyler during a match in March 2014?

12. Which common domestic pet is known in French as 'une araignée'?

13. The original 'Call of Duty' video game was set during which conflict?

14. Which English football team has the Latin motto 'Consilio et animis'?

15. With a capacity of 150,000, the massive Rungnado May Day Stadium is in which Asian capital city?

16. The Nobel prize is named after a Swedish industrialist and inventor. What was his first name?

17. How long in yards is a cricket pitch?

18. Musophobia is the fear of what type of animals?

19. East London is a major seaport in which Commonwealth country?
    a) Australia
    b) New Zealand
    c) South Africa

20. The rugby stadium Thomond Park is in which Irish city?
    a) Cork
    b) Killarney
    c) Limerick

Answers to Quiz 154: Television part 1

1. The Apprentice
2. As Time Goes By
3. Manchester
4. £250.00
5. Avoid
6. Are You Being Served?
7. Rugby league
8. Alan Partridge
9. Daybreak
10. The Big Bang Theory
11. Nine
12. Cluedo
13. Alan Carr
14. 1982
15. Brush Strokes
16. Mrs Brown's Boys
17. The Bill
18. 1930s
19. Edith
20. The Fall

DIFFICULT

Quiz 156: Chris Cross

1. Which film maker received his first Oscar nomination in 2012 for his film 'The Help'?

2. Which Mancunian comedian and actor played Ollie Reeder in the political comedy 'The Thick of It'?

3. Who scored a century off just 30 balls during an Indian Premier League cricket match in April 2013?

4. Who was the only British cyclist to win a medal at the 1992 Olympic Games in Barcelona?

5. Which Liberal Democrat MP was jailed in March 2013 after admitting perverting the course of justice?

6. Which celebrity won the reality TV show 'I'm a Celebrity... Get Me Out of Here' in 2007?

7. Who was the first winner of the BBC Sports Personality of the Year Award?

8. Which name is shared by the tennis player who finished runner-up at Wimbledon in 1983 and an England cricket all-rounder who won 32 Test caps in the 1990s?

9. 'Unbelievable, Jeff' is the catchphrase of which TV football pundit?

10. Who sang the theme song to the 2006 James Bond film 'Casino Royale'?

11. Which Bristol-born comedian and satirist directed the 2010 film 'Four Lions'?

12. Which Australian actor played racing driver James Hunt in the 2013 film 'Rush'?

13. Who played Francisco Scaramanga in the James Bond film 'The Man with the Golden Gun'?

14. Which producer and reggae connoisseur was founder of the Island Records label?

15. Which wife of a former British MP has a career as a broadcaster and tweets under the name @brit_battleaxe?

16. In 2012, who succeeded Gary Speed as manager of the Welsh national football team?

17. Which former SAS soldier wrote the 'Agent 21' and 'Alpha Force' series of books?

18. Which boxer was the first ambassador for the problem gambling charity Gamcare?

19. Who starred alongside Jackie Chan in the 'Rush Hour' films?

20. Penelope Cruz won her first Oscar in 2009 for her performance in which Woody Allen-directed film?

Answers to Quiz 155: Pot Luck

1. Gandhi
2. David Dimbleby
3. Javier Bardem
4. Best in show
5. NATO
6. George Cross
7. Mad Men
8. Pope John Paul II
9. Push the Button
10. 3m

11. Alan Pardew
12. Spider
13. World War II
14. Sheffield Wednesday
15. Pyongyang
16. Alfred
17. 22
18. Mice
19. South Africa
20. Limerick

DIFFICULT

Quiz 157: Pot Luck

1. What are the seven categories in which prizes are awarded in the annual dog show Crufts?

2. Which hit West End musical was based on a novel by the French author Gaston Leroux?

3. In 2014, Jenny Jones became Britain's first Winter Olympic medallist in which sport?

4. A road called the Via Dolorosa is a famous feature of which city?

5. Which is the only book of the Bible in which God is not mentioned?

6. What is the name of the dance fitness programme created by Colombian dancer and choreographer Alberto 'Beto' Perez?

7. Which character has been played on film by Alec Baldwin, Harrison Ford, Ben Affleck and Chris Pine?

8. What fruit is the main ingredient in the liqueur maraschino?

9. In 2014, Heather Jacks was crowned the winner of which craft-based TV talent show?

10. The witness-protection drama 'In Plain Sight' is set in which American city?

11. Mexico shares land borders with which three countries?

12. The Belvedere is a famous building in which European capital?

13. Who was the first British-born world heavyweight champion of the 20th century?

14. The sponge dessert known as the Lamington originated in which country?

15. The classic crime book 'In Cold Blood' was written by which American author?

16. Lombard Street, the most crooked street in the world, is in which American city?

17. Dr Ivo 'Eggman' Robotnik is the main enemy of which video-game character?

18. Trypanophobia is the fear of what objects?

19. 'Morning Phase' was a 2014 album by which American artist?
a) Beck   b) Michael Stipe   c) Pharrell Williams

20. Complete the title of the 2013 Costa Prize-winning novel: 'The Shock of the...'
a) Fall   b) New   c) Old

Answers to Quiz 156: Chris Cross

1. Chris Columbus
2. Chris Addison
3. Chris Gayle
4. Chris Boardman
5. Chris Huhne
6. Christopher Biggins
7. Chris Chataway
8. Chris Lewis
9. Chris Kamara
10. Chris Cornell
11. Chris Morris
12. Chris Hemsworth
13. Christopher Lee
14. Chris Blackwell
15. Christine Hamilton
16. Chris Coleman
17. Chris Ryan
18. Chris Eubank
19. Chris Tucker
20. Vicky Cristina Barcelona

DIFFICULT

Quiz 158: Fictional Cars

Match these iconic cars to the fictional TV or movie characters:

1.	Red 1975 Ford Gran Torino	a) Crockett and Tubbs
2.	1972 Ferrari Daytona Spyder	b) Simon Templar
3.	1971 Plymouth Barracuda	c) Jim Rockford
4.	1959 Peugeot 403 convertible	D) Magnum
5.	1960 Mark II Jaguar	E) Bullitt
6.	Mystery Machine	F) Saga Noren
7.	1974 Pontiac Firebird Esprit	G) Jack Frost
8.	Ferrarri 308GTS	H) Nash Bridges
9.	977 US-spec Porsche 911S	I) The Fall Guy
10.	Ford XB Falcon Coupe	J) Jim Bergerac
11.	Ford Sierra Estate	K) Michael Knight
12.	1982 GMC Sierra Truck	L) Columbo
13.	DMC DeLorean	M) Terry McCann
14.	1982 Pontiac Trans Am	N) Dr Emmett Brown

15.	Triumph Roadster	O)	Starsky and Hutch
16.	White Ford Capri	P)	Mad Max
17.	Mini Cooper	Q)	James Bond
18.	1963 Aston Martin DB5	R)	Scooby Doo
19.	1962 Volvo P1800	S)	Mr Bean
20.	1968 Ford Mustang 390 GT 2+2 Fastback	T)	Inspector Morse

Answers to Quiz 157: Pot Luck

1. Working, Utility, Hound, Pastoral, Toy, Terrier and Gundog
2. The Phantom of the Opera
3. Snowboarding
4. Jerusalem
5. Esther
6. Zumba
7. Jack Ryan
8. Cherry
9. The Great British Sewing Bee
10. Albuquerque
11. USA, Guatemala and Belize
12. Vienna
13. Lennox Lewis
14. Australia
15. Truman Capote
16. San Francisco
17. Sonic The Hedgehog
18. Needles
19. Beck
20. Fall

DIFFICULT

Quiz 159: Pot Luck

1. The most retweeted photo of all time was a selfie posted by which comedian at the 2014 Oscars?

2. Robert Galbraith is the pseudonym of which best-selling author?

3. Which English footballer has a tattoo on his forearm that reads 'Just enough education to perform'?

4. The popular holiday resort of Sharm el-Sheikh lies on the coast of which body of water?

5. Dr Nikki Alexander, Dr Harry Cunningham and Professor Leo Dalton are characters in which medical/crime drama?

6. What is the surname of the singer Adele?

7. Which American author, who died in 1910, said 'Age is an issue of mind over matter. If you don't mind, it doesn't matter'?

8. The Battles of Lexington and Concord were the first military engagements in which war?

9. Which comedian won the Critics' Circle Theatre Award in 2014 for his portrayal of binman Troy Maxson in the American play 'Fences'?

10. Death Valley National Park is on the border of which two American states?

11. Aruba and Curucao are overseas territories of which European country?

12. Which controversial broadcaster delivers a 'Weekly Wipe'?

13. Vicar Adam Smallbone is the central character in which TV comedy?

14. The guarani is the currency of which South American country?

15. Footballer Nicolas Anelka caused controversy by making what gesture after scoring a goal for West Bromwich Albion against West Ham in December 2013?

16. Which five letter word, when written in capital letters, appears the same when upside down?

17. A football stadium called the Allianz Arena is in which European city?

18. Roger Moore made his debut as James Bond in which film?

19. Who played the title character in the 2013 film 'The Secret Life of Walter Mitty'?
    a) Jack Black   b) Adam Sandler   c) Ben Stiller

20. Which fictional detective features in the play 'Black Coffee'?
    a) Miss Marple   b) Hercule Poirot   c) Sherlock Holmes

Answers to Quiz 158: Fictional Cars

1.	O	11.	G
2.	A	12.	I
3.	H	13.	N
4.	L	14.	K
5.	T	15.	J
6.	R	16.	M
7.	C	17.	S
8.	D	18.	Q
9.	F	19.	B
10.	P	20.	E

DIFFICULT

Quiz 160: Movies

1. In 2010, Kathryn Bigelow became the first woman to win the Oscar for Best Director. For which film?

2. Complete the title of the 2014 Oscar-winning documentary – '20 Feet from...'?

3. Which Oscar-nominated British actor played a drag queen called Lola in the 2005 film 'Kinky Boots'?

4. Which father and son won the Razzies for Worst Actor and Worst Supporting Actor in 2014 for their performances in 'After Earth'?

5. 'Wittertainment' is the title of an award-winning radio show featuring Simon Mayo and which bequiffed film critic?

6. 'The Day of the Jackal' was about a plot to assassinate which political leader?

7. 'Don't let go' was the tagline to which hit 2013 film?

8. Which film was released first – 'Grease' or 'Saturday Night Fever'?

9. Which 1993 film became the first black-and-white film to win a Best Picture Oscar since 1960?

10. Which actor's star on the Hollywood Walk of Fame is situated at 7007 Hollywood Boulevard?

11. Tatooine, Hoth and Bespin are fictional planets in which film series?

12. Which American state was also the title of a film nominated for Best Picture at the 2014 Oscars?

13. What is the only monster with a star on the Hollywood Walk of Fame?

14. Which actress played Princess Grace in the 2014 film biopic 'Grace of Monaco'?

15. Running at just 93 minutes, which Woody Allen comedy is the shortest film to win a Best Picture Oscar?

16. Which veteran Hollywood actress is the co-owner of a New York ping-pong club called SpiN?

17. What are the first names of the film-producing Weinstein brothers?

18. Which actor holds the record for the most acting nominations at the Oscars?

19. Which film was named Best Picture at the 2014 Oscars?
    a) 12 Years a Slave   b) American Hustle   c) Gravity

20. What nationality is the award-winning film director Alfonso Cuaron?
    a) Brazilian   b) Colombian   c) Mexican

Answers to Quiz 159: Pot Luck

1. Ellen DeGeneres
2. JK Rowling
3. Wayne Rooney
4. The Red Sea
5. Silent Witness
6. Adkins
7. Mark Twain
8. The American War of Independence
9. Lenny Henry
10. California and Nevada
11. The Netherlands
12. Charlie Brooker
13. Rev
14. Paraguay
15. Quenelle
16. SWIMS
17. Munich
18. Live and Let Die
19. Ben Stiller
20. Hercule Poirot

DIFFICULT

Quiz 161: Pot Luck

1. The American state of New York shares a border with which two Canadian provinces?

2. What name describes a word with two opposite meanings, such as 'sanction'?

3. Which unit of capacity, equal to a quarter of a bushel, can also mean 'to give someone a light kiss on the cheek'?

4. Defenestration is the act of throwing something or someone out of what?

5. In which country was the British cycling champion Sir Bradley Wiggins born?

6. In relation to radio broadcasting, what do the initials 'DAB' stand for?

7. Which word describes the point on the Earth's surface that is directly above where an earthquake originates?

8. What type of animal is known in French as 'un singe'?

9. The 'Vyshcha Liha' is the name of the top-flight football competition in which European country?

10. What was Michael Jackson's only million-selling UK single?

11. What does the 'L' in the acronym 'laser' stand for?

12. The chart-topping singer Lorde is from which Commonwealth country?

13. Paramaribo is the capital city of which South American country?

14. The Victoria Cross was first awarded to combatants serving in which war?

15. Which South American country is some 2,610 miles long but only 112 miles wide at its widest point?

16. Lake Titicaca is in which continent?

17. In 2014, which supermarket became the official shirt sponsor of the England cricket team?

18. The FIVB is the international governing body for which Olympic sport?

19. Which film was nominated for a Razzie for Worst Picture in 2013?
    a) Movie 42
    b) Movie 43
    c) Movie 44

20. Saga Noren and Martin Rohde are characters in which Scandinavian drama?
    a) Borgen
    b) The Bridge
    c) Wallander

Answers to Quiz 160: Movies

1.	The Hurt Locker	11.	Star Wars
2.	Stardom	12.	Nebraska
3.	Chiwetel Ejiofor	13.	Godzilla
4.	Will and Jaden Smith	14.	Nicole Kidman
5.	Mark Kermode	15.	Annie Hall
6.	Charles de Gaulle	16.	Susan Sarandon
7.	Gravity	17.	Bob and Harvey
8.	Saturday Night Fever	18.	Jack Nicholson
9.	Schindler's List	19.	12 Years a Slave
10.	Sir Roger Moore	20.	Mexican

DIFFICULT

Quiz 162: Reality TV

1. Who won 'The X Factor' in the year that JLS finished second?

2. 'Big Brother' first aired in which European country?

3. Which actress was the first dancer to score a perfect 40 out of 40 on 'Strictly Come Dancing'?

4. Who was the host of the canine-inspired 2014 Sport Relief series 'Top Dog'?

5. The 2009 series of celebrity cooking show 'Hell's Kitchen' was won by which American soap star?

6. Who was the first winner of 'The X Factor'?

7. David Sneddon and Alex Parks were winners of which short-lived BBC musical talent show?

8. In 2014, Ping Coombes was crowned the winner of which TV talent show?

9. Leanne Mitchell and Andrea Begley were the first two winners of which TV talent show?

10. In 2012, which 74-year-old became the oldest competitor to take part in 'Strictly Come Dancing'?

11. Which actress was the first winner of 'Dancing on Ice'?

12. Which former 'Blue Peter' presenter also hosted 'The Xtra Factor'?

13. 'Dance of the Knights' by Russian composer Sergey Prokofiev is the theme song to which TV show?

14. Starring James Corden, the 2013 film 'One Chance' was a film about the life of which TV talent-show winner?

15. Which motoring journalist and broadcaster holds the record for the lowest score ever awarded on 'Strictly Come Dancing'?

16. Which 1980s singer caused controversy in the 'Celebrity Big Brother' house after claiming to wear a coat made from gorilla fur?

17. Who are the three sportsmen to have won 'Strictly Come Dancing'?

18. Which Scottish singer won 'Britain's Got Talent' in 2011?

19. Attraction, the winners of 'Britain's Got Talent' in 2013 are a shadow theatre from which country?
    a) Bulgaria
    b) Hungary
    c) Romania

20. In which year was 'The X Factor' broadcast for the first time?
    a) 2003
    b) 2004
    c) 2005

Answers to Quiz 161: Pot Luck

1. Quebec and Ontario
2. Contranym
3. Peck
4. A window
5. Belgium
6. Digital Audio Broadcasting
7. Epicentre
8. Monkey
9. Ukraine
10. Earth Song
11. Light
12. New Zealand
13. Surinam
14. The Crimean War
15. Chile
16. South America
17. Waitrose
18. Volleyball
19. Movie 43
20. The Bridge

DIFFICULT

Quiz 163: Pot Luck

1. Irene Adler is a character who appears in stories featuring which fictional sleuth?

2. Who was the first British footballer to receive a knighthood?

3. 'Artpop Ball' was the title of which female singer's 2014 world tour?

4. Who was the first American president whose Christian name started with a vowel?

5. Which neighbourhood of New York is an acronym of the Triangle Below Canal Street?

6. 'Bobo's in the Bush' is the Dutch version of which reality TV show?

7. In 2008, DJ Chris Evans paid a reported £5.6m at auction for a Ferrari formerly owned by which 'Magnificent Seven' actor?

8. The Philippines takes its name from a former king of which country?

9. The fairing cake originates from which English county?

10. Author Agatha Christie was born in which seaside town?

11. Which two politicians held the post of deputy prime minister during the Thatcher government?

12. In a men's 110m hurdles race, the athletes jump over how many obstacles?

13. In 2014, Jermain Jackman was crowned the winner of which TV talent show?

14. In which European city will you find a famous cemetery called Père Lachaise?

15. In which sport can a player be penalized for travelling?

Answers – page 333

16. NAPO is a trade union that represents workers in which occupation?

17. On a radio, what do the initials 'AM' stand for?

18. The Estádio da Luz is a sporting venue in which European city?

19. In which year were the Scots victorious over the English in the Battle of Bannockburn?
    a) 1313
    b) 1314
    c) 1315

20. The author Philip K Dick is most commonly associated with which genre of book?
    a) crime
    b) romance
    c) science fiction

Answers to Quiz 162: Reality TV

1. Alexandra Burke
2. The Netherlands
3. Jill Halfpenny
4. Gaby Roslin
5. Linda Evans
6. Steve Brookstein
7. Fame Academy
8. Masterchef
9. The Voice
10. Johnny Ball
11. Gaynor Faye
12. Konnie Huq
13. The Apprentice
14. Paul Potts
15. Quentin Wilson
16. Pete Burns
17. Darren Gough, Mark Ramprakash and Louis Smith
18. Jai McDowall
19. Hungary
20. 2004

DIFFICULT

Quiz 164: History

1. In which decade was the Nobel Prize awarded for the first time?

2. In early 20th-century America, what was banned by the Volstead Act?

3. Tanks were used in battle for the first time in which conflict?

4. Before becoming prime minister, Neville Chamberlain was the mayor of which English city?

5. Eleanor of Aquitaine was the wife of which English king?

6. In which decade did the first McDonalds restauarant open in the UK?

7. Which pope died in 1978, just 33 days after his election to the position?

8. Which English king was reportedly killed after a red hot poker was inserted in his bottom?

9. The remains of which king were discovered in a car park in Leicester in 2012?

10. In 1983, the USA invaded which tiny Caribbean island after a military coup?

11. In which year was Nelson Mandela released from prison?

12. Pu Yi was the last emperor of which country?

13. Who succeeded Queen Victoria as the British monarch?

14. Who was Britain's youngest 20th-century prime minister?

15. Which English king was killed during the siege of Chalus-Chabrol in France in 1199?

Answers – page 335

16. Britain was involved in a conflict known as the 'Cod Wars' with which country?

17. Boudicca was the queen of which Celtic tribe?

18. John F Kennedy defeated which Republican challenger in the 1960 US presidential election?

19. 'Longshanks' was the nickname of which English king?
    a) Edward I
    b) Edward II
    c) Edward III

20. How many American colonies declared independence from Britain in 1776?
    a) 12
    b) 13
    c) 14

Answers to Quiz 163: Pot Luck

1. Sherlock Holmes
2. Sir Stanley Matthews
3. Lady Gaga
4. Andrew Jackson
5. Tribeca
6. I'm a Celebrity ... Get Me Out of Here
7. James Coburn
8. Spain
9. Cornwall
10. Torquay
11. William Whitelaw and Geoffrey Howe
12. 10
13. The Voice
14. Paris
15. Basketball
16. Prison officers
17. Amplitude modulation
18. Lisbon
19. 1314
20. Science fiction

DIFFICULT

Quiz 165: Pot Luck

1. Paramatta is a city in which country?

2. Which American singer, rapper and producer is also the co-founder of the fashion label Billionaire Boys Club?

3. Rafiq Hariri, who was assassinated in 2005, was the prime minister of which Middle Eastern country?

4. 'Wolfie' is the nickname of which World Champion darts player?

5. Narita airport serves which Asian capital city?

6. What common English word contains five successive vowels?

7. Cross Fell is the highest peak in which range of English hills?

8. A lepidopterist is a person who studies what type of creatures?

9. The Wireless Music Festival moved to a new venue in 2014. In which London park did it take place?

10. The popular holiday island of Phuket is part of which country?

11. Which actor played Tonto in the 2013 film 'The Lone Ranger'?

12. EA is a major computer-game designer and creator. What do the initials EA stand for?

13. Which veteran American rock band signed a contract saying that they would never reform after The Final Tour of 2014?

14. The football club Lazio is based in which city?

15. Martin Scorsese won his first Best Director Oscar for which film?

16. The second largest city in the Australian state of New South Wales shares its name with a city in England. Which one?

17. 'Not I', 'Footfalls' and 'Rockaby' are works by which Nobel-Prize-winning Irish playwright, who died in Paris in 1989?

18. Which western American state is nicknamed 'The Beaver State'?

19. Whose law says that 'work expands so as to fill the time available for its completion'?
    a) Norton's Law
    b) O'Grady's Law
    c) Parkinson's Law

20. In which field of the arts is Matthew Bourne a notable name?
    a) dance
    b) painting
    c) sculpture

Answers to Quiz 164: History

1. 1900s
2. Alcohol
3. World War I
4. Birmingham
5. Henry II
6. 1970s
7. Pope John Paul I
8. Edward II
9. Richard III
10. Grenada
11. 1990
12. China
13. Edward VII
14. Tony Blair
15. Richard I (The Lionheart)
16. Iceland
17. Iceni
18. Richard Nixon
19. Edward I
20. 13

DIFFICULT

Quiz 166: Science

1. The stirrup, the smallest bone in humans, is found in which part of the body?

2. The ohm is a unit that measures what?

3. Which four planets of the Solar System have rings?

4. The name of which type of rock derives from the Latin for 'fire'?

5. Someone with anosmia is lacking what?

6. Which acid is also known as aqua fortis?

7. In 2013, Mark Cahill became the first Briton to undergo which pioneering medical operation?

8. What was the name of the first Space Shuttle?

9. True or false – more than a quarter of the bones in the human body are in the hands?

10. The first creature to be launched into space was called Laika. What type of animal was Laika?

11. In which decade was the world's first successful heart transplant carried out?

12. After nitrogen and oxygen, what is the third most common gas in the earth's atmopsphere?

13. The mobile-phone operating system Android was developed by which company?

14. The 19th-century naturalist Charles Darwin was born in which English Midlands town?

15. In 2013, which country launched 'Mangalyaan', a spacecraft that will orbit Mars?

16. Geothermal power is generated using heat energy from what?

17. What is the most abundant metal in the earth's crust?

18. In underwater navigation, what does the acronym 'Sonar' stand for?

19. Halley's comet is visible from earth every how many years?
    a) 57.3 years
    b) 73.5 years
    c) 75.3 years

20. How many eyes does a caterpillar have?
    a) 8
    b) 10
    c) 12

Answers to Quiz 165: Pot Luck

1. Australia
2. Pharrell Williams
3. Lebanon
4. Martin Adams
5. Tokyo
6. Queueing
7. The Pennines
8. Butterflies
9. Finsbury Park
10. Thailand
11. Johnny Depp
12. Electronic Arts
13. Mötley Crüe
14. Rome
15. The Departed
16. Newcastle
17. Samuel Beckett
18. Oregon
19. Parkinson's Law
20. Dance

DIFFICULT

Quiz 167: Pot Luck

1. The rock festival called 'Primavera Sound' is held in which major European city?

2. Yerevan is the capital city of which former Soviet Republic?

3. John Cusack played which US President in the 2013 film 'The Butler'?

4. In 2014, which European football club became the first to pass 50 million likes on Facebook?

5. Queen Elizabeth II has made the most official visits to which country?

6. Which name is shared by a film by the Coen brothers and the largest city in the US state of North Dakota?

7. Whose album 'Xscape' was posthumously released in 2014?

8. Who is older – actor Russell Crowe or singer Jon Bon Jovi?

9. Which British actor and comedian played baddie Dominic Badguy in the 2014 film 'Muppets Most Wanted'?

10. A phillumenist is a collector of what?

11. Which African country appeared in the title of a 2005 top-ten single by rapper Kanye West?

12. In which month do Americans commemorate Martin Luther King Day?

13. Which former codebreaker for the Royal Canadian Navy topped the UK singles chart in 2014 with 'Hideaway'?

14. Animated TV comedy 'South Park' is set in which American state?

15. Prior to Barack Obama, who was the last American President whose surname ended with a vowel?

16. In 2013, King Willem-Alexander became the monarch of which European country?

17. In 2014, Manuel Valls was appointed the prime minister of which European country?

18. Singers Cliff Richard and Engelbert Humperdinck were born in which country?

19. According to a 2014 survey, what was voted Yorkshire's greatest icon?
    a) Geoffrey Boycott
    b) the Yorkshire Dales
    c) the Yorkshire pudding

20. Football club Real Betis is based in which Spanish city?
    a) Barcelona
    b) Malaga
    c) Seville

Answers to Quiz 166: Science

1. The ear
2. Electrical resistance
3. Jupiter, Saturn, Uranus, Neptune
4. Igneous
5. The sense of smell
6. Nitric acid
7. A hand transplant
8. Columbia
9. True
10. Dog
11. 1960s
12. Argon
13. Google
14. Shrewsbury
15. India
16. Rocks in the Earth's crust
17. Aluminium
18. SOund Navigation And Ranging
19. 75.3 years
20. 12

DIFFICULT

Quiz 168: Music part 2

1. Andre 3000 played which legendary musician in the 2013 film biopic 'All Is By My Side'?

2. Nun Cristina Sciuccia set the record for the most hits for a YouTube clip after singing 'No One' on the Italian version of 'The Voice'. Who sang the original version?

3. Guy Garvey is the lead singer with which band?

4. Which Harry Belafonte song was the first Christmas song to sell over one million copies in the UK?

5. What was the biggest-selling UK single by The Beatles?

6. The Seekers were the first band from which country to have a UK number one single?

7. Which festive favourite is the biggest-selling single in the history of the UK charts that didn't reach number one?

8. Who were the first act to top the UK singles chart with their first six releases?

9. Which female singer represented the United Kingdom at the 2014 Eurovision Song Contest?

10. What is the biggest-selling single in the UK charts by a female solo artist?

11. In 1985, who became the first female solo act to have a million-selling UK single?

12. American actor Donnie Wahlberg was formerly a member of which boy band?

13. What was the only single by Oasis to sell one million copies in the UK?

14. Ray Parker Jr's biggest UK hit was the theme to which film?

15. What 1969 chart-topper was the last number one single by the Rolling Stones?

16. Which 1980s popsters were the first act to reach the top five of the UK singles chart with their first seven releases?

17. Who is the only solo act to have enjoyed a UK number one single and album after the age of 60?

18. Elliot Gleave is the real name of which British rapper who topped the charts with 'Changed the Way You Kiss Me' and 'Stay Awake'?

19. Which of the following is the name of a best-selling band?
    a) Abbot and the Makers
    b) Bishop and the Makers
    c) Reverend and the Makers

20. What is the surname of American musician Beck?
    a) Hansen
    b) Lawrenson
    c) Shearer

Answers to Quiz 167: Pot Luck

1.	Barcelona	11.	Sierra Leone
2.	Armenia	12.	January
3.	Richard Nixon	13.	Kiesza
4.	Barcelona	14.	Colorado
5.	Canada	15.	Calvin Coolidge
6.	Fargo	16.	The Netherlands
7.	Michael Jackson	17.	France
8.	Jon Bon Jovi	18.	India
9.	Ricky Gervais	19.	Yorkshire pudding
10.	Matchboxes	20.	Seville

DIFFICULT

Quiz 169: Pot Luck

1. 'Nadolig Llawen' is 'Merry Christmas' in which language?

2. Which singer 'flipped the bird' to the 'suits' at the 2012 Brit Awards ceremony?

3. St Domingo's was the former name of which Premier League football club?

4. Who was the Roman governor of Judaea at the time of the execution of Jesus?

5. In computing, what does the acronym 'GIF' stand for?

6. The popular online games Chefville and Farmville were created by which technology company?

7. Based on an Italian semi-operatic song, what was Elvis Presley's only million-selling UK single?

8. The National Railway Museum is in which English city?

9. Ayda Field is the wife of which British pop superstar?

10. The surname of which former England striker is also the name of a town and province in western Spain?

11. In the music business, what do the initials 'A&R' stand for?

12. Which children's TV show featured a housekeeper called Noo Noo?

13. Jack Dawson and Rose DeWitt Bukater are the central characters in which hit 1997 film?

14. Dave Murdoch led the British team to an Olympic silver medal in 2014 in which sport?

15. Who are the five Oscar-winning actors and actresses to have topped the UK singles chart?

16. 'Symphonica' was a chart-topping 2014 album by which male singer?

17. Valentino Rossi was a multiple world champion in which sport?

18. Who is Queen Elizabeth II's eldest grandchild?

19. A hat belonging to which member of the Royal Family was sold for £81,000 at auction following the wedding of Prince William and Catherine Middleton?
    a) Princess Beatrice
    b) Princess Eugenie
    c) Zara Phillips

20. The Isle of Skye is the largest island of which group?
    a) Inner Hebrides
    b) Orkney
    c) Shetland

Answers to Quiz 168: Music part 2

1. Jimi Hendrix
2. Alicia Keys
3. Elbow
4. Mary's Boy Child
5. She Loves You
6. Australia
7. 'Last Christmas' by Wham
8. The Spice Girls
9. Molly Smitten-Downes
10. 'Believe' by Cher
11. Jennifer Rush
12. New Kids on the Block
13. Wonderwall
14. Ghostbusters
15. Honky Tonk Woman
16. Culture Club
17. Tom Jones
18. Example
19. Reverend and the Makers
20. Hansen

DIFFICULT

Quiz 170: Sport part 1

1. Which was the first British football club to win a European trophy?

2. Which US Open golf winner took part in 'Strictly Come Dancing' in 2013?

3. Which American man lost in the Wimbledon final in 2004, 2005 and 2009?

4. Who was Britain's first black world boxing champion?

5. Which event took place first – the Rugby League World Cup or the Rugby Union World Cup?

6. Which Central American country was in the same group as England at the 2014 World Cup?

7. Ayrton Senna died during a Formula One race at which circuit?

8. The Pichichi Trophy is awarded to the leading goal-scorer in which European country's football league?

9. Which actor played South African sportsman Francois Pienaar in the 2009 film 'Invictus'?

10. Sopot, the venue for the 2014 World Indoor Athletics Championships, is in which country?

11. Who is the only Dutch winner of the Men's Singles at Wimbledon?

12. Which course is longer – the Boat Race or the Grand National?

13. Yorkshire Jets, Hertfordshire Mavericks and Loughborough Lightning are teams in which sport's Premier League?

14. Which Frenchwoman won her first Wimbledon Ladies Singles title in 2013?

15. Which Formula One Grand Prix is hosted at the Marina Bay Street Circuit?

16. James Brian Hellwig was the real name of which American wrestler, who died in April 2014?

17. What are the four teams from Yorkshire to have won English football's top flight?

18. What nationality is the 2011 Wimbledon winner Petra Kvitova?

19. Which cricketer declared 'you guys are history' after being hit on the head while batting, then went on to take 9 for 57 for England against South Africa in 1994?
    a) Darren Gough
    b) Dean Headley
    c) Devon Malcolm

20. Which West Indian fast bowler was knighted in February 2014?
    a) Curtly Ambrose
    b) Michael Holding
    c) Courtney Walsh

Answers to Quiz 169: Pot Luck

1. Welsh
2. Adele
3. Everton
4. Pontius Pilate
5. Graphics Interchange Format
6. Zynga
7. It's Now or Never
8. York
9. Robbie Williams
10. Zamora
11. Artists and repertoire
12. The Teletubbies
13. Titanic
14. Curling
15. Frank Sinatra, Lee Marvin, Barbra Streisand, Cher and Nicole Kidman
16. George Michael
17. Motor cycling
18. Peter Phillips
19. Princess Beatrice
20. Inner Hebrides

DIFFICULT

Quiz 171: Pot Luck

1. What type of metal provided David Guetta with the title of a 2011 chart topper?

2. 'Tears' was a million-selling single in 1965 for which British comedian?

3. Located 3,640m above sea level, what is the highest capital city in the world?

4. Which female singer had to wait over 25 years from her chart debut in 1965 for her first UK number-one single in 1991?

5. In which year did Queen Elizabeth II become a grandmother for the first time?

6. 'Pitbull' is the nickname of which former rugby player-turned-journalist and commentator?

7. How many fences must a horse jump to finish the Grand National?

8. Cricketing knights Sir Viv Richards and Sir Andy Roberts are from which Caribbean island?

9. Which veteran heavy rock band had a UK number-one album in 2013 with '13', 43 years after 'Paranoid' topped the charts?

10. Bush is one of five surnames that has been shared by two US presidents. What are the other four?

11. In 2011, who became the first British singer to sell one million digital copies of a single in the UK?

12. Who was the last British prime minister to preside over an exclusively Liberal Party government?

13. The classic Alfred Hitchcock thriller 'Vertigo' was set in which American city?

14. The so-called 'Long Parliament' occurred in England during which century?

Answers – page 349

15. Which BBC sports broadcaster was appointed Chancellor of Leeds Trinity University in January 2013?

16. Five of Northern Ireland's six counties have a shore on which large freshwater lake?

17. Which two cities are divided by the River Irwell?

18. Which London landmark can be found at the junction of Oxford Street, Park Lane, Edgware Road and Bayswater Road?

19. Pteromerhanophobia is the fear of what?
    a) dinosaurs
    b) flying
    c) sheep

20. What is the English equivalent of the Spanish name Iago?
    a) James
    b) John
    c) Julian

Answers to Quiz 170: Sport part 1

1. Tottenham Hotspur
2. Tony Jacklin
3. Andy Roddick
4. Randolph Turpin
5. Rugby League World Cup
6. Costa Rica
7. Imola
8. Spain's
9. Matt Damon
10. Poland
11. Richard Krajicek
12. The Grand National
13. Netball
14. Marion Bartoli
15. Singapore
16. The Ultimate Warrior
17. Huddersfield Town, Leeds United, Sheffield United and Sheffield Wednesday
18. Czech
19. Devon Malcolm
20. Curtly Ambrose

DIFFICULT

Quiz 172: Art and Architecture

1. Which Italian city hosts a major art exhibition known as the Biennale?

2. Which abstract impressionist's 1955 painting 'Untitled (Red, Blue, Orange)' was sold at auction for $56.2 million in May 2014?

3. The English artist George Stubbs was best known for his paintings of what?

4. 'The Kiss' and 'The Thinker' are works by which French sculptor?

5. The Lascaux caves, the site of cave paintings thousands of years old, are in which country?

6. What did the initials 'LS' stand for in the name of the artist LS Lowry?

7. William Holman Hunt, John Everett Millais and Dante Gabriel Rossetti were members of which 19th-century artistic movement?

8. Which Spanish artist said, 'It took me four years to paint like Raphael, but a lifetime to paint like a child'?

9. Which American state is home to the J Paul Getty Museum?

10. What was the first name of the Dutch painter Mondrian?

11. 'Everyone I Have Ever Slept With 1963–1995' is a work by which controversial British artist?

12. The Rijksmuseum is in which European city?

13. In 2013, the Turner Prize was held outside England for the first time. Which city hosted the ceremony?

14. What famous school of design was founded in Weimar Germany in 1919?

15. What nationality was the noted surrealist Magritte?

16. In 2011, the Turner Contemporary gallery opened in which English seaside resort?

17. Which artist is best known for his landscape paintings of Dedham Vale?

18. The Uffizi is a famous museum and gallery in which Italian city?

19. What was the first name of the Spanish romantic painter Goya?
    a) Felipe
    b) Fernando
    c) Francisco

20. The Burrell Collection is situated in which city?
    a) Aberdeen
    b) Edinburgh
    c) Glasgow

Answers to Quiz 171: Pot Luck

1. Titanium
2. Ken Dodd
3. La Paz (Bolivia)
4. Cher
5. 1977
6. Brian Moore
7. 30
8. Antigua
9. Black Sabbath
10. Adams, Harrison, Roosevelt and Johnson
11. Adele
12. Herbert Asquith
13. San Francisco
14. 17th century
15. Gabby Logan
16. Lough Neagh
17. Manchester and Salford
18. Marble Arch
19. Flying
20. James

DIFFICULT

Quiz 173: Pot Luck

1. Estádio José Alvalade is a football ground in which European city?

2. A bucket of water was thrown over which politician at the 1998 Brit Awards?

3. On which card do playing-card manufacturers usually display their company and trademark information?

4. Which British singer was the first woman to have three singles in the US Billboard 100 chart at the same time?

5. The headquarters of the CIA are named after which American president?

6. Footballer Gareth Bale started his professional career with which English club?

7. Which actor played Gregory in the 1981 film 'Gregory's Girl'?

8. In which year did women compete in the Olympic Games for the first time?

9. What type of animal is known in French as 'un dauphin'?

10. Released in 2014, 'Everyday Robots' was the title of the debut solo album by which former Britpop star?

11. Burghley House, home of the famous horse trials, is in which English county?

12. Catherine Hogarth was the wife of which famous 19th-century author?

13. If all of America's presidents were listed alphabetically, who would be last on the list?

14. 'Don't You Want Me' by the Human League returned to the charts in 2014 after being adopted by followers of which Scottish football club?

Answers – page 353

15. Someone suffering from nyctophobia fears what?

16. What was the first name of the French artist Matisse?

17. Alexandria is the second-largest city in which country?

18. Which national radio station celebrated its 20th anniversary in March 2014?

19. In 2014, a British man won £108m on the EuroMillions lottery. What was his name?
    a) Neil Fawlty
    b) Neil Steptoe
    c) Neil Trotter

20. What image appears on the flag of Turkmenistan?
    a) bicycle
    b) carpet
    c) plough

Answers to Quiz 172: Art and Architecture

1. Venice
2. Mark Rothko
3. Horses
4. Auguste Rodin
5. France
6. Lawrence Stephen
7. Pre-Raphaelite Brotherhood
8. Pablo Picasso
9. California
10. Piet
11. Tracey Emin
12. Amsterdam
13. Derry / Londonderry
14. Bauhaus
15. Belgian
16. Margate
17. John Constable
18. Florence
19. Francisco
20. Glasgow

DIFFICULT

Quiz 174: Books

1. What do the authors Harper Lee, Emily Bronte, Boris Pasternak and Oscar Wilde have in common?

2. What word is missing from the title of the novel by Sylvia Plath – 'The ____ Jar'?

3. Which sporting figure was the author of the biggest-selling autobiography of 2013?

4. Holden Caulfield is the most famous creation of which reclusive American author?

5. Which hit TV series is based on the novels of George RR Martin?

6. The novels featuring the forensic psychologist Alex Cross are set in which American city?

7. Which world leader's autobiography was called 'The Long Walk to Freedom'?

8. 'All children, except one, grow up' is the opening line to which novel?

9. 'The Selfish Gene' is the best-known work by which evolutionary biologist?

10. The novels featuring Inspector Montalbano are set on which Mediterranean island?

11. Which crime writer wrote the series of thrillers known as the 'Millennium Trilogy'?

12. Which 1925 novel is set in the fictional American town of West Egg?

13. Complete the title of the best seller by Markus Zusak – 'The Book ____'.

14. Which author wrote the series of novels featuring the magical nanny Mary Poppins?

15. Ronald Reull are the middle names of which famous writer?

16. 'Tackling My Demons' was the title of which controversial footballer's 2013 autobiography?

17. Which fictional detective returned to duty in the 2013 novel 'Saints of the Shadow Bible'?

18. 'The No. 1 Ladies' Detective Agency' novels by Alexander McCall Smith are set in which African country?

19. Which notorious double agent was the subject of the 2014 biography 'A Spy Among Friends'?
    a) George Blake   b) Guy Burgess   c) Kim Philby

20. Complete the title of the classic novel by John Kennedy Toole – 'A Confederacy of...'?
    a) Dunces   b) Idiots   c) Morons

Answers to Quiz 173: Pot Luck

1. Lisbon
2. John Prescott
3. Ace of spades
4. Adele
5. George H W Bush
6. Southampton
7. John Gordon Sinclair
8. 1900
9. Dolphin
10. Damon Albarn
11. Lincolnshire
12. Charles Dickens
13. Woodrow Wilson
14. Aberdeen
15. The dark
16. Henri
17. Egypt
18. BBC Radio 5 Live
19. Neil Trotter
20. Carpet

DIFFICULT

Quiz 175: Pot Luck

1. Who was assassinated by Nathuram Godse on 30 January 1948?

2. Pecorino cheese is made from the milk of which animal?

3. Which British politician was nicknamed the 'Chingford Skinhead'?

4. In which year was the first 'Now That's What I Call Music!' compilation album released?

5. 'Unicorn' is the US Secret Service codename for which member of the British Royal Family?

6. Bechuanaland is the former name for which southern African country?

7. The 1989 novel 'A Time to Kill' was the debut from which American thriller writer?

8. Italian football club Fiorentina is based in which city?

9. 'Quercus' is the Latin name for which common tree?

10. The Open University is based in which English city?

11. Eric Blair was the real name of which English writer, who died in 1950?

12. Bart Simpson's hair has how many spikes?

13. Jan Hoch was the real name of which media mogul, who died in mysterious circumstances in 1991?

14. Which Disney cartoon character is known in Sweden as 'Musse Pigg'?

15. 'Don't ask the price, it's a penny!' was the original slogan of which high-street shop?

16. Which country in Africa is home to the largest population?

17. In which year was the breathalyser test introduced on Britain's roads?

18. The Mendip Hills are in which English county?

19. The continent of Africa covers approximately what percentage of the Earth's land area?
    a) 15%
    b) 20%
    c) 25%

20. In 2014, Twitter and YouTube were banned in which country?
    a) Greece
    b) Israel
    c) Turkey

Answers to Quiz 174: Books

1. They only wrote one novel
2. Bell
3. Sir Alex Ferguson
4. JD Salinger
5. Game of Thrones
6. Washington DC
7. Nelson Mandela
8. Peter Pan
9. Richard Dawkins
10. Sicily
11. Stieg Larsson
12. The Great Gatsby
13. Thief
14. PL Travers
15. JRR Tolkien
16. Stan Collymore
17. Inspector Rebus
18. Botswana
19. Kim Philby
20. Dunces

DIFFICULT

Quiz 176: Places

1. The name of which African country means 'lion mountains' in English?

2. Bharat Ganrajya is an alternative name for which country?

3. 'MINT' is an acronym used to describe a group of countries with emerging economies. What country is represented by the letter 'M'?

4. The Brenner Pass lies on the border of which two countries?

5. Abyssinia is the former name of which country?

6. Which European country's name translates into English as 'light stone'?

7. The ski resort Tromsø is in which country?

8. Norman Manley Airport is in which Commonwealth country?

9. In which American city can the Space Needle be seen?

10. Thames House in London is the headquarters of which organization?

11. The Diana, Princess of Wales memorial and the Holocaust Memorial can be found in which London park?

12. Which European city is served by Ciampino Airport?

13. 8–10 Broadway, London SW1H 0BG is the address of which famous headquarters?

14. Which small Welsh town is home to the Royal Mint?

15. Willerby Road, Anlaby Road and Bransholme are areas of which English city?

16. Which English Midlands city was known in Roman times as Ratae Corieltauvorum?

17. The football match known as the 'superclasico' takes place in which city?

18. The giant Gateway Arch, the tallest man-made monument in America is in which city?

19. The world's first official football international took place in which city?
    a) Dublin
    b) Glasgow
    c) London

20. What is the largest of the Balearic Islands?
    a) Ibiza
    b) Majorca
    c) Menorca

Answers to Quiz 175: Pot Luck

1. Gandhi
2. Sheep
3. Norman Tebbit
4. 1983
5. Prince Charles
6. Botswana
7. John Grisham
8. Florence
9. Oak
10. Milton Keynes
11. George Orwell
12. Nine
13. Robert Maxwell
14. Mickey Mouse
15. Marks and Spencer
16. Nigeria
17. 1967
18. Somerset
19. 20%
20. Turkey

DIFFICULT

Quiz 177: Pot Luck

1. In which year were the Commonwealth Games held in India for the first time?

2. British actor Alan Rickman played which American President in the 2013 film 'The Butler'?

3. Cagliari is the capital city of which Mediterranean island?

4. While accepting a Brit Award in 2001, which singer offered to have a fight with Oasis frontman Liam Gallagher?

5. Which Premier League football club was formerly known as Dial Square?

6. Which female singer duetted with Jack White on the theme to the James Bond film 'Quantum of Solace'?

7. The 2014 album 'GIRL' was the first to top the charts for which American singer and rapper?

8. Bangui is the capital city of which African country?

9. In which year was the first Tour de France held?

10. The River Danube flows through which four European capital cities?

11. Which continent was named after a figure in Greek mythology who was abducted by the god Zeus?

12. 'Il Divin Codino' (in English, 'The Divine Ponytail') was the nickname of which European footballer?

13. Mount Pinatubo is an active volcano in which Asian country?

14. H'Angus the Monkey is the mascot of which northern English football club?

15. Former UN Secretary General Kofi Annan is from which African country?

16. Which landlocked body of water, located between Israel and Jordan, lies 400m below sea level?

17. The Black Caps is the nickname of the cricket team of which country?

18. In UK law, the initials 'DPP' refer to the holder of which post?

19. The Union Jack does not appear on the flag of which of these countries?
    a) Fiji
    b) Tuvalu
    c) Papua New Guinea

20. Which of the following countries does not share a land border with Russia?
    a) Finland
    b) Norway
    c) Sweden

Answers to Quiz 176: Places

1. Sierra Leone	11. Hyde Park
2. India	12. Rome
3. Mexico	13. New Scotland Yard
4. Italy and Austria	14. Llantrisant
5. Ethiopia	15. Hull
6. Liechtenstein	16. Leicester
7. Norway	17. Buenos Aires
8. Jamaica	18. St Louis
9. Seattle	19. Glasgow
10. MI5 (The Security Service)	20. Majorca

DIFFICULT

Quiz 178: Anagrams part 1

Rearrange these groups of letters to make the name of a well-known TV soap character:

1. Gill Charm Tent (EastEnders)

2. Mad Zinc Doll (Coronation Street)

3. Merry Chin Balsam (Home and Away)

4. Drank Keenly (Neighbours)

5. Earwig Hemlines (Coronation Street)

6. Nun Chiming Candy (Hollyoaks)

7. Bang Ran Minx (EastEnders)

8. Warbler Poet (Coronation Street)

9. Capri Rolled (Emmerdale)

10. Opulent Racer (Neighbours)

11. Tersely Bawls (Coronation Street)

12. Staler Waft (Home and Away)

13. Limy Lilt Belch (EastEnders)

14. Snorer Broaden (Hollyoaks)

15. Hooded Mamas (EastEnders)

16. Worrier Balded (Coronation Street)

17. Labours On Pin (Neighbours)

18. Darling Melon (Emmerdale)

19. Toner Berries (Home and Away)

20. Waved Cork Thru (Coronation Street)

Answers to Quiz 177: Pot Luck

1. 2010
2. Ronald Reagan
3. Sardinia
4. Robbie Williams
5. Arsenal
6. Alicia Keys
7. Pharrell Williams
8. Central African Republic
9. 1903
10. Vienna, Bratislava, Budapest and Belgrade
11. Europe
12. Roberto Baggio
13. The Philippines
14. Hartlepool United
15. Ghana
16. The Dead Sea
17. New Zealand
18. Director of Public Prosecutions
19. Papua New Guinea
20. Sweden

DIFFICULT

Quiz 179: Pot Luck

1. The name of which one-word African country contains all five vowels?

2. Which Hollywood superstar was given the codename 'Zorro' by the US Secret Service after the actor hosted a fund-raising event for President Obama?

3. 'Iranalamadingdong' was the title of the 2014 tour by which actor and comedian?

4. What is the Republic of Ireland's smallest county?

5. What is Robbie Williams' biggest-selling UK single, despite it only reaching number four in the charts?

6. Which Britpop band declared that 'Modern Life Is Rubbish' in a 1993 album?

7. Bill Murray, Jon Voight and Alan Cumming have all played which US president in films?

8. Which was the last team to win English football's top flight that did not have red, white or blue in their home kit?

9. In 1901, Annie Edson Taylor became the first person to survive a trip over Niagara Falls in what?

10. Which piece of household furniture was the nickname of former Premier League footballer Papa Bouba Diop?

11. The Yomiuri Shimbun is a best-selling newspaper in which country?

12. Which Antipodean film star keeps his Best Actor Oscar in a chicken coop on his ranch?

13. In measurement, a quart is equal to how many pints?

14. Which English city is situated approximately midway between London and Edinburgh?

15. Which country won the most medals at the 2014 Winter Olympics?

16. The flag of Monaco is identical to that of which Asian country?

17. The port of Piraeus is in which European city?

18. In the film 'The Lion King', what type of animal was Timon?

19. Gideon is the real first name of which British politician?
    a) David Cameron
    b) Boris Johnson
    c) George Osborne

20. Prior to finding pop fame, what was the occupation of 'X Factor' winner Sam Bailey?
    a) chef
    b) lawyer
    c) prison officer

Answers to Quiz 178: Anagrams part 1

1. Grant Mitchell	11. Sally Webster
2. Liz McDonald	12. Alf Stewart
3. Marilyn Chambers	13. Billy Mitchell
4. Karl Kennedy	14. Darren Osborne
5. Eileen Grimshaw	15. Masood Ahmed
6. Cindy Cunningham	16. Deirdre Barlow
7. Max Branning	17. Paul Robinson
8. Peter Barlow	18. Marlon Dingle
9. Eric Pollard	19. Irene Roberts
10. Lou Carpenter	20. Vera Duckworth

DIFFICULT

Quiz 180: Fill in the Blank

1. Mexico City, Munich, ____, Moscow

2. Louis Oosthuizen, ____, Ernie Els, Phil Mickelson

3. ____, Harry Redknapp, Andre Villas Boas, Tim Sherwood

4. ____, Al Gore, Dick Cheney, Joe Biden

5. New Zealand, Australia, ____, Australia

6. Sir Winston Churchill, Sir Anthony Eden, Harold Macmillan, ____

7. The Motion Picture, The Wrath of Khan, ____, The Voyage Home

8. Paris, ____, Berlin, Johannesburg

9. Norma, Cherie, ____, Samantha

10. Albino Luciani, Karol Wojtyła, ____, Jorge Mario Bergoglio

11. Identity, Supremacy, ____, Legacy

12. Carlo Ancelotti, Roberto Mancini, ____, Roberto Martinez

13. Coca Cola, ____, Carling, Capital One

14. Robin Cook, Jack Straw, ____, David Miliband

15. Natalie Portman, Meryl Streep, ____, Cate Blanchett

Answers – page 367

16. John Carmel Heenan, Basil Hume, Cormac Murphy O'Connor, ____

17. Andrew Flintoff, Andrew Strauss, ____, Alastair Cook

18. ____, Ron Atkinson, Sir Alex Ferguson, David Moyes

19. ____, Jacques Chirac, Nicolas Sarkozy, François Hollande

20. Serena Williams, Petra Kvitova, ____, Marion Bartoli

Answers to Quiz 179: Pot Luck

1. Mozambique
2. Antonio Banderas
3. Omid Djalili
4. Louth
5. Angels
6. Blur
7. Franklin D Roosevelt
8. Wolverhampton Wanderers
9. A barrel
10. The Wardrobe
11. Japan
12. Russell Crowe
13. Two
14. York
15. Russia
16. Indonesia
17. Athens
18. Meerkat
19. George Osborne
20. Prison officer

DIFFICULT

Quiz 181: Pot Luck

1. In 2013, who became the first British female solo artist to have eight UK top-five singles?

2. Conductor Simon Rattle and actors Tom Baker and Jason Isaacs were all born in which British city?

3. 'The greatest trick the devil ever pulled was convincing the world he didn't exist. And like that – poof – he's gone!' are the last lines of which 1995 thriller?

4. Which Oscar-winning actor owns an Italian restaurant in New York called Locanda Verde?

5. Diana Prince is the alter ego of which comic-book superhero?

6. In mobile-phone technology, what do the initials 'WAP' stand for?

7. The flag of which European country features a double-headed black eagle?

8. In the Batman film series, what is the full name of Bruce Wayne's butler?

9. Which sportsman wrote a 2013 novel entitled 'Taking the Fall'?

10. What is measured using a Brannock Device?

11. Which British actor played the title character in the 2014 film 'Locke'?

12. The miniature pots known as 'netsuke' originate from which country?

13. In which field is the Robert Capa Gold Medal awarded?

14. Which popular British TV detective drama is based on a series of novels by Caroline Graham?

15. Rene Lacoste, founder of the fashion label Lacoste, was a world-class performer in which sport?

16. In the 'Jeeves and Wooster' books, what is the first name of Jeeves?

17. The Ferens Art Gallery and a large aquarium called The Deep are in which northern English city?

18. In which month do Americans mark Labor Day?

19. Which British actor was crowned 'King Bacchus' as part of the 2014 Mardi Gras celebrations in New Orleans?
    a) Hugh Bonneville   b) Hugh Grant   c) Hugh Laurie

20. Which US pop star has a quote from US president Teddy Roosevelt tattooed on her forearm?
    a) Christina Aguilera   b) Miley Cyrus   c) Katy Perry

Answers to Quiz 180: Fill in the Blank

1. Montreal (Summer Olympics host cities 1968 to 1980)
2. Darren Clarke (winners of golf's Open Championship 2010 to 2013)
3. Juande Ramos (Tottenham Hotspur managers)
4. Dan Quayle (US vice presidents)
5. South Africa (the first four winners of the Rugby World Cup)
6. Sir Alec Douglas-Home (British prime ministers 1945 to 1964)
7. The Search for Spock (Star Trek films)
8. Yokohama (World Cup final host cities 1998 to 2010)
9. Sarah (first names of the spouses of British prime ministers)
10. Joseph Ratzinger (Real names of the four most recent popes)
11. Ultimatum (Bourne films)
12. Roberto Di Matteo (FA Cup-winning managers 2010 to 2013)
13. Worthington (sponsors of football's League Cup)
14. Margaret Beckett (UK foreign secretaries)
15. Jennifer Lawrence (Best Actress Oscar winners 2010 to 2013)
16. Vincent Nichols (Archbishops of Westminster)
17. Kevin Pietersen (captains of the England Test cricket team 2006 to present)
18. Dave Sexton (Manchester United managers)
19. François Mitterand (presidents of France)
20. Serena Williams (Wimbledon champions 2010 to 2013)

DIFFICULT

Quiz 182: Cricket

1. In which year was the first Cricket World Cup held?

2. Who captained England to their first global limited-overs tournament win?

3. Only two matches in the history of Test cricket have been tied. Which team was involved in both matches?

4. Who was the first England batsman to score 8000 Test runs?

5. England have played the most matches in Test cricket history, followed by Australia. Who comes third on the list?

6. Which portly Pakistani confronted a spectator at a 1997 One Day International after being called a fat potato?

7. 'Shrek' was the nickname of which England bowler?

8. Which actor, comedian and panel-show regular masqueraded as a cricket journalist on a tour of India, later turning his experiences into a book and stand-up show?

9. The Sunrisers is the nickname of the IPL franchise based in which Indian city?

10. In which year did the first One Day International take place?

11. Arundel Castle is an occasional home of which English county cricket team?

12. Who are the two West Indian batsmen to have scored over 10,000 Test runs?

13. A cricket match between All-Muggleton and the Dingley Dell Cricket Club features in which novel by Charles Dickens?

14. The first Test match in England was held at which ground?

15. Who are the three Indians to have taken 400 Test wickets?

16. St George's Park is a Test match venue in which South African city?

17. Which spin bowler holds the record for scoring the most Test runs for England without making a century?

18. Which English county plays its home games at the St Lawrence ground?

19. How many Test wickets did Sir Ian Botham take?
    a) 381
    b) 382
    c) 383

20. Ronald is the middle name of which England batsman?
    a) Ian Bell
    b) Alastair Cook
    c) Joe Root

Answers to Quiz 181: Pot Luck

1. Leona Lewis
2. Liverpool
3. The Usual Suspects
4. Robert De Niro
5. Wonder Woman
6. Wireless Application Protocol
7. Albania
8. Alfred Pennyworth
9. Tony McCoy
10. Feet
11. Tom Hardy
12. Japan
13. Photography
14. Midsomer Murders
15. Tennis
16. Reginald
17. Hull
18. September
19. Hugh Laurie
20. Miley Cyrus

DIFFICULT

Quiz 183: Pot Luck

1. 'Always Managing' was the title of the 2013 autobiography by which English football manager?

2. Which comic-book superhero celebrated his 75th birthday in May 2014?

3. What was the first name of the Italian classical composer Vivaldi?

4. What object, often found in a tool box, is also the name of a measurement equal to 5.715cm?

5. In which country are fervent sports fans, especially football supporters, are known as 'tifosi'?

6. Which fictional character rode a horse called Rocinante?

7. On 1 January 2014, which country became the 14th to adopt the euro as its currency?

8. 'Zalig Kerstfeast' is Merry Christmas in which language?

9. Who was the first non-European player to score 20 goals in a Premier League season?

10. What nationality is the author Margaret Atwood?

11. In the board game Monopoly, what is the name of the person in jail?

12. Patrick Grant and May Martin are the judges in which TV talent show?

13. Which artist survived an assassination attempt in 1968 after being shot by Valerie Solanis?

14. Who was Chelsea's last permanent English manager?

15. The first Football League game held under floodlights took place in which decade?

16. In which month do Americans observe Memorial Day?

17. What is the nickname of Brazilian footballer Givanildo Vieira De Souza?

18. Fashion retailer Gap launched its first store in 1969 in which American city?

19. How much prize money was awarded to the winner of the 2014 World Cup?
    a) $25m
    b) $30m
    c) $35m

20. Complete the title of a 2012 Sherlock Holmes novel by Anthony Horowitz: The House of ...
    a) Daggers
    b) Musk
    c) Silk

Answers to Quiz 182: Cricket

1. 1975
2. Paul Collingwood
3. Australia
4. Geoffrey Boycott
5. West Indies
6. Inzamam-ul-Haq
7. Matthew Hoggard
8. Miles Jupp
9. Hyderabad
10. 1971
11. Sussex
12. Brian Lara and Shivnarine Chanderpaul
13. The Pickwick Papers
14. The Oval
15. Kapil Dev, Anil Kumble and Harbhajan Singh
16. Port Elizabeth
17. John Emburey
18. Kent
19. 383
20. Ian Bell

DIFFICULT

Quiz 184: Sport part 2

1. In which sport are the brothers Andy and Frank Schleck notable performers?

2. The first World Athletics Championships were hosted in which city?

3. Which footballer's 2014 autobiography was called 'How Not to be a Football Millionaire'?

4. In greyhound racing, which colour vest is worn by a dog running from trap two?

5. Briton Alison Williamson competed at the Olympic Games six times between 1992 and 2012 in which sport?

6. The French Derby horse race takes place at which track?

7. In 1867, Welshman John Graham Chambers defined the rules for which sport?

8. Who is the youngest footballer to have won a full cap for England?

9. In which sport do teams compete for the Lamar Hunt Trophy?

10. Which cult 1996 film contains the line, 'I haven't felt that good since Archie Gemmill scored against Holland in 1978'?

11. In which event is Russia's Yelena Isinbayeva a multiple gold medallist?

12. The record for the longest ever televised putt wasn't set by a golfer but by a multiple Olympic gold medallist. Who sank the 150-foot monster in 2012?

13. Which broadcaster was the unlikely holder of the old record after sinking a 100-footer in 1981?

14. Brian Lara scored his record-breaking innings of 501 not out at which cricket ground?

15. Champion jockey Tony McCoy rode his 4000th winner at which racecourse?

16. By what name is the Portuguese footballer Luis Carlos Almedia Da Cunha better known?

17. In which sport did Britain's Carl Hester win an Olympic gold medal in 2012?

18. Which Australian bowler scored a double century in his final Test match innings against Bangladesh in 2006?

19. In which year was the Football League founded?
    a) 1888   b) 1889   c) 1890

20. What was the name of the all-conquering Australian racehorse that retired in 2013?
    a) Black Caviar   b) Black King   c) Black Orchid

Answers to Quiz 183: Pot Luck

1. Harry Redknapp
2. Batman
3. Antonio
4. Nail
5. Italy
6. Don Quixote
7. Latvia
8. Dutch
9. Dwight Yorke
10. Canadian
11. Jake the Jailbird
12. The Great British Sewing Bee
13. Andy Warhol
14. Glenn Hoddle
15. 1950s
16. May
17. Hulk
18. San Francisco
19. $35m
20. Silk

DIFFICULT

Quiz 185: Pot Luck

1. True or false – Sherlock Holmes creator Sir Arthur Conan Doyle also played football professionally?

2. What nationality is the film director James Cameron?

3. Which 1970s TV sitcom was set at 46 Peacock Crescent, Hampton Wick?

4. The 'Eroica Symphony' is a work by which composer?

5. The artist Pablo Picasso was born in which Spanish city?

6. The strength of what is measured using the Scoville scale?

7. Which British prime minister coined the phrase 'the unacceptable face of capitalism'?

8. Named after the highest peak in Alaska, 'Denali' was the US Secret Service codename for which controversial American politician?

9. Stretching some 185 miles, what is the third-largest river in England?

10. Which three counties of the province of Ulster are in the Irish Republic?

11. In 2013/14, which English football club was forced to play its home games 35 miles away at Northampton, after a row between the club and stadium owners?

12. The first album to top the UK album chart in 1956 was 'Songs for Swingin' Lovers'. Who recorded it?

13. Which contemporary British artist opened a restaurant in Notting Hill called 'Pharmacy'?

14. What is the third largest city in Scotland?

15. Which Labour MP for Ashfield in Nottinghamshire used to be a newsreader on the breakfast TV show 'GMTV'?

Answers – page 377

16. What was Michael Jackson's only UK Christmas number-one single?

17. Which 'Doctor Who' actor played for the youth teams of Leicester City and Nottingham Forest before turning to acting?

18. Which American rockers topped the UK album charts in 2013 with 'Mechanical Bull'?

19. The talus is the technical name for which bone?
    a) ankle
    b) elbow
    c) shin

20. Which unit of measurement is equal to 7.92 inches?
    a) a chain
    b) a link
    c) a nail

Answers to Quiz 184: Sport part 2

1. Cycling
2. Helsinki
3. Keith Gillespie
4. Blue
5. Archery
6. Chantilly
7. Boxing (Marquess of Queensberry rules)
8. Theo Walcott
9. American football
10. Trainspotting
11. Pole vault
12. Michael Phelps
13. Terry Wogan
14. Edgbaston
15. Towcester
16. Nani
17. Dressage
18. Jason Gillespie
19. 1888
20. Black Caviar

DIFFICULT

Quiz 186: Television part 2

1. In 2009, politician John Prescott made a guest appearance in which TV sitcom?

2. Played by Douglas Henshall, detective Jimmy Perez is the central character in which British crime drama?

3. What were the first names of the TV detectives Randall and Hopkirk?

4. In 'The Simpsons', what is the character Robert Underdunk Terwilliger better known as?

5. Which actress plays DCI Sasha Miller in crime drama 'New Tricks'?

6. Played by Brenda Blethyn, what is the surname of the TV detective 'Vera'?

7. Which actor and comedian plays Geoff 'The Oracle' Maltby in TV comedy 'Benidorm'?

8. Who was the original host of the panel show 'Room 101'?

9. Which high-street retailer was also the name of the holiday camp in 1980s comedy 'Hi-De-Hi'?

10. Geraldine Granger, David Horton and Alice Tinkle were characters in which sitcom?

11. True or false – former prime minister Margaret Thatcher wrote a sketch for the hit TV comedy 'Yes, Minister'?

12. Mental Agility, Observation, Assault Course and General Knowledge were rounds in which TV game show?

13. In the sitcom 'Allo Allo', what was René's surname?

14. In 'Only Fools and Horses', what was the name of Del and Rodney's father?

15. In the American soap 'Dynasty', which actress played Krystle Carrington?

16. Danny Latimer was the murder victim in which 2013 British crime drama that starred a former Dr Who?

17. Which spy series starring Claire Danes was based on an Israeli drama called 'Prisoners of War'?

18. Which British prime minister once made a guest appearance on the 'Morecambe and Wise Show'?

19. The hit crime drama 'The Killing' was set in which country?
    a) Denmark
    b) Norway
    c) Sweden

20. Royston Vasey, the name of the village in 'The League of Gentlemen', is the real name of which stand-up comedian?
    a) Roy 'Chubby' Brown
    b) Bernard Manning
    c) Charlie Williams

Answers to Quiz 185: Pot Luck

1. False
2. Canadian
3. George and Mildred
4. Beethoven
5. Malaga
6. Chilli peppers
7. Edward Heath
8. Sarah Palin
9. Trent
10. Cavan, Donegal and Monaghan
11. Coventry City
12. Frank Sinatra
13. Damien Hirst
14. Aberdeen
15. Gloria de Piero
16. Earth Song
17. Matt Smith
18. Kings of Leon
19. Ankle
20. A link

DIFFICULT

Quiz 187: Pot Luck

1. Ellis Bell was the pseudonym of which Yorkshire-born 19th-century writer?

2. Captain Marvel was the nickname of which former England footballer?

3. Every computer that is used to go online has an IP address. What do the initials 'IP' stand for?

4. With 51.8 million followers, which female singer is the most followed person on Twitter?

5. The Ring Cycle is a series of operas by which German composer?

6. Which Oscar-winning Hollywood actor and director said in 2013, 'If I could be somebody, it'd definitely be Brad Pitt. I love the way he looks'?

7. In the human body, which lung is larger – the left or the right?

8. 'All Things Must Pass' was the only UK number-one solo album by which former Beatle?

9. Which Asian city was the first from outside Europe to host the World Athletics Championships?

10. The soundtrack to which 1992 film is the biggest-selling soundtrack album of all time?

11. Which indie rock band won their third Best Album award at the 2014 Brit Awards for 'AM'?

12. The Jacks is the nickname given to followers of which British football team?

13. Which race is finished in the quicker time – the Boat Race or the Grand National?

14. The 2012 Oscar-winning film 'Silver Linings Playbook' was set in which American city?

15. Actor and comedian Russell Brand is the owner of a cat named after which controversial British singer?

16. Newton Heath is the former name of which English football club?

17. Tim Wonnacott succeeded David Dickinson as the host of which long-running TV show?

18. Which politician was awarded the highest possible ranking by the president of the World Taekwondo Federation on a 2013 visit to South Korea?

19. What does 'nano-' indicate?
    a) a thousandth b) a millionth c) a billionth

20. Lexington, the scene of a famous battle, is in which American state?
    a) Illinois b) Massachusetts c) New Jersey

Answers to Quiz 186: Television part 2

1. Gavin & Stacey
2. Shetland
3. Jeffrey and Martin
4. Sideshow Bob
5. Tamzin Outhwaite
6. Stanhope
7. Johnny Vegas
8. Nick Hancock
9. Maplin
10. The Vicar of Dibley
11. True
12. The Krypton Factor
13. Artois
14. Reg
15. Linda Evans
16. Broadchurch
17. Homeland
18. Harold Wilson
19. Denmark
20. Roy 'Chubby' Brown

DIFFICULT

Quiz 188: Natural World

1. Approximately half of the world's cork is harvested in which European country?

2. Self, fancy and picotee are varieties of which flower?

3. Which deadly tree condition is caused by the fungus 'Ophiostoma ulmi' and is spread by dark beetles?

4. The climbing plant sweet pea is native to which European country?

5. Dartford, barred and Cetti's are types of which bird?

6. Mulhacén is the highest mountain on the mainland of which European country?

7. The Adélie is the most common species of which bird?

8. 'Panthera leo' is the scientific name for which creature?

9. True or false – the puffin is native to Antarctica?

10. Which country's coastline is the longest in the world?

11. The giant Angel Falls are in which continent?

12. What type of creature lives in a holt?

13. The dodo, which became extinct in the 17th century, lived on which island in the Indian Ocean?

14. What is the smallest of the world's five oceans?

15. Excluding Russia, what is Europe's leading oil-producing country?

16. The rock formation known as the 'Twelve Apostles' lies off the coast of which country?

17. Mount Elbrus is the highest peak in which Eurasian mountain range?

18. What type of bird can be great spotted, green or pileated?

19. Which of the following mammals has the longest pregnancy?
    a) elephant
    b) giraffe
    c) rhino

20. What is a ginkgo?
    a) bird
    b) plant
    c) reptile

Answers to Quiz 187: Pot Luck

1. Emily Bronte
2. Bryan Robson
3. Internet protocol
4. Katy Perry
5. Richard Wagner
6. Ben Affleck
7. The right lung
8. George Harrison
9. Tokyo
10. The Bodyguard
11. Arctic Monkeys
12. Swansea City
13. Grand National
14. Philadelphia
15. Morrissey
16. Manchester United
17. Bargain Hunt
18. Vladimir Putin
19. A billionth
20. Massachusetts

DIFFICULT

Quiz 189: Pot Luck

1. What unit of area is equal to 4,840 square yards?

2. Which Yorkshire TV detective duo were based on a series of novels by Reginald Hill?

3. Ardwick FC is the former name of which Premier League football club?

4. Argentina shares land borders with which five countries?

5. The Sounders are an American soccer team based in which city?

6. The name of which animal is also a unit of measurement used in chemistry to express amounts of a chemical substance?

7. True or false – there is a place in Canada called Uranium City?

8. Up to the 2013/14 season, which were the only two clubs to have won the old top-flight title who had not played in the Premier League?

9. Which team were runners-up in the first season of football's Premier League?

10. Which English rock star invited the unlikely duo of Sir Cliff Richard and Sir Tom Jones to join him at a 2014 concert in New York?

11. The jazz musician Stan Getz played which instrument?

12. Who was the first dart player from outside Britain to win the World Championship?

13. Which 20th-century British prime minister served under three monarchs?

14. Elise Christie was disqualified three times at the 2014 Winter Olympics. In which sport was the British athlete competing?

Answers – page 385

15. What are the four Michael Jackson top-ten hits that have a name in their title?

16. Bruce Lee was born in which American city?

17. Which two European football teams meet in a derby match called 'De Klassikier'?

18. Which city is closer to London – Dubai or Toronto?

19. Which of these clubs was not a founder member of the Football League?
    a) Aston Villa
    b) Tottenham Hotspur
    c) West Bromwich Albion

20. Which country singing legend had a brief spell playing tennis professionally in the late 1970s?
    a) Johnny Cash
    b) Kris Kristofferson
    c) Kenny Rogers

Answers to Quiz 188: Natural World

1. Portugal
2. Carnation
3. Dutch elm disease
4. Italy
5. Warbler
6. Spain
7. Penguin
8. Lion
9. False
10. Canada
11. South America
12. Otter
13. Mauritius
14. Arctic
15. Norway
16. Australia
17. Caucasus Mountains
18. Woodpecker
19. Elephant
20. Plant

DIFFICULT

Quiz 190: Connections

1. Which 2014 Oscar-nominated film was based on a memoir by Jordan Belfort?

2. Which Hollywood A-lister is the daughter of a German opera singer called Helga Meyer?

3. What was the title of American rocker Meat Loaf's debut album?

4. Robert De Niro won an Oscar in 1981 for his performance in which film?

5. What was the name of the character played by David Duchovny in the TV drama 'The X Files'?

6. 'Mummy's Boy' is the title of the autobiography of which former 'EastEnders' actor?

7. 'Do You Really Want to Hurt Me' was the first UK number one for Culture Club. What was their second chart-topper?

8. Who is the British host of the American TV talent show 'So You Think You Can Dance'?

9. Which American artist, noted for his drip style of painting, was the subject of a 2000 film biopic starring Ed Harris?

10. Who sang the theme song to the James Bond film 'Tomorrow Never Dies'?

11. Who was the first English footballer to score a Premier League hat trick?

12. Brad Pitt was nominated for his first Oscar for which 1995 sci-fi film?

13. What is the nickname of Leicestershire County Cricket Club?

14. Who featured on the reverse of the Bank of England £10 note between 1975 and 1994?

15. In America, what name is used to describe an unidentified male corpse?

16. Which actor was married to Uma Thurman between 1998 and 2005?

17. The Bills is the name of an American football team in which city?

18. By what name is Michael Balzary, bass player with the Red Hot Chili Peppers more commonly known?

19. TV make-up artist Lisa Armstrong is the wife of which British TV presenter?
    a) Declan Donnelly
    b) Ant McPartlin
    c) Ben Shepherd

20. What is the connection between all the answers?

Answers to Quiz 189: Pot Luck

1. One acre
2. Dalziel and Pascoe
3. Manchester City
4. Bolivia, Brazil, Chile, Paraguay, Uruguay
5. Seattle
6. Mole
7. True
8. Preston North End and Huddersfield Town
9. Aston Villa
10. Morrissey
11. Saxophone
12. John Part (Canada)
13. Stanley Baldwin
14. Speed skating
15. Rockin' Robin, Ben, Billie Jean and Dirty Diana
16. San Francisco
17. Ajax and Feyenoord
18. Dubai
19. Tottenham Hotspur
20. Kenny Rogers

DIFFICULT

Quiz 191: Pot Luck

1. What do the initials of the bank HSBC stand for?

2. Mount Cook is the highest peak in which Commonwealth country?

3. Stomatology is the study of diseases that affect which part of the body?

4. Which country did England beat in the semi-final of the 1966 World Cup?

5. Which contemporary football manager said that 'football is the most important of the less important things in life'?

6. Who is the oldest member of the boy band One Direction?

7. The Knavesmire is the name of the racecourse in which English city?

8. Which opened first – the Panama Canal or the Suez Canal?

9. Which Premier League football club was originally known as St Mary's Young Men's Association?

10. 'Fantasy', 'Believe' and 'Curious' are fragrances created by which female pop star?

11. The first British motorway was a bypass around which Lancashire town?

12. Who is Britain's longest-reigning male monarch?

13. What was the name of the official mascot for the 2014 World Cup?

14. Between 2001 and 2010, who were the two Scots to win the World Snooker Championship?

15. What is tested using a Snellen chart?

Answers – page 389

16. Which city is closer to London as the crow flies –
Los Angeles or Seoul?

17. Which British band topped the US charts in 1985 with songs
called 'Shout' and 'Everybody Wants to Rule the World'?

18. In which country may a Member of Parliament put the
letters TD after his or her name?

19. What animal appears on the logo of the Asian car
manufacturer Proton?
a) lion
b) snake
c) tiger

20. The first branch of the bookshop WH Smith opened in
1848 at which London railway station?
a) Euston
b) Victoria
c) Waterloo

Answers to Quiz 190: Connections

1. The Wolf of Wall Street
2. Sandra Bullock
3. Bat Out of Hell
4. Raging Bull
5. Fox Mulder
6. Larry Lamb
7. Karma Chameleon
8. Cat Deeley
9. Jackson Pollock
10. Sheryl Crow
11. Mark Robins
12. 12 Monkeys
13. The Foxes
14. Florence Nightingale
15. John Doe
16. Ethan Hawke
17. Buffalo
18. Flea
19. Ant McPartlin
20. They all contain an animal

DIFFICULT

Quiz 192: World Cup Football

1. Who is the only England player to be the leading goal-scorer at a World Cup finals?

2. Which country hosted the World Cup for the first time in 1938?

3. Which was the first European country to win the World Cup?

4. In which year was the World Cup expanded to 32 teams?

5. Which award is given to the best player at each World Cup?

6. In which year did England take part for the first time?

7. Which five African countries took part in the 2014 World Cup?

8. True or false – England, Scotland, Wales and Northern Ireland all reached the 1958 World Cup finals?

9. Which country was runner-up in the 1934 and 1962 World Cups?

10. Who was the first English player to be sent off in a World Cup finals match?

11. Which African country was banned from wearing sleeveless shirts at the 2002 World Cup?

12. Which two teams took part in the match known as 'The Battle of Nuremberg' in 2006, where the referee dished out 16 yellow cards?

13. What unwanted record was created by Argentina's Pedro Monzon at the 1990 tournament?

14. True or false – the only team that ended the 2010 World Cup unbeaten was New Zealand?

15. Which two players captained England at both the 1986 and the 1990 World Cup finals?

16. Zakumi was the mascot of the World Cup held in which country?

17. What was the first country to lose two World Cup finals?

18. Which South American country was scheduled to host the 1986 tournament but bowed out because of financial difficulties?

19. Which was the first African country to win a game at the World Cup?
    a) Algeria
    b) Tunisia
    c) Zaire

20. How many teams took part in the first World Cup?
    a) 13
    b) 15
    c) 17

DIFFICULT

Quiz 193: Pot Luck

1. CBI are the initials of which business organization?

2. The Indomitable Lions is the nickname of which national football team?

3. Prince George's first foreign tour was to which Commonwealth country?

4. Which planet of the Solar System has moons including Oberon and Titania?

5. Which Scottish city is home to cathedrals called St Andrew's, St Machar's and St Mary's?

6. Who was Britain's first Christian martyr?

7. Who was the only Englishman to win the World Snooker Championship in the 1990s?

8. Chief Inspector Frank Haskins was a character in which 1970s police drama?

9. Which British singer's 2014 tour was called '20 Years of Dreaming'?

10. The British and World Championship in which game takes place every year at the Greyhound pub, in Tinsley Green, Crawley?

11. The famous grave-robbers Burke and Hare had the same Christian name. What was it?

12. In which decade was The Highway Code first published?

13. Which English football club was formerly known as Small Heath Alliance?

14. Which city is closer to London as the crow flies – Buenos Aires or Tokyo?

15. Which television character's 1981 Daimler Sovereign was sold at auction in April 2014 for over £15,000?

16. In 1944, Helen Duncan became the last person to be jailed for which offence?

17. By what name is Sirius, the brightest star in the night sky colloquially known?

18. A notaphilist is a collector of what?

19. What was the cost of the first television licence?
    a) £1
    b) £2
    c) £3

20. Westminster Abbey in London is dedicated to which saint?
    a) St Mark
    b) St Matthew
    c) St Peter

Answers to Quiz 192: World Cup Football

1. Gary Lineker
2. France
3. Italy
4. 1998
5. The Golden Ball
6. 1950
7. Cameroon, Ivory Coast, Nigeria, Ghana and Algeria
8. True
9. Czechoslovakia
10. Ray Wilkins
11. Cameroon
12. Holland and Portugal
13. He was the first player to be sent off in a World Cup final
14. True
15. Bryan Robson and Peter Shilton
16. South Africa
17. Hungary (1938 and 1954)
18. Colombia
19. Tunisia
20. 13

DIFFICULT

Quiz 194: Sport part 3

1. Which is the only Scottish football team to have won two European trophies?

2. What nationality are boxing's Klitschko brothers?

3. In pounds, what is the minimum weight for a male boxer to be classed as a heavyweight?

4. Cricket's 2014 World T20 competition was hosted in which country?

5. Which team did Liverpool beat to win their first European Cup?

6. In 2014, England's Laura Massaro won the world championship in which sport?

7. Who was the first English batsman to score a century in a T20 cricket international?

8. Which rugby team was punished for its involvement in the scandal known as 'Bloodgate'?

9. David Moyes started his football management career with which club?

10. True or false – boxing champ Manny Pacquiao has a daughter named after Queen Elizabeth II?

11. Newbold is the middle name of which British Olympic gold-medal-winning runner?

12. Which is the only English football club to have won the FA Cup and promotion to the top flight in the same season?

13. England's Trina Gulliver is a multiple world champion in which sport?

14. What nationality is the tennis major-winner Victoria Azarenka?

15. What was historic about Edin Djeko's goal for Manchester City against Cardiff City on 18 January 2014?

16. Who in 2010 became the first Italian woman to win a Grand Slam tennis tournament?

17. 'I Think Therefore I Play' is the title of the 2014 autobiography of which elegant Italian midfielder?

18. Which was the first Asian country to take part in the World Cup finals?

19. Prince Obolensky was an England international in which sport?
    a) cricket
    b) football
    c) rugby union

20. The Rapids is the nickname of the T20 team of which English cricket county?
    a) Hampshire
    b) Northamptonshire
    c) Worcestershire

Answers to Quiz 193: Pot Luck

1. Confederation of British Industry
2. Cameroon
3. New Zealand
4. Uranus
5. Aberdeen
6. St Alban
7. John Parrott
8. The Sweeney
9. Gabrielle
10. Marbles
11. William
12. 1930s
13. Birmingham City
14. Tokyo
15. Arthur Daley
16. Witchcraft
17. The Dog Star
18. Banknotes
19. £2.00
20. St Peter

DIFFICULT

Quiz 195: Pot Luck

1. Which actor and James Bond baddie represented Spain at rugby at under-21 level?

2. 'Tumbler' and 'Trailblazer' were the US Secret Service codenames for which American president?

3. The song 'Everything Is Awesome' features heavily in which 2014 movie animation?

4. Which former soap star played King Edward VIII in the 2010 film 'The King's Speech'?

5. What common two-word Latin phrase translates into English as 'to a sickening degree'?

6. Which football club was formed following the merger of Christ Church Rangers (1882) and St Jude's Institute (1884)?

7. In 2014, which film became the highest grossing animation in movie history?

8. In 2012, which 'Blue Peter' presenter became the first person to reach the South Pole on a bike?

9. What connects country singer Johnny Cash and South African golfer Gary Player?

10. Which actress, best known for playing Caress Morrell in 'Dynasty' and Laura Wilde in 'Howards' Way', died in March 2014?

11. Margarita Carmen Cansino was the real name of which Hollywood star, who was briefly married to Orson Welles?

12. Which boy-band star made his footballing debut for Doncaster Rovers reserves against Rotherham United reserves in February 2014?

13. Von Reibnitz was the maiden name of which member of the British Royal Family?

14. Which sitcom character drove a red Austin 1100 Estate, registration WLG 142E?

15. The Dante Stakes is a horse race run at which English racecourse?

16. The Kyalami Grand Prix circuit is in which country?

17. Which geologic period came between the end of the Triassic and the beginning of the Cretaceous?

18. What is the lightest metal in the periodic table of elements?

19. There are approximately how many postcodes in use in the UK?
    a) 1.6 million
    b) 1.8 million
    c) 2.0 million

20. England were shockingly beaten by which country in the 2014 World T20 cricket competition?
    a) Hong Kong
    b) The Netherlands
    c) Ireland

Answers to Quiz 194: Sport part 3

1. Aberdeen	11. Sebastian Coe
2. Ukrainian	12. West Bromwich Albion
3. 200lb	13. Darts
4. Bangladesh	14. Belarussian
5. Borussia Mönchengladbach	15. It was the first decided using goal-line technology
6. Squash	16. Francesca Schiavone
7. Alex Hales	17. Andrea Pirlo
8. Harlequins	18. Indonesia
9. Preston North End	19. Rugby union
10. True	20. Worcestershire

DIFFICULT

Quiz 196: Sport part 4

1. Which World Cup winner was the manager of Chelsea between 1979 and 1981?

2. In 2005, Michael Campbell became the second golfer from which country to win a major title?

3. In a Formula One race, what colour flag is flown to show a driver that he is about to be lapped?

4. Belgian Olivier Marteel and Dutchman Jan Verhaas are referees in which sport?

5. In 2013, James Dasaolu became only the fourth British athlete to do what?

6. Who was the first left-handed player to win the World Snooker Championship?

7. Who was the first left-handed player to win the BDO World Darts Championship?

8. Which boxer, who died in 2014, was the subject of the 1999 film 'The Hurricane'?

9. On an Olympic archery target, what colour ring lies between the red and the black rings?

10. The Birmingham Road End is a feature of which English football ground?

11. Which country finished third at the 2002 FIFA World Cup in only its second appearance in the competition?

12. In 1983, Jarmila Kratochvílová set a women's world record that still stands today. In which track event?

13. Which is the only country to have won at least one gold medal at every Summer Olympic Games?

14. True or false – Hollywood star Hugh Jackman is a follower of Norwich City?

15. The Chiefs and the Royals are professional sports teams based in which American city?

16. Which is the only country to host football's World Cup that has been eliminated in the opening round of the tournament?

17. Fill in the blank – Sharp, ____, AIG, AON

18. The 2014 Cheltenham Festival featured how many races in total?

19. Which of the following drivers has started the most Formula One races?
    a) Jenson Button
    b) David Coulthard
    c) Nigel Mansell

20. In which country was the England cricketer Ben Stokes born?
    a) Australia
    b) New Zealand
    c) South Africa

Answers to Quiz 195: Pot Luck

1. Javier Bardem
2. George W Bush
3. The Lego Movie
4. Guy Pearce
5. Ad nauseam
6. Queens Park Rangers
7. Frozen
8. Helen Skelton
9. They were both known as 'The Man in Black'
10. Kate O'Mara
11. Rita Hayworth
12. Louis Tomlinson from One Direction
13. Princess Michael of Kent
14. Basil Fawlty
15. York
16. South Africa
17. Jurassic period
18. Lithium
19. 1.8 million
20. The Netherlands

DIFFICULT

Quiz 197: Pot Luck

1. Highfield Road is the former ground of which English football club?

2. In 1959, the first postcodes were trialled in which English city?

3. Benjamin Disraeli was preceded by and succeeded as British prime minister by which politician?

4. Which Paralympic cyclist was named Celebrity Mum of the Year for 2014?

5. UMIST is an educational establishment in which northern English city?

6. Triton is the largest moon of which planet of the Solar System?

7. 'The Darlin' of Dublin' is the nickname of which snooker player?

8. Who was the first footballer to score 30 goals in a Premier League season?

9. By what name is the online blogger and gossip columnist Mario Armando Lavandeira, Jr better known?

10. Recep Tayyip Erdoğan was the long-time prime minister of which country?

11. A bichon frise is a breed of which animal?

12. Terry Biddlecombe, who died in 2014, was a notable name in which sport?

13. True or false – in 1814, British troops burnt down the White House?

14. Which online fashion retailer was founded in 2000 by businesswoman Natalie Massenet?

15. Which ruthless leader said, 'If you had not committed great sins / God would not have sent / A punishment like me upon you'?

16. As the crow flies, which city is closer to London – Sao Paulo or Bangkok?

17. How much did Prince George weigh at birth?

18. The Nobel Peace Prize-winning organization OPCW aims for the prohibition of what?

19. In a cycle race, what name is given to the stage that features the highest point of the race?
    a) king stage
    b) prince stage
    c) queen stage

20. Prior to entering politics, what was the occupation of Conservative MP Liam Fox?
    a) doctor
    b) lawyer
    c) soldier

Answers to Quiz 196: Sport part 4

1. Sir Geoff Hurst
2. New Zealand
3. Blue
4. Snooker
5. Run 100m in under 10 seconds
6. Mark Williams
7. Les Wallace
8. Rubin Carter
9. Blue
10. The Hawthorns
11. Turkey
12. 800m
13. Great Britain
14. True
15. Kansas City
16. South Africa
17. Vodafone (Manchester United shirt sponsors)
18. 27
19. Jenson Button
20. New Zealand

DIFFICULT

Quiz 198: Anagrams part 2

Identify an American state from each of the anagrams below:

1.   Airfoil Can

2.   Had Oak Stout

3.   Sin In Cows

4.   Lo Oar Doc

5.   Wearing Visit

6.   Sauna I Oil

7.   No Inmates

8.   Cow Mine Ex

9.   Hewn Seraphim

10. Cut Cent Coin

11. Ale Wader

12. Hogan Twins

13. Laddies Horn

14. Halo Amok

15. Corn Inhalator

16. Chase Stat Sums

17. Nip Nasal Envy

18. Lardy Man

19. I Own Gym

20. Urinals Cahoot

Answers to Quiz 197: Pot Luck

1. Coventry City
2. Norwich
3. William Gladstone
4. Dame Sarah Storey
5. Manchester
6. Neptune
7. Ken Doherty
8. Andy Cole
9. Perez Hilton
10. Turkey
11. Dog
12. Horse racing
13. True
14. Net-a-Porter
15. Genghis Khan
16. Sao Paulo
17. 8lb 6oz
18. Chemical weapons
19. Queen stage
20. Doctor

DIFFICULT

Quiz 199: Pot Luck

1. A street called Whip-Ma-Whop-Ma-Gate can be found in which northern English city?

2. What motor manufacturer was founded as the Swallow Sidecar Company in 1922?

3. The famous 'St Crispin's Day' speech appears in which play by Shakespeare?

4. EC4M 8AE is the postcode of which London landmark?

5. Annapolis, home of the US Naval Academy, is in which American state?

6. Which British star won his first Oscar in 2011 for his performance in 'The Fighter'?

7. 'Kevin, what did you do to my room?' is the closing line of which festive film?

8. What type of animal was the cartoon character Foghorn Leghorn?

9. What does the 'E' in the acronym 'laser' stand for?

10. Which current Hollywood A-lister played Randy in the US soap 'Dallas'?

11. Kimberley is the middle name of which actor and comedian, who first found fame in the drama 'Fat Friends'?

12. Which fruit is the main ingredient in the liqueur quetsch?

13. The Brewers and the Bucks are professional sports teams based in which American city?

14. Manchego cheese originates from which country?

15. Which car manufacturer takes its name from the Japanese for the star-cluster Pleiades?

16. The name of which famous Italian opera house translates into English as 'The Staircase'?

17. Who was the only prime minister to have previously held the other three great offices of state?

18. Which two states joined the USA in 1912?

19. On average, one postcode covers how many residential addresses?
    a) 7
    b) 17
    c) 27

20. Snake eyes is a term used in which gambling game?
    a) blackjack
    b) craps
    c) poker

Answers to Quiz 198: Anagrams part 2

1.	California	11.	Delaware
2.	South Dakota	12.	Washington
3.	Wisconsin	13.	Rhode Island
4.	Colorado	14.	Oklahoma
5.	West Virginia	15.	North Carolina
6.	Louisiana	16.	Massachusetts
7.	Minnesota	17.	Pennsylvania
8.	New Mexico	18.	Maryland
9.	New Hampshire	19.	Wyoming
10.	Connecticut	20.	South Carolina

DIFFICULT

Quiz 200: New and Old

1. Who is the famous brother of 'EastEnders' actress Laila Morse?

2. Nell Trent is the central character in which novel by Charles Dickens?

3. Which club returned to the Football League in 2013 after an absence of 25 years?

4. What is the cheapest property on a London Monopoly board?

5. 'You Got It (The Right Stuff)' and 'Hangin' Tough' were UK number ones for which American boy band?

6. Manchester is the largest city in which American state?

7. Which comedy duo played TV's 'Old Gits'?

8. The New Meadow is the home ground of which English football club?

9. Who appeared on the reverse of the Bank of England £1 note from 1978 until they went out of circulation in 1988?

10. Pine Villa is the former name of which English football club?

11. Which weekly music magazine was published for the first time in March 1952?

12. Which actress and singer, best known for her performance in a hit film musical, represented the UK in the 1974 Eurovision Song Contest?

13. Newell's Old Boys is a football club based in which South American country?

14. The Lockinge Stakes are run each May at which English racecourse?

15. Which area of London is known colloquially as Silicon Roundabout owing to the number of technology companies based nearby?

16. 'Better late than never' was the tagline to which 2005 comedy starring Steve Carell?

17. Fredericton is the capital city of which Canadian province?

18. Which actor won his only Best Actor Oscar for his performance in 'The Color of Money'?

19. Which of the following is a nickname for the devil?
    a) Old Barry
    b) Old Garry
    c) Old Harry

20. What is the oldest university in America?
    a) Brown
    b) Harvard
    c) Yale

Answers to Quiz 199: Pot Luck

1. York	11. James Corden
2. Jaguar	12. Plum
3. Henry V	13. Milwaukee
4. St Paul's Cathedral	14. Spain
5. Maryland	15. Subaru
6. Christian Bale	16. La Scala
7. Home Alone	17. James Callaghan
8. Chicken	18. Arizona and New Mexico
9. Emission	19. 17
10. Brad Pitt	20. Craps

DIFFICULT

Get quizzical with the Collins quiz range

Available in paperback and ebook.

Available in paperback.

Available in paperback.

Available in paperback and ebook.

Available in paperback and ebook.

Available in paperback and ebook.

Available in paperback and ebook.

Available in paperback and ebook.

All **Collins** quiz range titles in paperback are RRP £6.99. Ebook prices may vary.

Available to buy from all good booksellers.

Follow us on Twitter 🐦 @collinsdict | Like us on Facebook 🅕 facebook.com/CollinsDictionary